BONNIE KIME SCOTT

# Refiguring Modernism

VOLUME TWO

# Postmodern Feminist Readings of Woolf, West, and Barnes

INDIANA UNIVERSITY PRESS

*Bloomington and Indianapolis*

The paper used in this publication
meets the minimum requirements of American National Standard
for Information Sciences—Permanence of Paper
for Printed Library Materials,
ANSI Z39.48-1984.

Manufactured in the United States of America

Library of Congress Cataloging-in-Publication Data

ᵀᴹ

Scott, Bonnie Kime, date
      Refiguring modernism / Bonnie Kime Scott.
          p.   cm.
      Includes bibliographical references (p.   ) and index.
      Contents: v. 1. Women of 1928—v. 2. Postmodern feminist
   readings of Woolf, West, and Barnes.
      ISBN 0-253-32936-1 (v. 1 : cl : alk. paper).—ISBN 0-253-20995-1 (v. 1 : pa : alk. paper).
      —ISBN 0-253-32937-X (v. 2 : cl : alk. paper).—ISBN 0-253-21002-X (v. 2 : pa : alk. paper)
      1. English fiction—20th century—History and criticism.
   2. Modernism (Literature)—Great Britain.
   3. Feminism and literature—Great Britain—History—20th century.
   4. Feminism and literature—United States—History—20th century.
   5. Women and literature—Great Britain—History—20th century.
   6. Women and literature—United States—History—20th century.
   7. Woolf, Virginia, 1882–1941—Criticism and interpretation.
   8. West, Rebecca, Dame, 1892—Criticism and interpretation.
   9. Barnes, Djuna—Criticism and interpretation.
   10. Modernism (Literature)—United States.   I. Title.
   PR888.M63S43   1995
   823'.91099287—dc20          95-3579

   1 2 3 4 5   00 99 98 97 96 95

For
Tom

my lasting attachment

# Contents

# Acknowledgments

I should like to thank the following institutions for access to their collections and permission to quote from manuscripts and reproduce images: BBC Written Archives Centre for quotations from letters by Christopher Salmon and Charles Bridge; British Library for letters of Rebecca West to George Bernard Shaw (Add MS 50519 f 228 and 50522 ff 169–172) and a letter from Shaw to West (Add MS 50518 ff 211–213) in the Shaw papers; Musée Carnavalet, Paris, for Romaine Brooks's painting of Natalie Barney; Cornell University Library for a photo of Violet Hunt, Ford Madox Ford, and Rebecca West; University of Delaware Library, Newark, for letters of Emily Coleman and Djuna Barnes and a photograph of Coleman in the Emily Coleman Papers; Jacques Doucet Library for letters of Djuna Barnes and Natalie Barney in its Natalie Barney Collection; The Houghton Library, Harvard University, for a letter of Rebecca West to Alexander Woollcott (bMS Am 1449 (485)–(494)); House of Lords Record Office for letters of Rebecca West and Lord Beaverbrook in the Beaverbrook Collection; Special Collections, University of Maryland at College Park Libraries (cited in this volume as Maryland), for letters and drawings of Djuna Barnes and drawings by Thelma Wood in the Papers of Djuna Barnes, for a photograph of Zadel Barnes Gustafson in the Barnes Family Papers, and for drawings by Thelma Wood in the Papers of Saxon Barnes; The National Portrait Gallery for a photograph of Virginia Woolf (NPG P221) and a Wyndham Lewis sketch of Rebecca West (NPG 5693; The New York Public Library, Astor, Lenox and Tilden Foundations for letters by T. S. Eliot and John Quinn in the Henry W. and Albert A. Berg Collection; The Manuscripts Division, Department of Rare Books and Special Collections, Princeton University Libraries, for letters of Rebecca West in Box 1, Folder 26 of the Dora Marsden Collection (cited in this volume as Princeton) and a photograph of Djuna Barnes and Mina Loy; University of Reading Library for letters of Leonard Woolf and Rebecca West in its Hogarth Press and Jonathan Cape collections; The Manuscripts Section, University of Sussex Library, for letters of Clive Bell and Leonard Woolf and scrapbooks in the Monk's House Papers; Harry Ransom Humanities Research Center of the University of Texas at Austin for letters of Rebecca

West and Ottoline Morrell; University of Tulsa for letters and manuscripts of Rebecca West in the Rebecca West Collection; The Beinecke Rare Book and Manuscript Library, Yale University, for letters of Rebecca West, a letter by Anthony West, and a sketch by H. G. Wells in the Rebecca West Collection. I am also grateful for the services of the Library of Congress, the British Council Archive, the Millicent Garrett Fawcett Library, the Lilly Library of Indiana University, the University of London Library, the University of Syracuse Library, and the Wellesley College Library.

I have made a concerted effort to contact holders of copyrights and apologize for any that are missing. Djuna Barnes extracts copyright by the Authors League Fund, 330 West 42nd Street, New York, NY 10036, as Literary Executor of the Estate of Djuna Barnes; Clerk of the Records, the House of Lords Record Office, acting on behalf of the Beaverbrook Foundation Trustees; Georgina Berkeley for the Literary Estate of Stella Benson; Joseph Geraci, Literary Executor of Emily Holmes Coleman; Quentin Bell for the literary estates of Clive Bell and Virginia Woolf; Valerie Eliot, Literary Executor for T. S. Eliot; Laurence Pollinger Limited for the Literary Estate of D. H. Lawrence; Harold Ober Associates for permission to quote Naomi Michison; the literary executors of Ottoline Morrell; Artists Rights Society (ARS), New York, as agents for the Man Ray Trust, Paris, for photographs of Djuna Barnes and Barnes with Mina Loy; A. P. Watt Ltd. on behalf of The Literary Executors of the Estate of H. G. Wells; Lily West for permission to quote from a letter by Anthony West; Peters Fraser & Dunlop Group Ltd. for permission to publish extracts from Rebecca West; M. T. Parsons, Literary Executor for Leonard Woolf; Roma Woodnut for The Society of Authors for the Literary Estates of Clive Bell, G. B. Shaw, G. B. Stern, and Virginia Woolf; Ezra Pound Letter to Dora Marsden, copyright 1995 by the Trustees of the Ezra Pound Literary Property Trust, used by permission of New Directions Publishing Corporation, agents. I should also like to acknowledge permission to reprint passages from the published works of Virginia Woolf by Harcourt Brace Jovanovich and Hogarth Press.

Excerpts from *Mrs. Dalloway* by Virginia Woolf, copyright 1925 by Harcourt Brace & Company and renewed in 1953 by Leonard Woolf, reprinted by permission of the publisher.

Excerpts from *To the Lighthouse* by Virginia Woolf, copyright 1927 by Harcourt Brace & Company and renewed in 1954 by Leonard Woolf, reprinted by permission of the publisher.

Excerpts from *A Room of One's Own* by Virginia Woolf, copyright 1929 by Harcourt Brace & Company and renewed in 1957 by Leonard Woolf, reprinted by permission of the publisher.

Excerpts from *The Waves* by Virginia Woolf, copyright 1931 by Harcourt Brace & Company and renewed in 1959 by Leonard Woolf, reprinted by permission of Harcourt Brace & Company.

Excerpts from *Between the Acts* by Virginia Woolf, copyright 1941 by Harcourt Brace & Company and renewed in 1969 by Leonard Woolf, reprinted by permission of the publisher.

Excerpts from *Moments of Being* by Virginia Woolf, copyright © 1976 by Quentin Bell and Angelica Garnett, reprinted by permission of Harcourt Brace & Company.

Excerpts from *The Diary of Virginia Woolf*, Volume III: 1925–1930, copyright © 1976 by Quentin Bell and Angelica Garnett, reprinted by permission of Harcourt Brace & Company.

Excerpts from *The Diary of Virginia Woolf*, Volume V: 1936–41, copyright © 1984 by Quentin Bell and Angelica Garnett, reprinted by permission of Harcourt Brace & Company.

Several essays published previously are reworked here, and I thank the publishers for permitting me to draw from this material: "Jellyfish and Treacle: Joyce, Lewis, Gender and Modernism," published in *Coping with Joyce: Essays from the Copenhagen Symposium*, ed. Morris Beja and Shari Benstock, Ohio State University Press; " 'The Look in the Throat of a Stricken Animal': Joyce as Met by Djuna Barnes," published in *Joyce Studies Annual 1991*, University of Texas Press; "Refiguring the Binary, Breaking the Cycle: Rebecca West as Feminist Modernist," *Twentieth Century Literature* 37.2 (Summer 1991), Hofstra University; " 'The Word Split Its Husk': Woolf's Double Vision of Modernist Language," *Modern Fiction Studies* 32.3 (1988), Purdue University.

I am grateful to the University of Delaware for awarding me a year to work on this project as a fellow in its Center for Advanced Study. Archival research was made possible by travel grants from the Dean of Arts and Science and the General University Research Fund.

Finally, I am appreciative of colleagues who have provided resources, criticism, and encouragement: Jane Marcus, who shares a fascination with all three of my central authors, a depth of wisdom about them, and her own West archive; Mary Lynn Broe and Phil Herring for consultations on Barnes; Carl Rollyson, Victoria Glendinning, Loretta Stec, and Margaret Stetz as consultants on West; and Suzette Henke and Ann Ardis for reading early drafts. I thank Wayne Craven, who identified Zadel Gustafson's illustrator, and my brother, Milford Burton Kime, who restored a family photograph. I am grateful to all of the contributors to an earlier project, *The Gender of Modernism: A Critical Anthology,* who prepared the wider context I needed as a basis. Finally, my graduate students and honors students, including Shirley Peterson, Patience Phillips, Marylu Hill, Judith Allen, Justyna Kostkowska, Donald Brown, and Jennifer Johnson, have traversed little-read texts with me, casting their own light upon them.

# Abbreviations

# Introduction:
# Feminist/Modernist Attachments

In this second volume of *Refiguring Modernism,* the generative metaphor of the web finds further elaboration. I opened volume 1 with figurative web work by Virginia Woolf. The famous quotation begins, "Fiction is like a spider's web, attached ever so lightly perhaps, but still attached to life at all four corners" (*Room* 43). Woolf's simile has helped establish my method for both volumes of this work. The spider's actions of repeatedly attaching, launching out into the unknown, and landing for the next anchoring point suggest agency, polyvalence, and the ability to make selective use of existing structures, or to seek new ones—not all of them manmade. It allows us to think of an emerging design, and the process that produces it—figures that encompass both traditional modernist and postmodern modes. Webs and comparable textiles worked by women have regularly aided feminist theory as it has sought alternatives and appropriations of linguistic and psychoanalytic theories that premise language upon relations to patriarchy.[1] Like the largely contextual work of volume 1, the close readings that follow benefit from leads provided by Julia Kristeva, Luce Irigaray, Toril Moi, Jane Marcus, Sandra Gilbert and Susan Gubar, Judith Butler, and Pamela Caughie—to mention but a few feminist revisionists writing on both sides of the Atlantic.

While the first volume explored the selective and sometimes coinciding attachments of Virginia Woolf, Rebecca West, and Djuna Barnes to a number of supportive scaffoldings, this volume turns more to the web of their fiction. Some of the anchoring "corners" of their webs were found in dysfunctional families, influential Edwardian men of letters, fostering literary women of that era, adventurous and brash suffragettes, and the "men of 1914," traditionally accepted as the framers of modernism (see separate chapters of volume 1). I found through Woolf, West, and Barnes a second flourishing of modernism around 1928, with works such as Woolf's *Orlando,* West's *The Strange Necessity,* and Barnes's *Ladies Almanack.* By the late 1920s they had a developing sense of their identities as professionals in a changing field of enterprise capitalism. They addressed the pressing question of censorship in their own work, and in the crisis posed by the trial of Radclyffe Hall's lesbian novel, *The Well of Loneliness.*

This second volume of *Refiguring Modernism* endeavors to follow the creative lines of Woolf, Barnes, and West, in turn, as each negotiates modernist questions of enduring importance to postmodern readers. Woolf departs from expected modernist norms of masterful, experimental use of language and patterned unities, giving way instead to a rapture with words. In rewriting the concept of character, Woolf is shrewdly sensitive to personal politics and new possibilities for relationship. Her creative protagonists concentrate—however painfully—on the process of discovery, where the written results are often fragmentary and tentative but occasionally visionary and enabling. Barnes plays with acts of representation, whether taking a stitch in nature or staging woman in the controversial role of primitive. She restages the abuses of the dysfunctional family encountered in volume 1, using unexpected players and vantage points. West seeks out the underlying assumptions, including divisive binaries, that have driven the repetition of destructive cycles, on both domestic and political fronts. Her merger of the domestic and the political in surprising analogies gives authority to female experience. West tangles with the very forms and forces she seeks to de-authorize. The network of connections with Edwardians and modernists of both genders, made for Woolf, West, and Barnes in volume 1, is reinforced in volume 2, with specific examples of contact. Though I concentrate on one issue per author, I also attempt to show where Woolf, West, and Barnes resonate with one another in their interests and strengths.

## Postmodern Concerns

In choosing to trace what I do in the writing of Woolf, West, and Barnes, I manifest postmodern attachments to new historicist, deconstructionist, and feminist theories and a set of postmodern conflicts and concerns. By doing so, I test the terms of the present era's relation to modernism, and the limitations of the questions we are posing.

Chapter 1, "Woolf's Rapture with Language," interrogates the emphasis on language mastery and experimental form in new critical discussions of modernism, and the continuing obsession with language in postmodernism. It studies Woolf's experience of words, both in her criticism of modernist texts and in her own works, where I develop a model of rapture with language. As noted in her reading of Percy Lubbock, Woolf expressed ambivalence in discussing the method of her contemporaries. Yet she was exultant when unconsciously she hit upon the right working method for a project. Despite her fame for experimentation, culminating in *The Waves,* Woolf oscillated between abstraction and realism within and between projects. She is more interested in problems with language than in its mastery. Woolf struggles with the instability of words and the inadequacy of rhetorical phrases, both in her personal writing and through her characters in fiction. Gaps and pauses rival words. The metaphor and the moment offer only illusions of order and wholeness.

The second modernist problem, addressed through Djuna Barnes in chapter 2, is the fascination with the "primitive," one aspect of essentialism expressed in modernist texts from Conrad's *Heart of Darkness* to Lawrence's *Lady Chatterley's Lover.* Barnes offers highly charged interactions between humans and animals, from her early drawings through the most puzzling passages of *Nightwood,* and even in her last poems. Through this focus it will be possible to address problems of essentialism, occasioned by the traditional equation of woman with nature and by a consideration of maternal origins and roles. The animal "other" bears comparison to racial, anti-Semitic, and gendered patterns of marginalization. Furthermore, Barnes presents her animals as fabrications or crafted representations, enhancing our sense of the web.

The authority of the binary in Western thinking will be tested through Rebecca West's politically charged modernism in chapter 3, "West's Sense of Scaffolding." West repeatedly works with Augustinian categories of good and evil in sketching character and in the operation of political forces. She is regularly identified with Manichaeanism and refers to it deliberately as an abiding philosophy in many cultures. She detects mixed elements in other modern writers, such as Wyndham Lewis and D. H. Lawrence. West calls for an escape to another mind frame, which female characters such as Harriet Hume occasionally express. West's tone of writing and her political essays have been called masculine, but hers is no simple crossover or reversal. Her authority diminishes the power of cultural dualism by confusing its location in gender.

### The Sense of an Ending

Volume 1 pivoted from 1914, the privileged date in accounts of modernism focused upon James Joyce, T. S. Eliot, Ezra Pound, and Wyndham Lewis, to 1928, as an era of achievement for Woolf, West, and Barnes.

This volume closes with 1939, a date situated toward the end of the modernist era, as demarcated in most accounts. The final chapter, "1939 and the Ends of Modernism," briefly investigates the sense of community and relation to tradition arrived at in works either written or situated in 1939. At that time, fascism impended upon Woolf, West, and Barnes, but unlike many of their celebrated male modernist colleagues, they would have none of it. By 1939, the fragility of the scaffoldings that modernists had attached to in one way or another was all too obvious. Political forces were closing in, demanding new forms of response.

Heeding the crafts of these three women of modernism yields unexpected results with lasting strategic value. I am not suggesting that Woolf, West, and Barnes all wove the same modernist web at a given time. But, as with the larger female population of *The Gender of Modernism,* the critical anthology I edited in 1990, I find that cooperatively these writers fill important gaps in my satisfaction with and understanding of modernism. Their works strain at traditional categories and take on problems not examined in male-centered visions of modernism.

Refiguring Modernism

# 1  Woolf's Rapture with Language

> "Yes," said Jinny, "our senses have widened. Membranes, webs of nerve that lay white and limp, have filled and spread themselves and float round us like filaments, making the air tangible and catching in them far-away sounds unheard before."
>
> —*The Waves* 135

> It is as though there were two faces to every situation; one full in the light so that it can be described as accurately and examined as minutely as possible; the other half in shadow so that it can be described only in a moment of faith and vision by the use of metaphor.
>
> —"Phases of Fiction" 139, in a section on Proust

The mastery and, indeed, the revolution of the word were accomplishments prized among male modernists and the critics who canonized them, as shown in volume 1. Woolf was more skeptical: "Do I fabricate with words, loving them as I do?" she asked in her diary (2 D 248). She was also wary of facility with images. In reviewing Edith Sitwell's poetry, she was concerned that Sitwell was relying too much on visual imagery. Woolf feared that, like the male word-crafters, her poet friend might become "prematurely imprisoned within the walls of her own style" (2 E 309). Woolf's formal experimentation was aimed, beyond words and images, at a new relation to tradition and audience. She recognized the gender-weighted politics of language, and made this a theme in her essays and fiction. Woolf challenged the exclusionary sentencing of females by pontificating authorities such as Charles Tansley in *To the Lighthouse* and the Bishop and even Dr. Johnson in *A Room of One's Own*. She studied the untroubled inheritance of literary traditions and archives by young university men of her creation—St. John Hirst in *The Voyage Out* and Jacob Flanders in *Jacob's Room*—and the ways that they exercised this proprietorship over young women when offering them home education. Her relation to tradition was variable and thereby rich in perspective.

In *A Room of One's Own*, as she strolls by the architecture of the London military establishment, Woolf's persona makes the famous observation, "If one is a woman one is often surprised by a sudden splitting off of consciousness, saying in walking down Whitehall, when from being the natural inheritor of that civilisation she becomes, on the contrary, outside of it, alien and critical" (169). By late 1940, she saw the word-proof structures of her male contemporaries as defensive shelters, unable to withstand the assault of her understanding:

> These queer little sand castles, I was thinking. . . . Little boys making sand castles. . . . Each is weathertight, & gives shelter to the occupant. . . . But I am the sea which demolishes these castles. . . . What is the value of a philosophy which has no power over life? I have the double vision. I mean, as I am not engrossed in the labour of making this intricate word structure. I also see the man who makes it. I should say it is only word proof not weather proof. We all have to discover the natural law & live by it. . . . I am carrying on, while I read, the idea of women discovering, like the 19th century rationalists, agnostics, that man is no longer God. (5 *D* 340)

She refused the authoritarian tradition of *logos* that was the cultural inheritance of the young James Joyce. The little boys she had in mind for the above quotation included T. S. Eliot. She expressed her assessment of the next male generation in "The Leaning Tower," invoking a metaphor of exalted architecture, already tilting from new social and political forces of the 1930s (2 *CE* 170–72). Through such complex figures, Woolf could declare that, as a woman, she had a different, more varied relation to language than many of her male contemporaries. Her female critical persona might assume the position and strength of a natural demolishing agent, the sea. Or she could visit the leaning tower, but unlike its inhabitants, she need not, she must not, remain. She has her own philosophy that valorizes life, and she is able to read the word-builder as well as the word; her "natural law" enveloping "watertight" or inescapable constructions becomes not simply an opposed alternative but a new process, a "double vision" of modernist language.[1] Consonant with *Three Guineas,* in which she develops the idea of an outsider's society, Woolf reminds herself in the same journal entry that it is "essential to remain outside" (5 *D* 340).

This "double vision" is consistent with Woolf's sensitivity to multiple states of mind, frequently discussed in her essays, and most notably in "Phases of Fiction." As a reader of fiction, Woolf identified different "phases" of the mind that made it desirable to move from one tradition to another, revising categorization itself.[2] A preference for variable critical positions or phases also supports her view of character, as she studies its being shaped by personal relations and cultural forces. The New Critics and the prefeminist historians of modernism typically erected secure structures that explained away the originally disruptive forms and denied the political implications of the small foothold on modernism they promoted. Woolf provides both matter and method for the ongoing work of revision.

There has been considerable feminist discussion of the relation of the woman writer to language. The tidal assault evoked by Woolf's diary entry prefigures some of the imagery of French deconstruction. Along lines that would be suggested by Jacques Derrida and Julia Kristeva, Woolf challenges the static, retentive qualities of phallogocentrism, disrupting the "phallic position" in cultures where "speaking subjects are conceived of as masters of their speech" (Kristeva, "Oscillation" 165). Kristeva's depiction of woman's sense of self in relation to language is only partially adequate, however, given Woolf's accomplishments and recent feminist renegotiations of the postmodern and the self. Woman's creation of "an imaginary story through which she constitutes an identity" (ibid. 166) could serve to describe Woolf's repeated creation of fantasy illustrations of creative women in process, in both her diary and her essays. Gilbert and Gubar have seen Woolf's concept of "woman's sentence" provisionally as a productive fantasy: "Woolf used what was essentially a *fantasy* about a utopian linguistic structure—a 'woman's sentence'—to define (and perhaps disguise) her desire to revise not woman's language but woman's relation to language" (1 *No Man's Land* 230). Woolf's invoking of "fantasy" need not be taken as a negative symptom, or an evasion of politics. Kristeva's statement that in women's writing "language seems to be seen from a foreign land . . . from the point of view of an asymbolic, spastic body" ("Oscillation" 166) is useful for its contribution of "asymbolic" as a form, and its focus on the female body as a basic site of language, providing its own rhythm and distance for action. Woolf's concept of the outsider is accommodated, though the turning of it to a strategy needs to be stressed. Woolf comes close to the concept of a "spastic body" when she registers "spasmodic" reactions, as when she reports that she read *Ulysses* "with spasms of wonder, of discovery" (5 D 353). But any implication of physical abnormality and nonnative facility should be rejected, as these miss the mobility and power of the metaphors and fantasy-making processes that we shall be examining, including their historical and political connections.[3] Although she writes of aspiring to wholeness, Woolf does not develop a static or achieved sense of the whole or of selfhood, but instead she continuously deploys techniques aimed at bringing a fuller and more adequate sense of life into writing. She envelops like a tide that quickly withdraws and later returns, never in exactly the same form. Woolf is the woman writer in process—an adaptation from Julia Kristeva's definition of "woman as process" that has proven attractive to postmodern feminists.[4]

### "A Sketch" as Scaffolding

We find in Woolf's earliest recollections that she was enraptured and empowered by words. This personal history emerges from childhood "moments of being" recorded in her late memoir, "A Sketch of the Past." These "moments" have been heralded as one of Woolf's greatest experimental contributions to modernism. In some of their qualities—radiance, fragility, commonplace sources—they are comparable to Joycean "epiphany," though Woolf's concept lacks voyeuristic, religious, and retentive aspects present in Joyce's. Woolf's admiration for his "spiritual" qualities, expressed in her essay "Modern Fiction," was in effect a detection of the Joycean epiphany, which was not available as a concept during her lifetime.[5] Woolf suggests that moments of being stand out against the "cotton wool" of daily routine and serve as her "scaffolding in the background" ("Sketch" 73). This is a very different structure from the depersonalized, classicist scaffolding erected by T. S. Eliot in his explanation of Joyce's *Ulysses,* and relied upon in other criticism, including his appreciations of Djuna Barnes's works. Eliot sought modernist elements that he could align with established literary traditions. Woolf's scaffolding, on the other hand, arises in personal rapture and present history. It provides a base for a rich web of narrative attachments and returns.

Woolf's first memory, as recorded in "A Sketch of the Past," is of the red and purple flowers on her mother's dress, observed as she sat on her lap returning to London from St. Ives. Woolf modifies the sequence of her story, reversing the direction to arrive at St. Ives for "artistic purposes." St. Ives was her artistic origin. Louise DeSalvo has suggested that this place serves further to unlock familial dysfunction, which affected Woolf's literary strategies. In a second early memory recorded in "A Sketch," young Virginia is lying half-asleep in the St. Ives nursery. She hears waves breaking, watches movement of a yellow blind in the wind, listens to the tapping of an acorn on the shade pull, and feels "it is almost impossible that I should be here." It is "the purest ecstasy I can conceive" (*MB* 64–65). In further textual work, Woolf repeats and expands these moments, labels them as color-and-sound memories, and imagines them transformed into a "picture that was globular; semi-transparent . . . of curved petals; of shells. . . . " She was "drawing in such ecstasy as I cannot describe" (66). DeSalvo encourages us to distrust this set of moments, finding the images typical of children who have been "sexually or incestuously abused" (106–107).[6] Woolf's disbelief of being there has suggested to some readers that she has already imbibed the asymmetrical politics of gender and suspects that a little girl is undeserving of such ecstasy. Yet Woolf's memories present a combination of security and awareness. She senses her political vulnerability, but is catching on to the conditions enabling survival and even rapture. The womblike, cradling space (comparable to natural materials such as flowers, shells, and grapes, whose semi-transparency permits access by the senses) cannot be held or inhabited continually, but it can be made to come again.

Later memories take her out to the family and into a garden that is humid with generation, a setting for violence, and often the source of despair. Woolf records feelings of powerlessness because of male-induced terror—Gerald Duckworth's probing of her genitals when she was only a few years older (*MB* 69), the decision to endure a pummeling from Thoby because it no longer made sense to hurt another individual (71),[7] and news of a man's suicide (71). Woolf performs auto-analysis based on these experiences. Although the memoir was written toward the end of her life, she implies that the analysis of her feelings began contemporaneously with the events. She theorizes: "This seems to show that a feeling about certain parts of the body; how they must not be touched; how it is wrong to allow them to be touched; must be instinctive. It proves that Virginia Stephen was not born on the 25th January 1882, but was born many thousands of years ago; and had from the very first to encounter instincts already acquired by thousands of ancestresses in the past" (69). This female ancestral taboo, breeding guilt in the victim, joins the "dumb and mixed" feeling "resenting, disliking" which she directs at his violating hand, unable, perhaps, to take on the whole relation to her half-brother. The instinct to control access to her body transcends her own lifespan, merging her with stern ancestresses. It took a more mature Woolf to assess the ways that, in the names of protection and chastity, woman's body had been denied to herself. Woolf's reactions to the suicide and the pummeling also suggest a refusal of boundaries between herself and others, which would endure. Little Virginia also begins to read antithetical cultural attitudes, inherited from the maternal and paternal sides of her family.[8]

In "A Sketch," Woolf works over one moment which, unlike the incidents of male violence, is emotionally satisfactory and becomes a paradigm for structuring experience in language. "I was looking at the flower bed by the front door; 'That is the whole,' I said. I was looking at a plant with a spread of leaves; and it seemed suddenly plain that the flower itself was a part of the earth; that a ring enclosed what was the flower; and that was the real flower; part earth; part flower." Even as a small child she puts this thought away "as likely to be useful later" (71). It gives her the power of reason and explanation which will increase over time, dulling the shocks and blows of adverse moments of being, giving them value. "I make it real by putting it into words. . . . The wholeness means that it has lost its power to hurt me. . . . It is the rapture I get when in writing I seem to be discovering what belongs to what" (72). Wholeness then is not mastery of an isolated form but understanding of contexts and interdependencies.

Jane Harrison, Woolf's friend and a revisionist of male-centered classical studies, offers a useful term in "holophrases." This describes verbalization by a healthy mind, which expresses its perception of experience without separating "emotion and reason, feeling and thought, self and non-self," as would be the usual case in linear, hierarchical Western languages.[9] Woolf's young persona ultimately feels freed of the strictures of male art and a patriarchal god. She is a part of the whole world as an element of art: "There is no Shakespeare, there is no Beethoven; certainly and emphatically there is no God; we are the words; we are the music; we are the thing itself" (72). For Woolf, using words is significant, though the exact word is not important; the ongoing process of long-term studying, discovering relationships by finding first one part, then another, making the connections, and coming back to what she has created in words and especially metaphors, assures a capacity for coping with shocks, recourse to potent images, and a spiritual sense of being in the world. This is different from the formation of the "damned egotistical self" which Woolf questioned in her contemporaries Joyce and Dorothy Richardson. The "different voice" of relational thinking that Carol Gilligan situates empirically with women is of course pertinent here. Woolf's goals for herself as a writer, expressed to Clive Bell in 1908 as she worked on *The Voyage*

*Out,* were to "re-form the novel and capture multitudes of things at present fugitive, enclose the whole, and shape infinite strange shapes." She encountered the right material on her walks, yet knew that "tomorrow . . . I shall be sitting down to the inanimate old phrases" (1 *L* 356). The sentence had to become a place of process worthy of her rapidly collecting, connecting mind.

Virginia Stephen seems to have taken in considerable language before she began her career of spirited conversation and storytelling. Her sister Vanessa reported that around two she "couldn't speak clearly," but not long after "speech became the deadliest weapon as used by her" (*Virginia's Childhood* 2). Woolf's prodigious consumption of literature as an adolescent is evident in her early journals, where, for example, she reports "reading four books at once—The Newcomers, Carlyle, Old Curiosity Shop, and Queen Elizabeth"—on her fifteenth birthday, and is delighted to have received Lockhart's ten-volume *Memoirs of the Life of Sir Walter Scott* as a present from her father (*PA* 22). As suggested in volume 1, it is likely that she read it for the sake of their relationship.

My suggestion at the start of this chapter that Woolf worked away from classical scaffolding would seem to be challenged by the emphasis she placed upon the Greek in her early education. It would be safe to say that *Antigone* was as much favored as a text for her as the *Odyssey* was for Joyce. Her training in classical languages certainly surpassed that of Barnes and West.[10] Woolf began Greek and history classes at King's College in 1897, despite family worries about her health. Her particular angle toward the study of Greek comes out in reports of her private lessons, first with Clara Pater and later with the more demanding Janet Case, whose emphasis on grammar was not always met with enthusiasm (1 Bell 68). The lessons with Case expanded into serious arguments about Greek culture and drama, eliciting from Virginia respect for a "valiant strong minded woman" who "had the rare gift of seeing the other side" (*PA* 181–84). Woolf's side was more emotional and literary—probably related to her early experiences of rapture with words. She mildly satirized Case's concern for grammar, particularly in passages where Virginia had found and reacted to the rapture of love.[11] Greek drama is clearly idealized in Woolf's essay "On Not Knowing Greek" (*CR* 24–39). But "knowing" Greek meant more than the words and poetry. Woolf is concerned in her essay with the commonplace context. She seeks to understand the traditional expectations of the audience.

Woolf's mature novels offer the best opportunity to study the shocks and raptures of moments of being, the challenge of expressing them in words, her striving for a sense of the contextual whole, and the double vision of writer as well as the intricate structure of words. In focusing upon the artist's relationships to words, it makes sense to draw upon the study of states of mind found in Woolf's essays. Her fiction offers characters who have visions of wholeness, unity, and retention; these must yield to ongoing experience as it widens, becomes more politically aware, and faces the changing demands of history. Her fictional form alters, correspondingly, in relation to her original scaffolding of moments.

## Digging out *Mrs. Dalloway*

Woolf's 1925 novel, *Mrs.Dalloway,* is often viewed as her most accomplished modernist work. As such, it has been compared, often to its disadvantage, with Joyce's *Ulysses*.[12] *Mrs. Dalloway* permits the study of various attitudes toward mastery with words—attitudes which often can be divided along gender lines. Authority figures, particularly men, are an important source of words, and only men engage in actual writing. Septimus is the novel's only poet. Lady Bruton must rely on her male luncheon guests, Hugh Whitbread and Mr. Dalloway, to write her emigration proposal to the newspapers. Mrs. Dalloway's first and most persistent memories of her former suitor Peter Walsh are his word performances. "It was his sayings one remembered" (4). In their early, failed relationship, Peter tried to supply Clarissa with her critical vocabulary, which came with his aesthetic and world visions subtly attached: "She owed him words: 'sentimental,' 'civilised'; they started up every day of her life as if he guarded her" (36). As "guards" Peter's words confined her and defined her, to some extent, for life, despite the fact that she resisted a marital alliance with him.[13] Thinking over their morning meeting, Peter disapproves of Clarissa's having grown "a trifle sentimental" (49). His "civilised" ideas had sent him to India, emerging in his work there. Peter narrates a traditional romantic ending to the novel that brings Clarissa to him in its final moment.[14]

Yet Clarissa Dalloway encourages us to look to other places than the ending for a climax—as Woolf does on a larger scale in her tunneling method for that novel. An interesting irony about Peter's supposedly memorable sayings is that Clarissa readily alters his words. A comment, "Musing among the vegetables?" shifts in her memory to "I prefer men to cauliflowers," and by the end of the paragraph the cauliflowers have become cabbages (4)—a plenitude of plant life, at least. Clarissa's looseness with words includes an amusing momentary difficulty recalling Peter's name and a failure to heed his letters. He muses defensively that she knows nothing of his contributions to his Indian district. He has introduced a special plow and the wheelbarrow, but the Indians contribute a source of irritation and humor that reinforces Clarissa's own rebellion— the coolies have declined to put these foreign implements to work (49). Peter's words are not always amusing; he worked horrors when his word "Stargazing?" interrupted Clarissa's overpowering feeling of love for Sally Seton at Bourton, as she still recalls. Woolf allows us to see how differing attitudes toward language and the emotions are accessed again and elaborated through memory over time.

One of the cardinal qualities of Mrs. Dalloway is her tendency to notice routine things as exceptional—a capacity to use the present that is missing in Peter. This noticing things creates metaphorical "buds on the tree of life" (29), potential to burst into full bloom, in ordinary situations such as her walking through London streets and park land, or her listening to typical noises in her household. Mrs. Dalloway's plunge into a beautiful morning draws her back in memory to early mornings at Bourton when she was eighteen. Typically Clarissa's memories of Bourton are of dramatic, rapturous moments, of shocks to the system, which provide the sort of reusable scaffolding that Woolf describes in "A Sketch of the Past." "Moments" are both felt and remade, though with far less rapture, in the later London phase of her life. In this London phase, Elizabeth Abel has seen suppression of an unresolved attachment to an adolescent female world experienced at Bourton.[15] At this phase in her life, having struggled with illness, she also works on the impending problem of her own dissolution. The increasingly elderly Clarissa is made to "shiver" like a plant in a river bed at the passing shock of an oar when events such as Lady Bruton's luncheon go on without her (30).

On her own scale of emotion, Mrs. Dalloway selects as the "most exquisite moment of her whole life" her kiss from Sally Seton in the garden at Bourton.

> Passing a stone urn with flowers in it. Sally stopped; picked a
> flower; kissed her on the lips. The whole world might have turned
> upside down! The others disappeared; there she was alone with
> Sally. And she felt that she had been given a present, wrapped up,

and told just to keep it, not to look at it—a diamond, something infinitely precious, wrapped up, which, as they walked (up and down, up and down), she uncovered, or the radiance burnt through the revelation, the religious feeling!—when old Joseph and Peter faced them. . . . (35–36)

This moment changes the orientation of the world and extracts a forbidden passion. The feeling can be expressed only through a series of phrases, building a compound metaphor that oscillates in its multiple dimensions. The metaphor becomes the narrative of a gift, further comprehended as a diamond, generalized to something infinitely precious, yet given with mystical restrictions. She must not unwrap it, but she is able to experience it further through uncovering, or its radiance burning through. "Religious" is a final approximation of the feeling before it is violated by the appearance of Peter Walsh and the elderly Jacob Breitkopf, and the shock of Peter's word. The effect is a stark simile of confinement: "It was like running one's face against a granite wall in the darkness" (36). As in a flash of lightning, she sees his "determination to break into their companionship" and is concerned for Sally, who is supposedly "mauled" by Peter's jealousy.

Peter has an equivalent moment at Bourton. His scene is by the fountain instead of on the terrace, and it involves an argument over Clarissa's attraction to Richard Dalloway, not her love of Sally. Peter is able to see Sally only as a co-conspirator against the elder generation at Bourton, not a rival in love—an emphasis shared in J. Hillis Miller's discussion of the novel.[16] Breitkopf interrupts Peter's moment, showing embarrassment that he lacked when he broke in on the female couple. Peter experiences the reverse equivalent of Clarissa's stone wall: "He felt that he was grinding against something physically hard; she was unyielding. She was like iron, like flint, rigid up the backbone" (64). Indeed, her "failure" with Richard and her own metaphors for her functioning in society invoke the same metaphors. Most of Peter's remembered moments are negative. He admits a critical tendency to "ticket" moments in which Clarissa disappoints him, as when her prim reaction to illegitimacy becomes "the death of her soul" (59).

We get a very different feeling in language from Mrs. Dalloway as she tunnels back to the "scaffolding" of her great moment with Sally in one of Woolf's most memorable expressions.[17] We learn that "yielding to the charm of a woman" has been a repeated experience. At first she conventionally centers in male sexuality: "She did undoubtedly then feel what men felt" (32). But as she moves deeper into that feeling, her account becomes boldly physical, unlike anything produced by the men she has known. Her first analogy begins as a localized blush, growing to a suggestion of genital engorgement, comparable to other forms of natural burgeoning—a bud bursting the calyx or a butterfly cracking from its chrysalis. The emerging figure is expressive of a healthy, moist, self-alleviating life system that she is both outside and increasingly inside of.

> It was a sudden revelation, a tinge like a blush which one tried to check and then, as it spread, one yielded to its expansion, and rushed to the farthest verge and there quivered and felt the world come closer, swollen with some astonishing significance, some pressure of rapture, which split its thin skin and gushed and poured with an extraordinary alleviation over the cracks and sores! Then, for that moment, she had seen an illumination; a match burning in a crocus; an inner meaning almost expressed. (32)

This unarticulated, semiotic, sexually suggestive, lesbian, and visionary moment offers immediacy of the world and promises access to the unknown. Inspired by another woman, and self-alleviating, it is preferable to anything Peter offered in words. It remains a pressure on her consciousness and a resource even amid the reassertion of heterosexual relations, and after Sally's mature transformation.

An older, dryer Mrs. Dalloway has a routine encounter with figures and words of authority on her morning walk—an errand in quest of flowers. During the composition process, Woolf worried about the adequacy of Clarissa Dalloway, suggesting that she was too "stiff-glittering and tinselly" (2 D 272). Her model in life was supposedly Kitty Manxe, a friend in pre-Bloomsbury days who inhabited a world closer to George Duckworth's society than to Woolf's mature sense of style and purpose. On her morning walk, Clarissa captures as much glitter as buds of life. "A disc, inscribed with a name," extended to a police officer by a chauffeur is "magical" to this Clarissa. It "burnt its way through . . . to blaze among candelabras, glittering stars, breasts stiff with oak leaves, Hugh Whitbread and all his colleagues, the gentlemen of England, that night in Buckingham Palace." Pretension and ostentation overtake this fantasy, which Clarissa identifies with the party she plans. "She stiffened a little; so she would stand at the top of her stairs" (MD 17). Thus the word affect of officialdom is just as inhibiting as Peter's labels. Clarissa's stiffness atop her tower of stairs has a phallic, monumental, architectural quality, suggesting artificial construction rather than emotional burgeoning. She is part of the support system of officialdom, appropriate to receive the prime minister and a would-be architect of empire, Lady Bruton. This posture also makes it appropriate for her to neglect her dull relative Ellie Henderson. In expressing her many aims for the novel as she was writing it, Woolf entertained an uncharacteristic quantity of ideas, ending with "I want to criticise the social system, & show it at work, at its most intense" (2 D 248).

The most remarkable word display in *Mrs. Dalloway* is the much-commented-upon skywriting—an event which escapes Mrs. Dalloway's recording yet produces a transition to Septimus Smith's moments of being in the novel.[18] The very process of writing words, as reported by the narrator, is alarming. It "bored ominously into the ears of the crowd" and depends upon a futuristic machine, an instrument of the recent war, the airplane, "dropping dead down." Among the observers are a "stiff white baby" and a woman who seems to be sleepwalking, suggesting stultification by the word (29). Efforts at decipherment produce ugly new coinages typical of trade names, "Glaxo" and "Kreemo" (20).[19] The narrator ambiguously reports that "the clouds to which the letters E, G, or L had attached themselves moved freely, as if destined to cross from West to East on a mission of the greatest importance which would never be revealed, and yet certainly so it was—a mission of the greatest importance" (21). Sustaining Woolf's criticism of the social system, the narrative suggests all-too-typical patterns of Western capitalist and imperial impositions upon the East. As in Woolf's diary entry on the sand castles, nature dissipates the word. Only in this dissipation is there "exquisite beauty." This is perceived by Septimus Smith, a man marginalized first by class and later by a war that deranged his brain. The narrator points out that he has become legion—"London has swallowed up many young men called Smith" (84). Having renounced his origins for the self-improvements of the city, Septimus might have become the successor to Mr. Brewer at Sibleys and Arrowsmiths, or an H. G. Wells. On a negative note, he could become a pawn of fascism, characterized as flourishing among the uprooted people of industrial cities by Rebecca West, as we shall see in chapter 3. He was susceptible to the charisma of his lecturer Isabel Pole, honoring her as his beloved muse, and was eager to carry on the traditions of Shakespeare, Keats, Shaw, and Darwin, as he extrapolated their visions. In the sky words he sees "signals" and relates them to his own "mission," but at this point he does not know the words and language that will elaborate this role. The sounds of letters read from the sky bring a second natural element into play—the fantasy of trees come to life. For the moment, the contact of his wife Rezia's hand puts down such hallucinations (22).

Like Clarissa Dalloway, Septimus has words of authority imposed upon him. The word "time" is uttered by Rezia to remind Septimus of his appointment with a medical authority, Dr. Bradshaw—a man who, coincidentally, arouses hostile feelings in Clarissa Dalloway when he later appears at her party. This physician will sentence Septimus to an institution (in effect, to death) with the authority of his word "proportion" and the threat of enforcement by law. It is remarkable that with "proportion," Woolf selects a word of broad cultural value rather than specialized medical jargon. This word is dangerous because it can be made into a goddess, worshipped, and defended. The constructed goddesses of this novel, including Miss Pole as inspiration for Septimus and Clarissa as goddess for Peter and her servant Lucy (30), are suspect as patriarchal products. Bradshaw is upset by what he calls Septimus's "educated" use of words. What Septimus actually does is more carnivalesque than educated. He puns "Holmes' homes" (147), creating an added dimension of metonymy, where Holmes becomes the confining architecture advocated by his profession to confine mental and verbal disorder. In his verbal play Septimus introduces an inaccuracy in ownership. The bourgeois, possessive Bradshaw corrects this: "One of *my* homes, Mr. Smith. . . . " Woolf's choice of Septimus as punster may indicate a connection of word play with male mastery, though his outsider status mitigates this. As noted in volume 1, Woolf could be equally subversive and playful in her letters, as when she turned back upon itself Wyndham Lewis's bullish attack on her feminine version of modernism.[20]

When Rezia utters the word "time" in the park, Septimus associates it with an apocalyptic event—the return of his slain soldier love, Evans, and his own mission. His apprehension of "time" presents a multiple metaphor suggestive both of burgeoning seed and of blasting shell. There is an explosion: "The word 'time' split its husk; poured its riches over him; and from his lips fell like shells, like shavings from a plane, without his making them, hard, white, imperishable words, and flew to attach themselves to their places in an ode to Time, an immortal Ode to Time." This is when Evans emerges: "But no mud was on him; no wounds; he was not changed" (105). Woolf took the simultaneous rendition of sane and insane views of the world as one of the major challenges of her novel (2 D 207). The spontaneous flowing and splitting resemble Mrs. Dalloway's unverbalized, burgeoning expression of lesbian love, cited earlier, a feeling comparable to Septimus's unacknowledged longing for Evans (Lilienfeld 3). The unuttered, emerging word articulates desire, as if it is escaping from the "undermind" repeatedly referred to in Woolf's essays. The split husk issues forth beautiful materials—shells and shavings. The figure of shells as protective, secreted forms, molded to life, recurs often in Woolf, as in the "scaffolding" moment of "A Sketch," or for Bernard in the final section of *The Waves* (255). But Septimus's shells and shavings are not living things; they remind us of gun shells and the war that shattered him; they are shaved off a tree, not planted, and they cannot grow, as a living seed would, or alleviate pain, as does the liquid of Mrs. Dalloway's rapturous vision. They attach to an established literary form, the ode, and have the hard, monumental immortality imagined in Keats's "Ode on a Grecian Urn." In discussions of the moderns with Eliot, Woolf had held up Keats as an ideal not to be matched by them, but she now presents Keats as a danger. The classic model of artistic achievement leads Septimus on to the delusion of becoming a God-like man with a divine mission or heroic quest before him; he is akin to Joyce's Stephen Dedalus. That Septimus hears Greek from sparrows (a symptom taken from Woolf's own illness [1 Bell 90]) suggests usurpation of nature's music by the classical tongue. In Septimus's hallucination, Evans comes forth, "unchanged" by regenerative, earthy ooze of mud. Septimus approaches an alternate process of word generation, but fails to couple this with desire. The word-giving mud will persist, however, for another tormented creator in *Between the Acts*. Septimus dies impaled on iron railings—a cultural outlaw on the scaffolding, a Christ figure run through with iron nails. He has hurled himself in defiance at a barrier—stating his protest at structures that, by claiming to protect, limit and stifle difference and desire.[21]

As if in antithesis to the word-generating airplane and Septimus's impaled desire, Woolf offers another odd source of the word by the Regent's Park tube station. Both Peter and Rezia Smith hear it:

> a frail quivering sound, a voice bubbling up without direction, vigour, beginning or end, running weakly and shrilly and with an absence of all human meaning into
>
> ee um fah um so
> fo swee too eem oo—

the voice of no age or sex, the voice of an ancient spring spouting from the earth. It is a lost song of love. (*MD* 80–81)[22]

Though initially ungendered, its singer is identified as a battered, primeval woman (81). Schlack associates her with Ceres (152–53). There is a form of eternity, not static permanence, but a natural cycle of compos[t]-ing here, as the figure witnesses "the passing generations—the pavement was crowded with bustling middle-class people—vanished, like leaves, to be trodden under, to be soaked and steeped and made mould of by that eternal spring" (82).[23]

Rezia Smith also plays briefly with words. Walking away from Septimus for a few minutes in the park, Rezia expresses words of longing that fall unheard: "Her words faded. So a rocket fades. Its sparks, having grazed their way into the night, surrender into it, dark descends, pours over the outlines of houses and towers; bleak hillsides soften and fall in." She cries to no one "by the fountain in Regent's park," and her darkness resembles the ancient England that preceded the advent of the Romans (23–24). Outcast women's words tend back to earth burial and the primordial. Septimus's deadly, ugly resting place on area railings is transformed by Rezia's imagination into "cornfields," a "hill, somewhere near the sea . . . stirrings among dry corn, the caress of the sea, as it seemed to her, hollowing them in its arched shell and murmuring to her laid on the shore, strewn she felt, like flying flowers over some tomb" (150). H. D. would perform a comparable transformation of London railings in "The Walls Fall Down"—her own response to the destructions of war. Schlack's identification of Rezia with Ceres is very appropriate here. The war had "smashed a plaster cast of Ceres" in the garden of Septimus's employer, who calculated this as one of the losses of war (85–86). Rezia makes up a maternal, mythic, protective space, comparable to Woolf's nursery space at St. Ives. In her ritual motions, she anticipates the mourners of Percival in *The Waves*—another casualty of patriarchal construction.

In the writing of *Mrs. Dalloway*, Woolf arrived at her "prime discovery so far," which she called the "tunneling process" (2 D 292). The discovery was not worked out deliberately, but it emerged in practice, as if from the "undermind"—the productive, word-packed unconscious frequently cited in her essays. Woolf's use of the "unconscious" is both unusual and crucial. It is not synonymous with a Freudian or Jungian unconscious, though its difficulty of access is comparable. For Woolf the unconscious harbors madness as well as the creative essentials—a combination that has gained in interest as feminists have theorized the concept of "hysteri-cal narrative" inherited from Freud.[24] Woolf's unconscious allows vision to mesh with emotional need, and even history. Woolf's tunneling process worked out the same thing that her early vision of the flower had sup-plied—a sense of what was connected to what, a process directed toward wholeness through inclusiveness. The tunnel metaphor and its applica-tion are spatial, temporal, aesthetic, interpersonal, and culturally aware. She digs back into the past in installments, getting at gold (2 D 292). I suspect the tunnel is one of the empowering figural resources taken from Woolf's childhood summers in St. Ives. Woolf's underground system of tunnels is the figural antithesis of the tower. Its very intricacy almost guarantees a collapse, undermining old systems of support, from the glib phrase to the architecture of Whitehall. A simpler form of tunneling is done in *Jacob's Room*, where we learn what Jacob is like as he is dug out on all sides by surrounding figures, many of them female, situated in dif-fering time frames and cultural territories.

As she worked on *Jacob's Room*, Woolf was having the mastery of Joyce's *Ulysses* impressed upon her by Eliot, as noted in volume 1. A now famous diary entry of September 26, 1920, describes her reflections that "what I'm doing is probably being better done by Mr Joyce" (2 D 69), though she is not specific about what either might be doing. She worries that "I have not thought my plan out plainly enough," perhaps with Eliot's sense of the Odyssean plan of *Ulysses* in mind. In *Jacob's Room* Woolf was actually ahead of Joyce in deconstructing the male plan that determined both Jacob and Stephen Dedalus. In *Mrs. Dalloway,* tunneling gives us a complex sense of Clarissa that moves around and through her life and mind. The greater access into her being was more satisfactory to readers than the remote sensing of Jacob had been. Woolf digs back into the past in installments (2 D 263), getting at gold (292). The "beautiful caves behind [her] characters" connect as they work on similar moments in the past and come "to daylight at the present moment" (263). The figure of the tunnel may well emerge from the scaffolding of moments set in the beach and garden at St. Ives—places where a first experience of tunneling is likely to have occurred, along with the notion of demolishing sand cas-tles. The tunneling process was a resource that Rachel Vinrace could not claim. To her the tunnel remained a nightmare, leading to sexual horrors.

The best illustration of the tunneled moment is an incident we have already noted, the rapture of Sally's kiss. Clarissa tunnels from her mature life as the wife of Richard Dalloway in London, back to her youth in

Bourton. This tunnel crosses one of Peter's experiences of the period—his own shock of disappointment in Clarissa. Tunneling back a little farther, we come to Clarissa's memory of descending the stairs to meet Sally at dinner in a white dress. She had just felt a moment of excitement over having Sally under her roof that night—a moment to which a hot-water can that Clarissa was holding still adheres. Her anticipation, descending the stairs in white, makes the young Clarissa think of retaining the moment in death; she recalls "Othello's feeling . . . if it were now to die 'twere now to be most happy" (MD 35). Additional elements of Clarissa's descending the stairs in a white dress are dug out by Peter, Sally, and the older Clarissa, now closer to actual death and concerned with Septimus's decision to "die . . . now." Clarissa's present dress is green and shows best in artificial light, though she still preserves virginal attitudes. Peter recalls the white dress when he hears the hostess-like bells of St. Margaret's, "like Clarissa herself, thought Peter Walsh, coming down the stairs on the stroke of the hour in white" (50). He is relieved that, though she has been ill, Clarissa is not dead. The moment looms behind his terror and ecstasy at Clarissa's reappearance, seemingly for him (though originally for Sally), at the end of her party and Woolf's novel. "For there she was" (194). She fulfills his fantasy of being a solitary traveler who rides into the wood to meet his own dissolution from a siren goddess "like one of those spectral presences which rise in twilight in woods made of sky and branches" (56–57).

Sally "still saw Clarissa all in white going about the house with her hands full of flowers" (188), but has no recollection of their kiss. The only kiss she recalls is an unwelcome one from Hugh Whitbread, given in his confrontation with her suffragist politics. In reciprocation for Clarissa's most exquisite moment, Sally considers Clarissa's friendship the thing she is most grateful for. Disappointingly, it is a consideration devoid of passion and replete with considerations of class. Seeing the mature Sally Seton, Clarissa is able to calmly set down her former excitement (memorialized in the hot-water can). Still clinging to Sally's hand, she takes in the buds of the present moment—the full rooms, the roar of voices, the blowing of curtains, and roses brought by Richard (171). She is not immune to shocks; the moment may shudder or stiffen and cannot remain whole. But the shower is nearly incessant. Mrs. Dalloway yields up her most exquisite moment with Sally in the garden. Her emotional treasure is dug out, unwrapped, through time and cultural compromise, but it has given needed support.

Septimus Smith provides the final perspective on Clarissa's white dress on the stairs and her sense of emotional treasures. Having heard of his suicide, she asks, "Had he plunged holding his treasure? 'If it were now to die, 'twere now to be most happy' she had said to herself once, coming down in white" (184). Removed to a room, alone with thoughts of him, Clarissa tries to merge with his being, reconstituting his suicidal gesture, despite their differences in age, class, and sex. Readers are entitled to skepticism about the possibility of merging such differences. But they are hardly larger than the ones between the young Clarissa and Othello that originally inspired her thoughts on emotional treasures and death. As she meditates, her metaphorical treasure takes on "life" as an equivalent; it must be kept from William Bradshaw. Her tunnel comes close to events. Shortly before his leap, Septimus had affirmed that "life was good" and held on until the final encroachment of Holmes. "I'll give it you" (149) is his final statement, and one not to be singularly interpreted. One candidate for "you" is the old man, staring opposite. In this case, giving life to him, Septimus connects with Clarissa, who is glad he has "thrown it away." She now derives a new sense of life from the old man's counterpart, an old woman going about her daily routine, opposite Clarissa's window (186). Clarissa has grown beyond the desire to retain one supreme treasure in sudden death. She began her day content to be dispersed—"laid out like a mist between the people she knew best, who lifted her on their branches as she had seen the trees lift the mist, but spread ever so far, her life, herself" (9). There is lyrical grace to this late view of life. But it is culturally limited. Clarissa's party was planned for this well-known set. She makes small progress in understanding the misfit Miss Kilman, whose feminist, nationalist, evangelical tunnel through the novel greatly enriches its cultural critique. By the end, Clarissa reaches for an understanding that goes beyond "the people she knew best," who with the exception of her husband have faded as they have given in to cultural compromise. Through Septimus and the old woman, Clarissa looks at the margins and into the darkness for a new means of preserving life, where culture threatens to define, confine, and kill it.

## T(w)o the Lighthouse

A three-part structure was a major strategy for newness of form in Woolf's next novel, *To the Lighthouse.* The midsection assaults the orders of both language and family with nighttime, wartime, architectural disintegration, babble, dirt, and death. Yet it prepares a place of rewriting and revision in the final section. Although Woolf herself credited Roger Fry with keeping her "on the right path" more than anyone else had with this book, they clearly had different views of its structure. Thinking in linear and symbolic terms (though questioning their appropriateness), Fry wanted to know a "symbolic meaning" for "arriving at the lighthouse." Woolf responded with thoughts about readers and by focusing differently upon "a central line down the middle of the book to hold the design together. I saw that all sorts of feelings would accrue to this (3 *l* 385 and n. 2). She did not want "a" symbol, nor could she direct her attention to the ending. Concepts of right and wrong and singular meaning made the process of reading "hateful" for her. Along with her three-part structure, Woolf sets up a cast of characters who allow us to dig around one another, as was the case with *Jacob's Room* and *Mrs. Dalloway*. Mrs. Ramsay, the most tunneled-about character, is a profound challenge, as she marks an essentialist, maternal origin for the artist Lily and the Ramsay children Cam and James, as well as Woolf, who was obsessed by her mother until she completed the novel ("A Sketch," *MB* 80–81). Mrs. Ramsay has a vision of wholeness that is neither sentimentalized nor maintained by her perceivers, though this has not been true of her humanistic critics. She tries to think of the individual needs of her guests, her children, and her husband, but they cannot all be satisfied. Her exhausting role in the first part would seem to contribute to her death in the second. Nor can she satisfy everyone: Mr. Carmichael would prefer to be left alone. Her daughters have "infidel ideas" (*TTL* 6) and object to her special protection of men. She cannot obviate James's moment of gloom, occasioned by her husband's need to proclaim the facts of the adverse weather, or the premonition that the mood will crystallize in his mind. She cannot retain her youngest children in the present, which is perhaps where only she wants them. Mrs. Ramsay would also like to retain the most complexly realized moment of this novel, when she feels herself "hover like a hawk suspended" over the evening meal. Like Mrs. Dalloway at her party, Mrs. Ramsay works with her dinner to make it finally hum and cohere (104), but the rapture is brief. By admitting inhuman, disintegrative forces to the central portion of her novel, Woolf underscores the fragility of human attempts to order their world, and the necessity of thinking, or painting, or writing things many times over. It is a view of family life and loss shared by Toni Morrison, and taken into a new register with her evocation of African American communities in novels such as *Sula* and *Beloved.*[25]

James makes the most obvious claim for Mrs. Ramsay's attention at the start of the novel. But Woolf matches him with Cam, his nearest sibling in age, offering the contrast in gender that she would pursue again, more fancifully, with Shakespeare's sister in *A Room of One's Own*. The novel starts with a "yes" endowing James with joy. It is the feminine word of affirmation that Joyce had chosen for Molly Bloom in *Ulysses*. Cam's claims for attention are less pronounced, and she is less frequently embraced in criticism.[26] Others express their needs: Mr. Ramsay penetrates with unspoken needs, carrying Mr. Tansley as an appendage. Lily has asked Mrs. Ramsay to pose for a picture. Mrs. Ramsay summons Cam for an errand to the cook, but succeeds only on a second call. Cam is a child of some independence. Like Virginia Stephen in "A Sketch of the Past," she takes interest in flowers and picks some that grow on the bank. But she will not relinquish one to Mr. Bankes, despite the nursemaid's suggestion (21). She streaks by on the lawn, a mysterious projectile to her mother, aimed perhaps at "a vision—of a shell, of a wheelbarrow, of a fairy kingdom on the far side of the hedge; or it might be the glory of speed" (54). All of this is far less tangible than James's culling of commercial images with scissors, or even the crystallizing of his emotions. Having delivered her report in singsong tones, Cam takes an interest in the Grimms' fairytale Mrs. Ramsay is reading to James. She is apparently poised at the door when her mother commands, " 'Come in or go out, Cam,' suspecting that Cam was attracted only by the word 'Flounder' and that in a moment she would fidget and fight with James as usual. Cam shot off. Mrs. Ramsay went on reading, relieved, for she and James shared the same tastes and were comfortable together" (56). Mrs. Ramsay has clearly designed a different relation to her son and daughter, attributing different tastes to them. She infers that Cam is more interested in language than in being together with her mother. While Mrs. Ramsay expects the moment to be crystallized in James's mind, she imagines distortions in Cam's: "The words seemed to be dropped into a well, where, if the waters were clear, they were also so extraordinarily distorting that, even as they descended, one saw them twisting about to make Heaven knows what pattern on the floor of the child's mind" (54–55). If Mrs. Ramsay's metaphor of watery depths is appropriate, we can construct a very different mind from James's. Both a creature of the bottom of the sea and an undirected action, the word "flounder" is appropriate to this watery mind. But clearly there is an undermind—the bed of creativity Woolf frequently refers to. Rachel Vinrace had tended toward this same watery underworld in *The Voyage Out*, sinking back into it rather than fulfill the marriage plot.

At bedtime Mrs. Ramsay mediates the wishes of James and Cam, covering the boar's skull that hangs in the nursery with her own shawl, yet assuring James that it is still there, untouched, as he has bidden. Whatever the real dimensions of the object, Cam had been troubled by "great horns," and had "thought it was a horrid thing, branching at her all over the room" (114). Mrs. Ramsay also considers it "horrid," and regrets having permitted it in the nursery. To calm Cam, she creates a fantasy surface narrative in which the swathed form becomes an enchanted terrain for birds and fairies: "Mrs. Ramsay went on speaking still more monotonously, and more rhythmically and more nonsensically, how she must shut her eyes and go to sleep and dream of mountains and valleys and stars falling and parrots and antelopes and gardens, and everything lovely" (115). She has sensed Cam's powers of imagination, diverting them to the surface for the moment. Yet she leaves her horrors and her mental depths unaddressed, in effect sending her away a second time.[27]

The evening meal, setting of her most exquisite moment, comes to us principally through Mrs. Ramsay's mind, which operates at many different levels: she worries about seating and her husband's behavior; she plans another marriage plot. She becomes increasingly detached toward the conclusion of the scene, even abstracting the words from it, experiencing them as her voice, outside herself. In order to construct the "element of joy" in which she briefly floats, Mrs. Ramsay invokes Platonic concepts, "helping Mr. Bankes to a specially tender piece of eternity." She has a desire to retain unity. The multiple conditions of that moment of the dinner, expressed in a syntax that makes exact referents impossible, "seemed now for no special reason to stay there like a smoke, like a fume rising upwards, holding them safe together . . . there is a coherence in things, a stability; something, she meant, is immune from change, and shines out (she glanced at the window with its ripple of reflected lights) in the face of the flowing, the fleeting, the spectral, like a ruby. . . . Of such moments, she thought, the thing is made that endures" (105). Like Clarissa Dalloway, Mrs. Ramsay makes a metaphorical jewel of the moment. Her apparent achievement is an interconnected community. Implicit is a celebration of the engagement of Paul and Minta, a marriage plot in which Mrs. Ramsay has conspired. Mrs. Ramsay disperses the dinner reluctantly, first allowing her husband to complete his stories, then pausing on the threshold: "She waited a moment longer in a scene which was vanishing even as she looked, and then, as she moved and took Minta's arm and left the room, it changed, it shaped itself differently; it had become, she knew, giving one last look at it over her shoulder, already the past" (111). Mrs. Ramsay thinks in terms of her own freedom of dispersal, which she identifies with the third stroke of the lighthouse; to readers this may suggest her death in the third part of the novel.

Toward the end of the evening, when left briefly to herself, Mrs. Ramsay has a disorderly, soothing experience with words of poetry recalled from the dinner and the words of one of Shelley's sonnets, which she glances at alternately as she continues her knitting project. In the first instance she is sinking deep, thinking of "something I have come to get." The words recalled from dinner "began washing from side to side of her mind rhythmically, and as they washed, words, like little shaded lights, one red, one blue, one yellow, lit up in the dark of her mind, and seemed leaving their perches up there to fly across and across, or to cry out and be echoed" (119). The effect might be compared to the night world of words treated most extensively in Joyce's *Finnegans Wake*. She reads Shelley's lines about "lives . . . full of trees and changing leaves" at random, finding a shelter rather like the one described in the nursery of "A Sketch of the Past": "She felt that she was climbing backwards, upwards, shoving her way up under petals that curved over her, so that she only knew this is white, or this is red. She did not know at first what the words meant at all" (119). Mr. Ramsay resists interrupting her in this state, though she is aware of his presence as he sits reading and enjoying Sir Walter Scott. She goes after and achieves the sonnet whole, and though the fragility of this cohesion is evident in its metaphors, this gives indirect coherence to her day:

> She read, and so reading she was ascending, she felt, on to the top, on to the summit. How satisfying! How restful! All the odds and ends of the day stuck to this magnet; her mind felt swept, felt clean. And then there it was, suddenly entire; she held it in her hands, beautiful and reasonable, clear and complete, the essence sucked out of life and held rounded here—the sonnet. (121)

Lily has her own version of Mrs. Ramsay's triumphant moment at the dinner table. Indeed there are multiple resistances to Mrs. Ramsay's ideal community, with contrary thoughts from Mr. Tansley and Mr. Bankes;

even Mrs. Ramsay senses that the children have some joke of their own to be hoarded for later discussion (109). Lily, seated by Paul Rayley, senses that Mrs. Ramsay had "brought this off—Paul and Minta, one might suppose, were engaged. Mr. Bankes was dining here. She put a spell on them all, by wishing, so simply, so directly" (101), and the spell comes over even Lily, who finds herself "ready to implore a share" in Paul's "glowing, burning" experience, his raptured moment of being in love. Her offer to help find Minta's missing brooch is greeted with indifference: "The odd chuckle he gave, as if he had said, Throw yourself over the cliff if you like, I don't care. He turned on her cheek the heat of love, its horror, its cruelty, its unscrupulosity" (102). Down the table, she reads Minta's "being charming to Mr. Ramsay" as exposure to "these fangs," and Lily is glad to be out of it. She turns her thought to the composition of her painting, assisted by "the salt cellar on the pattern" (102).

In Part III we are left with Lily, Cam, James, and Mr. Ramsay to rewrite Part I. Mrs. Ramsay was right about the moment of his father's denial crystallizing in James's mind. But the shocking incident has given him a first view of the lighthouse that he can summon back as scaffolding when ten years later he is compelled by his father to reach the real lighthouse:

> He could see the white-washed rocks; the tower, stark and straight; he could see that it was barred with black and white; he could see windows in it; he could even see washing spread on the rocks to dry. So that was the Lighthouse, was it?
>
> No, the other was also the Lighthouse. For nothing was simply one thing. The other Lighthouse was true too. It was something hardly to be seen across the bay. In the evening one looked up and saw the eye opening and shutting and the light seemed to reach them in that airy sunny garden where they sat. (186)

"They sat" is also indefinite, allowing it to be either the past experience with his mother or a renewable one with others, in that garden. There is an overwhelming temptation to read the drama in the boat as a fulfilling of the Oedipal scenario. The father, by reading his book, is in possession of the word throughout. He takes his son and daughter on his linear journey, to which both eventually consent. Woolf had begun *To the Lighthouse* not with a mother but with a father figure, an old man sitting in a boat, killing a mackerel (3 D 18–19). The killing is displaced to Macalister's son, who makes the deed more hideous by vivisecting the fish for bait. This is done under the watchful eye of Cam, who has already been associated with the flounder in Part I. She is able to set aside the despotism of father and brother, constructing her own watery composition:

> She was thinking, as the boat sailed on, how her father's anger about the points of the compass, James's obstinacy about the compact, and her own anguish, all had slipped, all had passed, all had streamed away. What then came next? Where were they going? From her hand, ice cold, held deep in the sea, there spurted up a fountain of joy at the change, at the escape, at the adventure (that she should be alive, that she should be there). And the drops falling from this sudden and unthinking fountain of joy fell here and there on the dark, the slumbrous shapes in her mind; shapes of a world not realised but turning in their darkness, catching here and there, a spark of light; Greece, Rome, Constantinople. Small as it was, and shaped something like a leaf stood on its end with the gold-sprinkled waters flowing in and about it, it had, she supposed, a place in the universe—even that little island? (*TTL* 188–89)

Cam tells the story of her own fragile survival, of a mind briefly illuminated in this adventure by the great sources of culture. She also presents a second Mr. Ramsay, seated in the library with his old male cronies in muddled discussion of the newspapers, emerging to ask, "Was there nothing he could give her?" (190). The books were his, but the stories were a mixture—part the great cities, part her mother's fairy tales and rarely explored depths (62), and part a fountain spouted from her own watery depths.

This leaves Lily to have her vision, in revision, of what went before. In Part III Lily is able to tunnel back to unreported events from the era of Part I. One is a genial beach scene with Mrs. Ramsay and Mr. Tansley, mitigating somewhat his previously recorded pronouncement, "Women can't paint; women can't write" (48). In Part III Lily recalls the salt cellar and the "exaltation" of escaping the marriage plot. Serious talk and the enduring friendship of William Bankes, "whom she loved," had become "one of the pleasures of her life" (176). But Mrs. Ramsay's plot to have them marry had failed. Looking out to sea, Lily superimposes the recollected scorching from Paul's cheek in a much more elaborate set of metaphors, bred from years of meditation:

> (Suddenly, as suddenly as a star slides in the sky, a reddish light seemed to burn in her mind, covering Paul Rayley, issuing from

him. It rose like a fire sent up in token of some celebration by savages on a distant beach. She heard the roar and the crackle. The whole sea for miles around ran red and gold. Some winey smell mixed with it and intoxicated her, for she felt again her own headlong desire to throw herself off the cliff and be drowned looking for a pearl brooch on a beach. And the roar and the crackle repelled her with fear and disgust, as if while she saw its splendour and power she saw too how it fed on the treasure of the house, greedily, disgustingly, and she loathed it. . . . ) (175–76)

Mrs. Ramsay had set the "ruby" in opposition to "the flowing, the fleeting, the spectral" qualities of lights reflected in the water out the window. Here we find, in echo, a savage fire that makes the sea run "red and gold" and a treasure consumed. Mrs. Ramsay's house (including guests such as Lily) had fed upon her treasure.

"Treasure" is a much-repeated word in this novel, as it was in *Mrs. Dalloway*. Lily's most erotic moment comes in her expectation of treasure from Mrs. Ramsay in Part I:

Sitting on the floor with her arms round Mrs. Ramsay's knees, close as she could get, smiling to think that Mrs. Ramsay would never know the reason of that pressure, she imagined how in the chambers of the mind and heart of the woman who was, physically, touching her, were stood, like the treasures in the tombs of kings, tablets bearing sacred inscriptions, which if one could spell them out, would teach one everything, but they would never be offered openly, never made public. What art was there, known to love or cunning, by which one pressed through into those secret chambers? What device for becoming, like waters poured into one jar, inextricably the same, one with the object one adored? (50–51)

Lily presses for an art that would achieve orgasmic influx of mind and body.

What Lily understands over time is that "love had a thousand shapes." She has a critical but no longer a cynical distance from marriages as practiced by the Ramsays and the Rayleys. She sees unity and permanence in love as no more than a remote possibility, and largely a fabrication: "There might be lovers whose gift it was to choose out the elements of things and place them together and so, giving them a wholeness not theirs in life, make of some scene, or meeting of people (all now gone and separate), one of those globed compacted things over which thought lingers, and love plays" (192).

Lily's painting is not a globed thing. She is not egotistical like James, Mr. Tansley, and Mr. Ramsay, or retentive like Mrs. Ramsay. It does not matter to her that her painting would be hung in the attics. This "blurred" canvas is not the final product, however. Lily acts "with a sudden intensity, as if she saw clear for a second." The line in the center has been read as a feminist centering of the self, a move into female artistry (Lilienfeld), a detachment from family (Pearce). The simple mark is also a fragment, an element, the end of previous labors, a bold new move in the continual, evasive, exhausting process of life and art. In order to make this stroke, Lily requires an accumulation of moments, and experience in handling them.

## Saturation in *The Waves*

In March 1927, Virginia Woolf set aside early ideas for the images, time scheme, and narrative structure of *The Waves*, explaining, "I feel the need of an escapade after these serious poetic experimental books whose form is always so closely considered. . . . I think this will be great fun to write: & it will rest my head before starting the very serious, mystical poetical work which I want to come next." She even planned to satirize her "own lyrical vein" (3 D 131).

Woolf leaves no evidence of having gone through struggles over the form of *Orlando,* though she did make substantial changes from an original plan involving two poor, solitary women, situated in Constantinople. The formal task was probably simplified by its origin in "a perfectly definite, indeed overmastering impulse" (3 D 203)—one connected with the external factor of her relationship to Vita Sackville-West, as discussed in volume 1. In November 1928, with *Orlando* complete, and fresh from the lectures on "Women and Fiction" that would become *A Room of One's Own,* Woolf was considering more work along the lines of Orlando— "perhaps a history of Newnham or the women's movement" (3 D 203). She was tempted by the "fame" secured from the success of *Orlando* to go on with work people considered "so spontaneous, so natural" (3 D 209).

Woolf's *Orlando* "escapade" has a lot of implications for feminist modernism. *Orlando* and *A Room of One's Own* saw publication before *The Waves.* These two titles and her later work *Three Guineas* have all assumed greater importance than *The Waves* in feminist criticism. In the liberal feminist tradition, these books assess and protest the limitations imposed on women by patriarchy, planning for better cultural arrangements. By the early 1980s, feminist readings of *The Waves* found patterns of regression in Woolf's presentation of women, as was also the case with *Mrs. Dalloway* and *To the Lighthouse*. *The Waves* has been treated as a "representative text of modernism" (*W:H* 13), whereas her most obviously feminist works have not been written into modernism. Still, *The Waves* has never rivaled Joyce's *Ulysses* or Eliot's *The Waste Land* for modernist prominence. It may assume greater importance as we move into a more complex vision of feminist modernism, challenging the traditional readings.

As she returned to her commitment to *The Waves,* Woolf assessed what she had learned by laying off of her "experimental books." She discussed her artistic self in terms of two different veins, impulses, or applications of her "gift." *Orlando* satisfied a "vein [that] is deep in me—at least sparkling, urgent." She listed the benefits expected from *Orlando*: "I want fun. I want fantasy. I want (and this was serious) to give things their caricature value" (3 *D* 203). Despite Woolf's own dualistic use of categories for "spontaneous" and "experimental" works, I think it useful to think about qualities that she brought to *The Waves* from her "escapade." The new category had introduced new forms to match her desires, and confuses Woolf's own binary concept of her gift.

Whereas "serious" is usually reserved for the experimental books, Woolf applies it to "caricature"—implying, perhaps, its usefulness in social satire. Woolf took caricature to *The Waves* through Louis, who can be seen as a mock T. S. Eliot—a topic opened by Doris L. Eder. Louis has elements of Leonard Woolf as well. One way of looking at the lady seen writing between tall windows in Elvedon is as a caricature of caricatures. She sends back the aloof, privileged Bloomsbury image projected on Woolf by the Leavis set, and less negatively by Dorothy Richardson.[28] In further caricature, Desmond MacCarthy and Lytton Strachey lurk, more in the spirit of the *roman à clef,* behind Bernard and Neville (see Eder). I suspect a jab at Ezra Pound and imagism in Neville's poetic theory. Caricature also enters into the presentation of Percival and the set of booming boys who surround him. Bernard, Louis, and Rhoda all caricature themselves. In her 1939–40 memoir "A Sketch of the Past," Woolf evokes older visitors the children had laughed at as caricatures (74). Caricature has become a tool of self-restorative humor in feminist writing. Of the three authors dealt with in this study, Djuna Barnes is probably the most adept at this form, both in drawings and in writing, as shown in the discussion of her *Ladies Almanack* (see volume 1).

Woolf's interest in fantasy, so obvious in *Orlando,* is sustained in the dreamlike excursions of several characters in *The Waves.* Despite huge differences in personality, Rhoda comes closest to Orlando in her fantasy of world travels. Rhoda relinquishes physical supports, whereas Orlando defies constraints of time and sex. Woolf's fantasy narratives contribute to a feminist/modernist genre that is still in the process of detection and definition. In chapter 3 we return to this genre in Rebecca West's *Harriet Hume,* a novel patterned partly on *Orlando.*

Woolf's desire for "fantasy" is related to another important formal experiment in *Orlando*—its travesty of genre. *Orlando* dramatizes the constraints imposed on the spontaneous poet by the favored genres of the literary periods s/he passes through, and the dismissive attitudes of successful writers such as Nick Greene. Its subtitle, *A Biography,* is one of its most provocative and (to Woolf) liberating features, though she once feared it might cost her sales, since bookstores failed to place the book with novels. *Orlando* also brings attention to the women's genre of travel writing, sustained into the twentieth century by its biographical subject, Vita Sackville-West, and also practiced by West and Barnes. Woolf's genre blending continued in the mixture of literary history, autobiography, and fantasy in *A Room of One's Own.*

Genre was a constant consideration in Woolf's formal conception of *The Waves.* She repeatedly discusses a blend of prose, poetry, and "play" (which I take to mean both dramatic forms and textual play). A diary entry from February 1927 is suggestive in its varied list of enactments and its rhythmic play with simple, declarative sentences. She asks herself,

> Why not invent a new kind of play—as for instance
> Woman thinks: . . .
> He does.
> Organ Plays,
> She writes.
> They say:
> She sings:
> Night speaks:
> they miss

Her goal is to get "away from facts: free; yet concentrated; prose yet poetry; a novel & a play" (3 D 128). Woolf's "and" construction breaks from a sense of binary choice to embrace the possibility of intermediate, doubled form. The extreme brevity of her lines is also notable—a move suggestive of fragmentation. As writing on *The Waves* progressed, she used the dramatic term "soliloquy" to describe the emerging discourse of her characters. The "relation of the mind to general ideas and its soliloquy in solitude" had been the function and form Woolf arrived at for a new novel of poetic drama in her essay "The Narrow Bridge of Art," published in August 1927.[29] The essay is largely concerned with adapting genre to the present "atmosphere of doubt and conflict" that fills the mind with "monstrous, hybrid, unmanageable emotions" (219). Though she praised the contemporary lyric, Woolf found a narrowness in its "channel of expression" that was inadequate to her generation or the next (219). This in effect pointed out the inadequacy of much of romantic tradition to contemporary problems. The dramatic poets of her age (including Eliot, whose *Waste Land* is hinted at) did no better, as they drew a curtain around "the thoughts, the visions, the sympathies and antipathies which were actually turning and tumbling in their brains" in order to preserve "the poetic decencies" (221). Thus instead of turning to the experimental poets of her own age, Woolf looked back to the poetic drama and attitude toward life of the Elizabethans—to Shakespeare's ability to make the drama "the perfectly elastic envelope of his thought" (221). Woolf also acknowledges the presence in *The Waves* of autobiography, which exists mainly in her own recycled moments of being. Elegy is an embedded genre, given in characters' reactions to the death of Percival.

Woolf tried to find a way of combining her "spontaneous and natural" *Orlando* orientation with her older experimental vein. One idea was simple alternation—"one relieves the other" (3 D 203)—and this was a survival strategy that she applied not just between "spontaneous" and "experimental" works but also with critical, polemical, and biographical studies, as noted in volume 1. The other strategy was to try to position herself so as to manage a formal "combination of both." She worried that the more recent "qualities were largely the result of ignoring the others. They came of writing exteriorly; & if I dig, must I not lose them?" But she probed another implicit difference between the two sets of work: "What is my position toward the inner and the outer?" (3 D 209).

> The idea has come to me that what I want now to do is to saturate every atom. I mean to eliminate all waste, deadness, superfluity: to give the moment whole; whatever it includes. Say that the moment

is a combination of thought; sensation; the voice of the sea. Waste, deadness come from the inclusion of things that dont belong to the moment; this appalling narrative business of the realist: getting on from lunch to dinner: it is false, unreal, merely conventional. (Ibid.)

As a figure, "saturation" carries fullness, moisture, and freshness from the outside in. Thus it works rather differently from the burgeoning of rapture detected in moments such as Mrs. Dalloway's kiss from Sally Seton. Woolf associates saturation with the method of poets, whose other formal virtue is selectivity. She continues her opposition to the nonselective, linear narrative of realist convention. Woolf's plan to "saturate every atom," relating inside to outside, posed new formal demands. We might say that *The Waves* is saturated with form, as she transformed and layered her previous experiments in *To the Lighthouse* and earlier novels and still remembered the valuable externals captured in the methods of *Orlando*.

Woolf supplies both inside and outside portrayals of character in *The Waves*. As many have noted, Percival is circled round by observers but remains lost at the center, much as Jacob had been in *Jacob's Room*. Though himself an empty cipher, Percival becomes a Rorschach test of other characters' sensibilities and values, a ploy in Woolf's cultural critique of quest and conquest, so central to the Western imperial endeavor that Percival joins. For each of the six speaking characters of *The Waves*, as with Mrs. Dalloway or Mrs. Ramsay, we have both the surrounding impressions of a set of friends and acquaintances and an internal report of the raptures and shocks that become their formative scaffolding of moments of being. Thus Woolf recycles with increased complexity the tunneling method, digging around each character, and as the novel progresses, tunneling back in time to a scaffolding of early moments, whose shock sets the characters' direction and their capacity to cope and create. "Moments of Being" was one of the titles Woolf had written on the title page of her first holograph draft. It is clear that the concept applies very richly to the structures of the novel.

Woolf's principle of selectivity in *The Waves* provides a variety of character types and constellations. She picks up from the variety offered in the Ramsay children, which both Mrs. Ramsay—in her distinct assignments for each child—and Mr. Bankes—in selecting names for them from the kings and queens of England—call attention to. Neville of *The Waves* links the sets of children in the two novels, as he starts the first holograph draft with Jasper's name and his violent tendencies (Jasper, shooting at the rooks; Neville, physically and mentally wielding his knife). The six characters present vastly different traits and combinations of extroversion vs. introversion, thinking vs. feeling, and modes of expression.[30] Woolf pairs her characters on the basis of contrasting, mutually beneficial, or common attitudes: the introverted, judgmental Louis is kissed by the extroverted, perceptually oriented Jinny. This shatters Louis's solitary contemplations of his place on earth, crystallizing one of his scaffolding moments of being. The extroverted Bernard, who uses feeling to make decisions, provides phrases as a diversion to Susan when she is overcome by hate at having observed the kiss. Susan is only mildly introverted, and she shares Bernard's tendency to make decisions on the basis of feeling. Rhoda and Lewis are both introverts; they become lovers and critical conspirators. In a rare dialogue toward the middle of the novel, they judge group values, finding much that is primitive in the rites of their contemporaries. Woolf sets up situations that involve trios of characters—as in the kiss that implicates Louis, Jinny, and Susan, and more remotely Bernard. Thus there is a web of relationships, a holistic view that obscures the supposed hero at their center.

The italic interludes of *The Waves* render poetically a stream of Darwinian and insentient natural forces from the sea and the garden while also recording the day cycle of changing light effects on objects in the house. This formal device also descends from *To the Lighthouse*—specifically its middle part. The interludes are themselves interrupted, and in their cycle run parallel in mood to the human cycle of the characters, who represent and live through a single generation. The interludes of *The Waves* are more atmospheric and deeply rhythmic in effect. Woolf frequently reports listening to Beethoven on the gramophone in her hours of relaxation while working on the book. This was the period of her intimacy with the composer Ethel Smyth, as noted in volume 1. Importantly, she said to Smyth, "The rhythmical is more natural to me than the narrative" (4 L 204).

As in *To the Lighthouse,* the poetic interlude is not just an exercise in modernist aesthetic form. The poetic stream encodes politics.[31] India was a distant political backdrop for *To the Lighthouse* and a more insistent one, as we have seen, in *Mrs. Dalloway.* The politics of empire resonate through the interludes of *The Waves,* and Jane Marcus senses the Indian gayatri in their form. Their images replay ruling-class expectations of mastery and fears of turbaned, armed warriors assaulting their shores. Woolf had humorously rendered periods of history and their effect upon creativity in

*Orlando.* In *The Waves,* she demonstrates that patterns of oppression and dread had sunk deeply into Western consciousness.

There are now a variety of ways to locate *The Waves* outside of the modernist traditions erected by Pound, Eliot, and the New Critics. But feminists who have examined the narrative and the female characters of *The Waves* through numerous versions have been disappointed. Eileen Sypher considers *The Waves* a work of "constricted female possibility" (191). She admires a more aggressive Rhoda present in the early versions, tracing the disappearance of a central female mind with regret. Madeline Moore pursues dual values of mysticism and politics in her analysis. She can situate the solar woman who holds the light of day in the interludes in the mystical tradition of Jane Lead, but she regrets that *The Waves* failed to deliver a model for women's politics and community.

Bernard has not been allowed to rest on androgyny, particularly as that position has become more generally suspect. He has been accused by Sypher and Marcus of co-opting the writing from female figures. His fantasy of a lady writing between tall windows in Elvedon, while served by men who sweep her lawn and frighten the children away, posed further difficulties. Marcus suggests that Bernard preserves British nationalism and class privilege in this representation of English culture "as an aristocratic female figure in a grand country house called Elvedon, leisure for creativity provided by the security of the fixed class position of servants" ("Britannia Rules" 139). Gilbert and Gubar acknowledge the children's anxiety, occasioned by the sweepers. Woolf thereby creates "a paradigmatic ambivalence toward female literary inheritance." But they also read Woolf's image intertextually, as a reversal of Oliphant's ghostly man writing in a library window, and as a response to Beerbohm's negative figure of a woman scribbling in a summer house (1 *No Man's Land* 194).[32]

The constitution of the self is a central enterprise of all the characters in *The Waves.* This sets it at odds with postmodernist accounts of the self, though not with feminists who seek women's self-actualization, or with the traditional modernist trope of the alienated self. Bernard's vision helps Makiko Minow-Pinkney work between the "extremes of feminist realism and modernist schizophrenia" (155). His alternation between assertion of identity and its dissolution is comparable to Kristeva's concept of alternation between identity and loss (158). Minow-Pinkney finds that he steers a middle course toward mastery of the symbolic order in his extensive narrative function in the novel. The importance of the symbolic order gives way to interest in silence and the body postures of the dream in the postmodernist/feminist blend of strategies used by Patricia Laurence. Her analysis makes way for a different assessment of Rhoda's creativity that requires an elaboration of Kristeva. Laurence posits a place between the symbolic and the semiotic. In her estimation, Bernard's extensive role at the end of the novel fulfills Woolf's own sense that she needs "a rope to throw the reader" (173). Her figure is highly compatible with my early conceptual figure of the web in the scaffolding. Though Woolf tends to characterize her own options or abilities in twos, she regularly discovers a third position in language.

Metaphors bear new political weight in the psychobiography of abuse detected by Louise DeSalvo, as in the postimperialist reading of Jane Marcus. The new controversies are not how Woolf stacks up against Joyce in the modernist mode, but how she deals with issues of authority in narrative, the effects of gender on creativity, and the rapture and horror that emerge from attempts at unity in relationships, art forms, and culture. According to Woolf's own account, *The Waves* originated in a state of depression that she related to mysticism. In September 1926, Woolf recorded an "impulse" toward the new novel: "In the midst of my profound gloom, depression, boredom, . . . One sees a fin passing far out" (3 D 113). She was set for a gradual revelation—to "watch & see how the idea at first occurs. I want to trace my process" (ibid.). The vision of a fin in the water was one she would pass on to both Rhoda and Bernard in *The Waves*. Rhoda identifies "life" as a meaning for the fin, which takes different, multiple forms for her. She observes, "With intermittent shocks, sudden as the springs of a tiger, life emerges heaving its dark crest from the sea" (W 64), and she feels doomed to ride it to the extremes of fear. At a time of youthful confidence, Bernard records "Fin in a waste of waters" under "F" in his alphabetical phrase book, for later "use." But late in the novel, he senses no fin in Neville's life. As he yields up his own self, he states in gloom, "No fin breaks the waste of this immeasurable sea" (284).

By June 1927 it was moths, rather than the fin, that began to fill out the scaffolding of Woolf's new work: "Slowly ideas began trickling in; & then suddenly I rhapsodised . . . & told over the story of the Moths. . . . Now the moths will I think fill out the skeleton which I dashed in here: the play-poem idea: the idea of some continuous stream, not solely of human thought, but of the ship, the night &c, all flowing together: intersected by the arrival of the bright moths" (3 D 139). She plans to have a man left rather dim and a woman who "might talk, or think, about the age of the earth: the death of humanity: then moths keep on coming" (139). The moths suggest distant places of the earth.

Nearly two years later, when she resumed work on *The Waves* after the *Orlando* interlude, Woolf was suffering from a lack of impulse and the "pressure of difficulty." Her diary entry of May 29, 1929, is scrambled; all she had written were little sketches that might have no final relevance to a work in which "I am not trying to tell a story." These exercises, which do not seem to have survived, were part of her usual goal of seeking to convey life. "They might be islands of light, islands in the stream that I am trying to convey: life itself going on." She then seems to describe one such island, a lighted room. Here we meet the woman, now designated "She," and the same stream of moths: "The current of moths flying strongly this way. A lamp & a flower pot in the centre. The flower can always be changing." The "mind thinking" in the room will act upon both the moths and the plant (3 *D* 229). Woolf planned that at the climax, "she opens the window & the moth comes in" (ibid.). It is in discussing "She" that Woolf calls *The Moths* "autobiography."

The proposal of a nameless, pronominal thinking mind poses challenges that have a lot to do with existing literary traditions:

> But who is she? I am very anxious that she should have no name. I dont want a Lavinia or a Penelope: I want "She." But that becomes arty, Liberty, greenery yallery somehow: symbolic in loose robes. Of course I can make her think backwards & forwards; I can tell stories. But that's not it. Also I shall do away with the exact place & time. (*w* 229–30)

"She" must not be associated with the traditions of "Penelope" and "Lavinia"—names that have burned like beacons in classical and patriarchal scholarship, to borrow a skeptical phrase from *A Room of One's Own*. Penelope's web has become a modernist and even a feminist trope for nonlinear, unraveling narrative. Joyce's Molly Bloom, as Penelope, reweaves the account of *Ulysses*, but with the controlling hand of a male modernist (see Norris, *Joyce's Web* and my *James Joyce*). Woolf seems to think that any name would bear undesirable associations. Both Brenda Silver and Maria DiBattista have demonstrated the increasing importance of "anon" as a revision of literary tradition, based on former literary relations. "Liberty" represents the cultural liabilities of goddesses co-opted for cultural control, as in the goddesses of proportion and conversion who haunted *Mrs. Dalloway.* The goddess Britannià does rule many characters in *The Waves,* as Jane Marcus has shown, but she serves Woolf's cultural critique, and not the "thinking mind." Woolf's concern about being "arty" and "yallery" distances her from *Yellow Book* decadence as well. Despite Rider Haggard's use of the same pronoun, his *She,* and the female essentialism it implies, would have been equally uncongenial. Thus both names and generalizing pronouns posed liabilities. Woolf takes for granted the capacity both to tell stories and to make this mind think backwards and forwards in the former discovery—her tunneling process.

More unique is the reception of the stream of moths by "She," and her perception of the changing plant. This is conducted in a cyclical set of events. "I shall have the two different currents—the moths flying along; the flower upright in the centre; a perpetual crumbling & renewing of the plant. In its leaves she might see things happen." In working with the plant, "She" does not define a whole system related to herself, as young Virginia had in her moment of being, but she searches in the leaves, as Mrs. Ramsay had searched leaves while reading a sonnet in *To the Lighthouse.* Both Jinny and Susan explore in the leaves, leading to their drama with Louis in the first chapter of the finished novel. Susan is the character most alert to things in nature; she sees a beetle with a leaf and insects in the grass and attaches only single words to them (15–16). She notes that Bernard slips away from her focus in his facility with phrases (16). Louis's fantasy, constructed while he is hidden in the hedge, is also related to the original plant. He imagines himself to be a yew tree: "My hair is made of leaves. I am rooted to the middle of the earth. My body is a stalk. I press the stalk. A drop oozes from the hole at the mouth and slowly, thickly grows larger and larger" (12). While it does produce a burgeoning, self-alleviating ooze, this masturbatory conclusion is typical of Louis's self-centered sources of satisfaction.

Moths at one time had enough importance to Woolf to command the title of her emerging work. Although the moths largely disappear from *The Waves,* they mark a different attitude toward the collection of life which has lasting formal manifestations. Butterflies and moths have flitted metaphorically through many of Woolf's writings, starting with *The Voyage Out.* In *Jacob's Room* butterflies and moths were sought at great distances, netted, and identified by Jacob with exactitude that challenged the experts. This exercise in natural history was shared in by the Stephen children, providing Woolf's entry into the patriarchal discourse of scientific classification. In treasured solitude and difference just before his shattering discovery and kiss, Louis notes the ongoing activity:

> Up here Bernard, Neville, Jinny and Susan (but not Rhoda) skim the flower-beds with their nets. They skim the butterflies from the nodding tops of the flowers. They brush the surface of the world. Their nets are full of fluttering wings. "Louis! Louis! Louis!" they shout. But they cannot see me. I am on the other side of the hedge. There are only little eyeholes among the leaves. Oh, Lord, let them pass. Lord, let them lay their butterflies on a pocket-handkerchief on the gravel. Let them count out their tortoise-shells, their red admirals and cabbage whites. But let me be unseen. . . . I am rooted to the middle of the earth. (12)

Netting is a prominent metaphor for Jinny, who casts her net of light over Louis (13). In later life she uses her scarf, her gaze, and her dancing to draw men in. She makes a metaphorical net of the developing substance of the brain: "Membranes, webs of nerve that lay white and limp, have filled and spread themselves and float round us like filaments, making the air tangible and catching in them far-away sounds unheard before" (135). In maturity Neville sees himself as "immeasurable; a net whose fibres pass imperceptibly beneath the world. . . . It lifts whales—huge leviathans and white jellies, what is amorphous and wandering." His knots have been made and brutally torn apart by love (214). Susan protects babies and fruits in netting, and provides the next generation with butterfly nets. Bernard views a fly caught in a spider's web with confusion, not knowing whether to empathize with the fly or the spider. But Louis takes no pleasure in nets. They serve him as metaphors for disgusting food. Rhoda goes forth to extremes; she does not net them in.

In the holograph draft, "She" waits for the moths rather than hunting them. Woolf uses the figure of moths to describe her own mental readiness for the task of writing *The Waves*. She decides in September 1928 that she will not begin on "the Moths . . . until I am pressed into it by those insects themselves" (3 D 198). In *Jacob's Room*, Jacob uses a lantern to lure moths to their capture in the forest. In *The Voyage Out*, a single moth bumbles among the hotel lamps, and one woman ventures the opinion that it would be kinder to kill it, though no one does. In the plan for *The Moths*, however, there is a visit, not a capture, and no thoughts of killing.

The attracting lamp might be the incandescent mind which becomes saturated in the surrealistic stream.

Both the moths and "She" become dispersed into other forms in the finished novel.[33] The moth remained a subject for meditation and empathy. "The Death of the Moth" (first published in 1942, in a volume that bore its title) uses the daytime visit of a moth in autumn to analyze the massed and indifferent force of death, and the possibility of facing it with dignity.[34] The mind that was disposed to receive the stream of moths in *The Waves*, however, began to receive other visitors. Most notably, barely into the first draft, children tumble into the mind from the waves that labor as their suffering, metaphorical mothers. The first listed title for the draft, *The Moths*, carries a question mark beside it. The first line is "An enormous moth had settled on the bare plaster wall." The crescent mark on its wings "made a mysterious hieroglyph, always dissolving" (w:H 2). Woolf thus registers a secret, fleeting language, brought from the far reaches of the world. Its dissolving purple crescent suggests Muslim Persia, the moon of the youthful goddess, and the color associated with Mrs. Ramsay's deepest thoughts.

It is Rhoda who is most like the moth, which I have used to suggest a new sensibility behind the conception of *The Waves*. Susan, who refers to moths more than any other character in her soliloquies, compares Rhoda's eyes with "those pale flowers to which moths come in the evening" (w 16).[35] Bernard says she is wild, not to be caught. As she bends, frustrated, over her mathematics, Louis thinks "her shoulder blades meet across her back like the wings of a small butterfly . . . her mind lodges in those white circles; it steps through those white loops into emptiness, alone" (22). Like a moth, Rhoda travels most by night, in surrealistic dreams that compare to the experience "She" had with the stream of moths. Early in the first holograph, when lying in bed, Rhoda is able to go among the leaves of rootless trees, and up pagodas (35). In this same early draft, Rhoda looks in a mirror and thinks that she has no face, which is a clinically disturbing sign. But a marginal note suggests that the mirror shows "no frilled moth, of which the actual body was but the chrysalis." The "frill," the wings giving the capacity for flight, and not the body, still resembling the container where dormant worm becomes moth, is what Rhoda seeks. The main text comments of the mirror view: "There was nothing there except the body—no phantoms, no emanation & possibility" (32). Thus Rhoda would seem to have the narrator's sanction for seeing blankness in the image of her face, and possibilities elsewhere.

Throughout the finished novel, Rhoda is sensitive to another winged creature—the bird. Her first perception is of the birds' rhythmic sounds: "cheep, chirp; cheep, chirp; going up and down" (9). She mentions them a second time when, having been startled by a door (as she would be, repeatedly), "off they fly like a fling of seed" (10–11). She regularly stocks her landscapes with birds, noting the dipping of their wings (105).

Of the three female minds rendered in *The Waves*, Rhoda's has elicited the greatest controversy among critics. She comes as a disappointment after the dynamic, articulate figure of Orlando, lending herself better to the psychoanalytic patterns of hysteria and victimization than to liberal feminist celebration. Minow-Pinkney finds her unable to enter symbolic and temporal orders, and personally incapable of maturation (160–62). Rhoda enacts hysteria and self-destruction, failing as a model of productivity in language and worldly progress for women, and sinking into suicide. But I concur with Patricia Laurence that "there is a need to de-pathologize readings of Woolf and to freely observe that the 'disembodied mood' of Rhoda is a narrative exploration of the temporary loss of what we ordinarily refer to as the 'self,' or Woolf 'the egotistical self': this is an exploration of mind and dream space" (Laurence 146).[36] Laurence offers an exciting intertextual consideration of the narrative "suspension" of Rhoda's dream states and Max Ernst's erotic collages of suspended women, "Une Semaine de Sante," based in turn on Jean Martin Charcot's studies of hysterical women. I think that Rhoda is best seen as a formal experiment with unexplored mental capacities, which the discourse of hysteria can serve. But I am fascinated by the presence of other cultural discourses in Rhoda's mental flights. These show the difficulty in moving outside the norms and traditions of symbolic language. Interestingly, both West and Barnes experiment with comparable extremes of feminine mental states— Barnes with "the beast turning human," Robin Vote of *Nightwood*, and West with the ultrafeminine, mind-reading title character of *Harriet Hume*, both encountered later in this volume. West also provides women who understand and confront poltergeists in *The Fountain Overflows*.

Jinny is the only female figure in *The Waves* who has a positive relation to language. The breeding and burgeoning of language within her throat coincides with courtship. "This is rapture; this is relief. The bar at the back of my throat lowers itself. Words crowd and cluster and push forth one on top of another. It does not matter which. They jostle and mount on each other's shoulders. The single and the solitary mate, tumble and become many. . . . Crowding, like a fluttering bird, one sentence crosses the empty space between us. It settles on his lips. . . . The veils drop between us" (104). Unlike the men in the book, Jinny has no thought of controlling or selecting words; she embodies a verbal process that gets the desired external result.

By contrast, in all the versions of *The Waves,* Rhoda experiences difficulty with "hostile and cruel figures" (*w:h* 84) and sequences of words. She works out the threatening nature of school and party situations in terms of placement. She is the outsider, not contained in the mirror like the other girls, or in the mathematical figure whose loop she closes when left behind as the slowest math student. "The world is entire, and I am outside of it, crying, 'O save me, from being blown forever outside the loop of time!' " (*w* 21–22). In the earlier version of this scene the sides of her throat stiffen, and she longs to be back inside her bedroom with its door closed. The door bursting open at a party is like the horror of having a tiger leap upon her: "The door opens and the tiger leaps. . . . I am afraid of the shock of sensation that leaps upon me, because I cannot deal with it as you do—I cannot make one moment merge in the next. To me they are all violent, all separate . . . I have no end in view" (130).

Rhoda finds some ways of overcoming her fears and existing within the loop of the outer world (things met in space, in G. E. Moore's categorization). She acts the parts she sees Jinny and Susan play, hoarding "names and faces . . . like amulets against disaster" (43). She overcomes her lapse of identity, manifested in her fear of crossing a puddle, by gradually pushing her foot across and touching a brick wall with her hand (64). Much later in the novel she emerges from a highly saturated and poetic fantasy of her own dissolution when, "putting my foot to the ground I step gingerly and press my hand against the hard door of a Spanish inn" (206).

In solitude, even as she anticipates the fluid rapture of her dream excursions, Rhoda typically reassures herself of the presence of solid objects before taking flight—a use of scaffolding before the leap that webs new spaces. Rhoda's fantasies are not clear-cut liberations from patriarchy, however. As narratives they often follow familiar patriarchal plots in which she has masculine and godlike powers that she has not been able to assume in life. For example, her first fantasy, enacted with petal boats in the garden, is premised on tales of adventure to the sort of exotic place that became the ground of empire:

I have picked all the fallen petals and made them swim. I have put raindrops in some. I will plant a lighthouse here, a head of Sweet Alice. And I will now rock the brown basin from side to side so that my ships may ride the waves. Some will founder. Some will dash themselves against the cliffs. One sails alone. That is my ship. It sails into icy caverns where the sea-bear barks and stalactites swing green chains. . . . They have scattered, they have foundered, all except my ship which mounts the wave and sweeps before the gale and reaches the islands where the parrots chatter and the creepers . . . (18–19)

Rhoda thinks competitively of reaching a goal first and alone, as godlike and indifferent she creates deadly turbulence. She lapses into the dots of an ellipsis. Rhoda is not unique among Woolf's characters in this sort of fantasy. Her management of the pool was pioneered by Nancy in *To the Lighthouse*. Cam showed a similar penchant for nautical adventure toward the end of that same work, and even Rachel Vinrace stoned the sea in *The Voyage Out*. With her feminine petal, Rhoda performs phallic movements: she mounts waves, penetrates internal spaces, and reaches an exotic goal. Her inventory of the island is elided in the text, and her intentions there are never stated, though an imperial theme asserts itself later when she labels her boats "my Armadas." Similarly, Rachel Vinrace fantasized escape to a feminine colony where she would be a Persian princess, sung to by her women. Although she anticipates replaying this fantasy when at last she is alone in bed, Rhoda dreads losing control, being put in the place of the petals she has sunk, or smashed upon the cliffs. Before she ventures forth, Rhoda must "reassure myself, touching the rail, of something hard. Now I cannot sink; cannot altogether fall through the thin sheet now. . . . Out of me now my mind can pour. I can think of my Armadas" (27). But hard objects do fail her, stretching, as she does, into elongated shapes, and allowing Mrs. Constable to take her by surprise, running out from behind imagined pampas grass, much as Helen springs on Rachel in *The Voyage Out*. Rhoda falls into her aunt's carriage. She is tossed and tumbled in the waves. The chapter ends with people "pursuing, pursuing" (29).

Several of Rhoda's other fantasies are just as treacherous to her and to others. In both the first holograph draft and the final novel, Rhoda is rocked by feelings of love for a girl she never speaks to. She romanticizes the girl's travels from the markings on her luggage. She dreams of leaping high to excite the admiration of "these nameless, these immaculate people." She plays St. Sebastian: In bed at night "I excite their complete wonder. I often die pierced with arrows to win their tears" (44). The playing at St. Sebastian was shared by the young T. S. Eliot, in "The Love Song of St. Sebastian." Eliot asks, "No one ever painted a female Sebastian, did they?" (1 *The Letters of T. S. Eliot* 44–47). Not until Rhoda, whose affinities to Louis, a caricature of Eliot, we have noted. It is also interesting that in the holograph draft, the desired young woman was named Alice, a name synonymous with excursions into the dreams of a young girl, a tumble beneath the world, and beyond the mirror. Alice would provide one of the scaffolding devices for Joyce's *Finnegans Wake,* which is a complementary text to the day world of *The Waves.*

The imperial fantasies suggested in Rhoda's initial voyage in her Armada reappear in many other visions. The hands of the clock in the mathematics classroom become convoys in the desert, and the shorter one (associated with Rhoda herself) stumbles, and will die (21). In dreams listed in the first holograph draft, she masters a hostile tribe and is a hero in the Black Hole of Calcutta (35). In all the versions, she dreams of herself as a veiled and jeweled empress and triumphs over her fear of people: "I am waving my fist at an infuriated mob. 'I am your Empress, people.' My attitude is one of defiance. I am fearless. I conquer" (*w* 56). But she gives this up as a "papery tree," a bit of scenery in danger of falling over (56). We will return to this sense of history as stage set in the next chapter, on Barnes.

Rhoda then turns to reading poetry. From this tradition, she gets a more sustaining fantasy of picking flowers and binding them into a garland. A question that occurs to her produces some suffering, then physical liberation and rapture: To whom should she present them?

> There is some check in the flow of my being; a deep stream presses on some obstacle; it jerks; it tugs; some knot in the centre resists. Oh, this is pain, this is anguish! I faint, I fail. Now my body thaws; I am unsealed, I am incandescent. Now the stream pours in a deep tide fertilising, opening the shut, forcing the tight-folded, flooding free. (57)

The impulse to give is a revolutionary one, opening out of the mind into rapture of the body. In this phase, I associate her thinking more with the mythos of H. D.'s poetry and her posing of a similar question in *The Gift.*[37] The gesture is also reminiscent of primitive religious rites, preceding the concept of gods but affirmative of life, discussed by Woolf's friend Jane

Harrison. Rhoda's question of a recipient remains unanswered at this stage, yet it is a fundamental question that stays with her and other characters.[38]

Rhoda elaborates her concept of this gift in the context of Percival's farewell and death. At the gathering in Percival's honor, just before his departure for India, Louis and Rhoda stand apart, critical outsiders who see primitive gestures in the forgathering of their group. Her participation in this critique is probably a survival of Rhoda's writing "bitterly in prose of the brutality of the rest" in the first holograph draft (*w:h* 32). Rhoda starts the notion with a comparison to "the dancing and the drumming of naked men with assegais." Louis has a more grotesque imagination of savages dancing by firelight, with painted faces, flapping bladders, and bleeding limbs "torn from the living body" (*w* 140). The savage is Louis's subject. Rhoda turns to a more classical scene of a procession worthy of Keats's Grecian urn, and probably derived from her reading of the Romantic canon. As part of the classic ritual, they "deck the beloved with garlands" (140). Rhoda has touched with a tradition that, in honoring Percival, she will sustain. The Greeks also erected columns and statues to honor their heroes, and these join the scenery of her dreams.

Rhoda's question about the gift of her twined garland of flowers traverses the text, approaching but not answering the question of her ending, and concluding the chapter on Percival's death. That Rhoda should commemorate Percival has always strained against my sense of probability, but it may help to see this as another attempt by Rhoda to connect with the loop of the world. She inserts Percival into one of her favorite images of reassurance, the statue against the sky, echoing the imagery of the solar woman: "Now the shadow has fallen and the purple light slants downwards. The figure that was robed in beauty is now clothed in ruin. The figure that stood in the grove where the steep backed hills come down falls in ruin" (159). Not unlike Mrs. Dalloway reacting to Septimus's fall, she sees Percival's fall as a gift.

> Percival by his death, has made me this gift, let me see the thing. There is a square; there is an oblong. The players take the square and place it upon the oblong. They place it very accurately; they make a perfect dwelling place. Very little is left outside. (163)

Rhoda is typically left outside. She is perhaps now able to see the set of booming boys who escorted Percival to the playing field, who constructed a precise and exclusive view of the world that was to be his dwelling place, and now make his grave. But she puts a spiral on top of this image and briefly inhabits the house with other people. Instead of avoiding the public, she flings herself against people, making her way through London streets as never before. She assembles not the classical garland but

> torn up by the roots from the pavement of Oxford Street, my penny bunch, my penny bunch of violets. . . . Now I will relinquish; now I will let loose. Now I will at last free the checked, the jerked back desire to be spent, to be consumed. We will gallop together over desert hills where the swallow dips her wings in dark pools and the pillars stand entire. Into the wave that dashes upon the shore, into the wave that flings its white foam to the uttermost corners of the earth I throw my violets, my offering to Percival. (166)

In her last fantasy of the novel, Rhoda reviews this episode, but says, "I seldom think of Percival now" (205). This is reminiscent of Woolf's seldom thinking of her parents after their exorcism in *To the Lighthouse*. Rhoda no longer resists falling through sheets, now spotted with yellow holes. Instead of being sprung upon by others' faces, a "good woman with a face like a white horse at the end of the bed makes a valedictory movement and turns to go." She makes flowers into a loose sheaf, gives them "Oh, to whom?" and "we" launch into the waves. "I touch nothing." She is shouldered by waves but is lulled, not tormented. "Everything falls in a tremendous shower, dissolving me" (206).

Rhoda is the novel's most gifted character when it comes to conceiving images to match ideas. She is able to look to great geographical distances, to conceive monsters, and to cast shapes as unsubstantial, or monumental, and as defiant of symbolic naming as the productions of the solar woman. In mid-novel, Neville senses the difference of her view: "Let Rhoda speak, . . . Rhoda whom I interrupted when she rocked her petals in a brown basin, asking for the pocket-knife that Bernard had stolen. Love is not a whirlpool to her. . . . She looks far away over our heads, beyond India" (138–39). I associate Neville's whittling of forms with the cutdown quality of imagism as defined by Ezra Pound; Neville's association of love with a whirlpool carries him into the vorticism of Pound and Wyndham Lewis. Neville's mention of India is significant. Others in the group strain for a sense of India on the eve of Percival's departure to it.

Rhoda agrees with Neville's assessment of her longer view. It is remarkable that, despite her silence, she has been understood.

> "Yes, between your shoulders, over your heads, to a landscape," said Rhoda, "to a hollow where the many-backed steep hills come down like birds' wings folded. There, on the short, firm turf, are bushes, dark leaved, and against their darkness I see a shape, white, but not of stone, moving, perhaps alive. But it is not you, it is not you, it is not you; not Percival, Susan, Jinny, Neville or Louis. When the white arm rests upon the knee it is a triangle; now it is upright—a column; now a fountain, falling. It makes no sign, it does not beckon, it does not see us. Behind it roars the sea. It is beyond our reach. Yet there I venture." (139)

She offers a miniature of the shapes, spaces, and rhythms of *The Waves*. There is a dark background, wings and leaves, a light shape rising, first triangle, then column, like the figure of the solar woman. There is the fountain where the group met, and the implication of the drop "falling," one of Bernard's mature images for his experience of life. In denying each of their names, Rhoda creates a rhythm, and behind all "roars the sea."

Louis is Rhoda's conspirator in discussing culture from the outsider's position, and in searching for alternate habitations for himself. His scheme is more time-driven than hers, though it has some of her visual richness—his image of the pyramid might be seen as a correlate to her column by the pool. Louis's disadvantage in language is more a matter of colonial accent than ineptitude, though he is ultrasensitive to his Australian, professional class standing. Louis has command of cases and genders early (20). He knows that he can fix into words the perceptions of the moment: "This I see for a second, and shall try tonight to fix in words, to forge in a ring of steel" (40). Louis's efforts are as much directed toward Percival as are Rhoda's and Bernard's, even though he realizes that Percival will destroy his well-wrought moments: "It is Percival I need; for it is Percival who inspires poetry" (40). Indeed, it was the Percival type who elicited "The Charge of the Light Brigade" (much repeated by Mr. Ramsay) and the flood of World War I soldier poems. Louis cannot be part of Percival's retinue, but he describes it well: "They are always forming into fours and marching in troops with badges on their caps; they salute simultaneously passing the figure of their general. . . . But they also leave butterflies trembling with their wings pinched off." Louis fancies that if he were one of them, he would have a different relation to language: "If I had been with them and won matches and rowed in great races, and galloped all day, how I should thunder out my songs at midnight! In what a torrent the words would rush from my throat" (47). This flow of language from the throat resembles Jinny's word rapture, noted above.

Like T. S. Eliot, Louis looks to earlier eras for a better order, setting himself in relation to great monuments of the past: "I become a figure in the procession, a spoke in the huge wheel that turning, at last erects me, here and now" (35). He begins his long sense of history with "Egypt, in the time of the Pharaohs, when women carried red pitchers to the Nile" (67). He summarizes his efforts with history: "A pyramid has been set on my shoulders. I have tried to do a colossal labour" (201). He also imagines his place "as the last scion of the great houses of France," as an Arab prince, and as a poet in the time of Elizabeth (170). In historical range and noble position, Louis takes us back to some aspects of *Orlando*. It is interesting that Louis sets as his achievement in life "some gigantic amalgamation between the two great discrepancies so hideously apparent to me." He defines these as the "windy and moonlit territories" noted above, as opposed to the "grained oak doors," which would seem to represent reality, defined as either his exploits in the business world (where he is successful) or his immersion in the seamy side of London. What he fails to see as a challenge is the real problems of gender, the flight from Jinny, the relief he felt that at a boys' school there is "no crudity . . . no sudden kisses" (35).

In his acquisition of the symbolic order of language, his need to be with others, his role as public presenter, and his expectations from gender, Bernard is extremely different from Rhoda and Louis. He becomes a focus for consideration of language, as he cultivates his own approach and is witnessed and critiqued by others.[39] Louis has been unmasked as a caricature of T. S. Eliot, and hence he can be taken as one representative of male modernism in the text. Bernard's use of language makes many more contacts with male modernist paradigms, raising the question, To what extent is this self-proclaimed androgynous being free from them?

Bernard's power with words is tested early in his approach with Susan to the woman writing between tall windows in Elvedon. An unsigned "ringed wood with the wall round it," Elvedon evokes the magic of a Celtic fairy circle. Its attractions—"sleeping daws" and "the flop of a giant toad"—are similar to those of the leafy island of Yeats's "The Stolen Child." There is also a common threat to the human child, in Woolf's case posed by the gardeners. Bernard warns that the gardeners would shoot them and nail them "like stoats to the stable door" (17). His story echoes the cautionary tale of Peter Rabbit. Though Farmer MacGregor fails to kill the venturesome Peter, he does hang up the clothing lost in Peter's escape under the garden gate. As the woman writes, the men sweep the lawn—a strange selection of verb, were not the fantasy moment so saturated. In India, untouchables sweep garden paths. Marcus has made subalterns of the sweepers, thus producing a social text of class privilege. The threat permits Bernard to be the man of action, sounding the alarm and instructing Susan in how to escape.[40] Removed to the beechwood, he can make his informed, rhythmic, metaphorical phrase on the wood-pigeon. "That is a wood-pigeon breaking cover in the tops of the beech trees. The pigeon beats the air; the pigeon beats the air with wooden wings" (18). Susan realizes that Bernard has escaped her, rising on his phrases, yet he also tugs at her skirts, needing her for his audience.

Bernard does not reach his lady writing. She is a scaffolding he returns to, saturated with significance. Bernard remarks in his final monolog that he cannot "dislodge" her and seems to classify her with "enemies" (241). It is interesting to me that, in the first draft, Susan's view of the excursion to Elvedon and her interactions with Bernard (then called John) are given. To her the lady was "not the memorable part of the expedition." Their talk of Louis and Jinny, their joining "the great conspiracy of civilized people . . . which is to communicate impressions of life," is more important. The lady is a subject of narration and conversation: "And they saw the lady writing; & her conservatory; & John described it all, even though it was before their eyes; a curious habit, since & also they imagined the ladies life, & her character. & how she was writing to her lover, no; she was too old; to her sailor son who was beyond the sea" (W:H 16). This makes the woman writer also the mother, Betty Flanders, or Mrs. Ramsay, a founding image of writing where love and relationship are at stake. She may also be the female author of the cautionary tale, Beatrix Potter, the Christina Rossetti of "Goblin Market," or Julia Stephen.

Bernard's mastery of language is his passport to a wide range of male fellowship at school. His experience of other writers, and theirs of him, help sketch varieties of male modernist language. Neville is his most incisive critic. Yet he falls under the spell of Bernard's phrases, as do the athletes, who even prefer the experience of his language to cricket: "When he makes his foolish comparisons a lightness comes over one. One floats, too, as if one were that bubble; one is freed; I have escaped, one feels" (*w* 38). Neville has an early sense of betrayal by Bernard, preserved as a moment of being. Bernard not only left their activity of carving to console Susan, but took Neville's knife with him, leaving him unable to carve a stabilizing keel. Neville expects Bernard to construct an imperial story about his knife blades: "The big blade is an emperor; the broken blade a Negro. I hate dangling things, I hate dampish things. I hate wandering and mixing things together" (19).[41] The story of emperor vs. Negro is more appropriate to Neville's division of culture and is not told by Bernard.

Bernard represents laxity and impurity, failing to provide the endings that Neville looks for. Neville decides "there is an order in this world; there are distinctions, there are differences in this world" (21). He is able to master tenses early, and likes the exactitude of the Latin language and the Roman air of the quadrangles at his school. The uncompromising Neville disparages the prosperous plumber or a horse-dealer whom Bernard takes as a subject for writing. Though he tries to rout the common man with his laughter, Neville predicts a narrow end for himself. He will have to retreat to one of the universities, to "run in and out of the skulls of Sophocles Euripides like a maggot, with a high-minded wife, one of those University women (71).

Neville would seem to be the inheritor of the tradition of poets who celebrate their own homoerotic world in Oxbridge colleges. Neville experiences a frenzy of inspiration, but as a perfectionist, he worries that its product is insincere, artificial: "Words and words and words, how they gallop—how they lash their long manes and tails, but for some fault in me I cannot give myself to their backs; I cannot fly with them, scattering women and string bags. There is some flaw in me—some fatal hesitancy, which, if I pass it over, turns to foam and falsity. Yet it is incredible that I should not be a great poet" (83). His sexually loaded equestrian metaphor is a blend of his need to relinquish mastery to words ("give myself to their backs") and a continuing attitude of superiority, now toward women, whom he would heedlessly scatter. The violence of this act continues in Neville's metaphors for his poem, given in love to Bernard. Neville is pessimistic, feeling doomed "to cause disgust," expecting again to be deserted by Bernard: "Take it. The desire which is loaded behind my lips, cold as lead, fell as a bullet, the thing I aim at shop-girls, women, the pretence, the vulgarity of life (because I love it) shoots at you as I throw—catch it—my poem" (88). The cold bullet would both shoot women as targets and fall harmless or impotent, to serve as a homoerotic gift. Bernard gives an apostrophe to Neville's poem in the name of "friendship." But he feels it with the impact of Cupid's arrows: "O friendship, how piercing are your darts."

Bernard works out his own tendencies in contrast to Lewis and Neville: "I cannot sit down to my book, like Louis, with ferocious tenacity. I must open the little trap-door and let out these linked phrases in which I run together whatever happens so that instead of incoherence there is perceived a wandering thread, lightly joining one thing to another" (49). Later he contrasts his incapacity for solitary reflection and lead-cold control with the precision and exactitude of Louis and Neville. It is a comic scene, set in a train, in which Bernard's mind runs helter-skelter summing up his impulses and incapacities. Like Woolf's persona in her essay "Mr Bennett and Mrs Brown," he wishes to catch in writing someone encountered on a train; the person he selects, however, is male and prosperous—no Mrs. Brown. When he says he must "furbish him up and make him concrete," Bernard partakes of the Edwardian materialist school. But Bernard also takes cues from conversation, inventing a name and an appropriate business trip, more in the spirit of Woolf's persona in "Mr Bennett and Mrs Brown." Despite his taste for the concrete, Bernard must admit that "a good phrase" has "an independent existence" (68). He thinks that phrases "require some final refrigeration" but cannot manage this "dabbling always in warm soluble words" (68–69).[42] Lacking the cool perfectionist selectivity of Neville, he will never "find some perfect phrase that fits the moment exactly." He must stop to search for a ticket and, lacking that, negotiate his escape on another phrase (69).

Bernard's inclination to enter other characters is matched by his tendency to put on various styles. This stylistic play brings him into a favorite pastime of modernism, best known perhaps in the writings of James Joyce, but abundantly present in Djuna Barnes's work as well. Like Bernard, Joyce was a teller of other people's tales. Most of the episodes of *Ulysses* take on a different style. Its "Oxen of the Sun" episode parodies a succession of literary styles, from the Romans onward, at the same time exposing the bravado of a group of young male students. Having disposed of various forms of symbolic language, Joyce ends with an appropriation of the feminine style of Molly Bloom, which is itself perhaps only a cultural performance. The young Bernard resembles the young Joyce and his youthful persona Stephen Dedalus in his system of preserving memorable phrases—the keeping of an alphabetical notebook. Many of Joyce's garnered phrases evoked a character, or the atmosphere of a place, as do Bernard's. Joyce's later notebooks, with their encyclopedic lists of foreign-language items and geographical names, used once and marked through, are in a different spirit. The businesslike Louis would be more capable of their systematic application, pedantry, and networking round the globe.

Among Bernard's stylistic ventures is the creation of a biographer to help in his construction of a self. The first function of the biographer is to attribute androgyny to Bernard: "But 'joined to the sensibility of a woman' (I am here quoting my own biographer) 'Bernard possessed the logical sobriety of a man' " (76). Toward the end of the novel Bernard claims to have outlived the biographer. But his memory is sufficient to resurrect a style "to tack together torn bits of stuff, stuff with raw edges . . . phrases laid like Roman roads across the tumult of our lives," admirable "since they compel us to walk in step like civilised people with the slow and measured tread of the policeman though one may be humming any nonsense under ones breath" (259). Bernard moves with little difficulty from his androgynous pose to an affectation of Byron, useful in a letter written to impress a young woman.[43] He later admits to having played characters from Meredith and Dostoyevsky as well (272).

At times Bernard demonstrates a conflict of styles. An example of this is his description of re-entering London at an important juncture in his life, when his marriage proposal has been accepted. His style ranges from the dreamy, distant prospect of one of Hardy's rural heroes, to the deadly violence against nature perpetrated by the futurists:

> "How fair, how strange," said Bernard, "glittering, many-pointed and many-domed London lies before me under mist. Guarded by gasometers, by factory chimneys, she lies sleeping as we approach. She folds the ant-heap to her breast. . . . The early train from the north is hurled at her like a missile. . . . We are about to explode in the flanks of the city like a shell in the side of some ponderous, maternal, majestic animal. She hums and murmurs; she awaits us." (111)

In addition to the extremes of style cited above, I see Wordsworth's unflattering view of London as the "huge fermenting Mass of human-kind" (see *The Prelude*, Book 7), H. G. Wells's fascination with technical improvements in the gasometers, and Ezra Pound's sexual metaphors for the modernist enterprise: "driving any new idea into the great passive vulva of London, a sensation analogous to the male feeling in copulation."[44] Once he must leave the train, however, Bernard is reluctant to part from his community of travelers. But changing again in the stream of London, he is content to be carried along.

When Percival dies a few years later, Bernard has relaxed his will to master words and has begun to yield up the sense that he can present a life as a whole. He holds himself "outside the machine" of the city (158) in the National Gallery. "Arrows of sensation strike from my spine," as they had when the bath water was flowed over his body by his nurse.

> Something lies deeply buried. For one moment I thought to grasp it. But bury it, bury it: let it breed, hidden in the depths of my mind some day to fructify. After a long lifetime, loosely, in a moment of revelation, I may lay hands on it, but now the idea breaks in my hand. Ideas break a thousand times for once that they globe themselves entire. They break; they fall over me "Line and colours they survive. . . . " (157–58)

Bernard continues to provide the phrases needed for public occasions. His is the charge of summarizing himself and the five other characters in his chapter-length final soliloquy. From our knowledge of Rhoda, we can test his competency:

> I went into the Strand, and evoked to serve as opposite to myself the figure of Rhoda always so furtive, always with fear in her eyes, always seeking some pillar in the desert, to find which she had gone; she had killed herself. "Wait," I said, putting my arm in imagination (thus we consort with our friends) through her arm. "Wait until these omnibuses have gone by. . . . These men are your brothers." In persuading her I was also persuading my own soul. For this is not one life; nor do I always know if I am man or woman, Bernard or Neville, Louis, Susan, Jinny or Rhoda—so strange is the contact of one with another. (281)

Bernard is aware of Rhoda's visionary landscape, and her intention to reach it. But his description is sketchy and his syntax unpoetic, compared to her final soliloquies, excerpted above. His impulse to save her is really an effort to save himself, returning to the notion that he can be all the members of the group, even his self-declared opposite, Rhoda. Though he claims not to know his own gender, he reassures her with a masculine reference—her brothers. This is very like using the name of the father; it denies Rhoda her own place in language.

In his final explorations of experience, Bernard in effect follows Rhoda into the waste of waters, experiencing the dissolution of the self. He drops his "book, stuffed with phrases," for a charwoman to dispose of, anticipating a time of dissolution: "when the storm crosses the marsh and sweeps over me where I lie in the ditch unregarded. I need no words." But this is not a lasting dissolution of the self. Toward the very end, Bernard takes charge again. He reseats Percival on a metaphorical horse—a heavenly refurbishment of the flea-bitten donkey that had toppled him to his death. Bernard rides wave words as Neville never could, in defiance of death: "It is death against whom I ride with my spear couched and my hair flying back like a young man's, like Percival's, when he galloped in India. I strike spurs into my horse. Against you I will fling myself, unvanquished and unyielding, O Death!" (297).

Thus Bernard provides a masculine ending to the novel. Woolf's diary account suggests that writing this ending had been a dangerous chase to Woolf, as she associated it with her dead brother. She reports "having reeled across the last ten pages with some moments of such intensity & intoxication that I seemed only to stumble after my own voice, or almost, after some sort of speaker (as when I was mad). I was almost afraid, remembering the voices that used to fly ahead. Anyhow it is done; & I have been sitting these 15 minutes in a state of glory, & calm, thinking of Thoby" (4 D 10). Ironically, Leonard Woolf chose this passage for Virginia Woolf's epitaph, when it deserved to be her brother's. The final italicized sentence, *The waves broke on the shore,* is a reminder of Rhoda dissolved in the waves, and of Woolf in the 1940 diary cited at the beginning of this chapter, where she saw herself as the waves that lay waste to masculine castles in the sand.

## Acts of Sliding between the Raw and the Lyrical

"Between" befits Woolf's creative process for *Between the Acts.* Her diary suggests working time composed of "intervals," taken most notably "in between" the factual labors of the *Roger Fry* biography "when the pressure was the highest" (5 D 340). It was "simply seized, one day, about April [1938], as a dangling thread: no notion what page came next. And then they came. To be written for pleasure" (193). But the "airy world" of the novel bred doubts. Woolf describes herself "in a dazed state, hovering between 2 worlds like a spider's web with nothing to attach the string to" (5 *D* 138). Historically, Woolf wrote between the acts of German air attacks, completing the work on a day when the domestic triumph was the production of a pat of butter—skimmed off in a time of rationing (340). I find in the "between" position commonplaces neglected in history and dramatic art, the passive "other" of action, and the dynamics of rupture.

As she worked, Woolf said, "I think I see a whole somewhere," but wholeness is not arrived at in this final work. Instead various figures of the artist must address themselves to a constant surfacing of cliché. She eventually sums up *Between the Acts* as "a medley" (193) or "a new combination of raw and lyrical" which forced her to find out "how to slide over" (259). Raw content had been separating itself out in recent years, as we know from the "novel-essay" portion pruned from *The Years*, published in 1937, and the self-standing argumentation of *Three Guineas*, published in 1938. She quotes "scraps, orts & fragments" as a useful genre for her diary, taking up a "scrap" description of fighting near Boulogne from a neighbor's gardener. The scraps of the diary become "finger exercises" for the book (290); its shorthand is useful as a new style to mix with others (331). Woolf proposed to write and collect "on the spur of the moment, as now, lots of little poems to go into P. H." (5 *D* 180), as one might store supplies for future use. In another account "PH poetry" is the product of a free and happy mood, possible when a solitary morning at Monk's House follows an interval of visitors and a protracted London air raid. Woolf pronounces these verses "not very good" (5 *D* 313). They are part of the pattern of cliché. But PH poetry gave Woolf pleasure and suited the 1930s text (5 *D* 313).

As noted in volume 1, "Phases of Fiction" was a troublesome work of 1928 for Woolf. In it "consistency" begins to take the place of wholeness as a literary achievement. Consistency, taken as texture, is a useful way of approaching *Between the Acts*. Its most "consistent" texture is this PH poetry. As an imaginative scheme, the collection of poetic bits is comparable to the "tunneling process" of *Mrs. Dalloway* and the soliloquies of *The Waves*. The "airy quality" of the novel was certainly a change from the "poison and excitement" of *Three Guineas* (141). But she argued that the new quality was in keeping with her "outsider" position, since it gave her the freedom not to repeat herself and not to care that it brought the critical pack down on her. Scraps of verse are pervasive in the dialogue, the pageant, and the thoughts of characters in *Between the Acts*. But it is Isa who was assigned the preponderance of "PH Poetry" collected in

Woolf's notebooks; Isa, whose artistry is typically neglected in favor of the flamboyant pageantry of Miss La Trobe.

A restless shifting of positions and a sifting through cultural fragments characterize the text of *Between the Acts,* whether we consider the setting of Pointz Hall, the several generations of characters who inhabit it, or the shifting account of a single day when Miss La Trobe's pageant of English history is performed by local villagers. The family home, Pointz Hall, is evolving architecture; hence the importance of its various wings and terraces is seen in the fact that Woolf's first draft bore subheadings that identify many of its parts. Like the "gigantic house" of *Orlando,* it is refocused and redesigned by each generation. Its chapel is now a larder. The wall of an unfinished wing shelters apricot trees. The "country gentleman's" library now houses shilling shockers deposited by urban visitors, who are habitually hounded by boredom. A century-old guidebook points out the advantageous views afforded at Pointz Hall. We enter monumental time with reference to the Roman road nearby, and the discovery that the ancient barn is a perennial habitation of swallows.

While Isa and Miss La Trobe are clearly the most important crafters of language in the novel, words and images are worked upon by the full array of characters, implicating differences in generation, gender, and social status in our understanding. Servants have their own language and perception. The cook, Mrs. Sands, uses kitchen, not dining room, names. She rechristens the cat Sunny (32) and helps him to Mrs. Oliver's fish fillet. A snatch of conversation picked up from the children's nurses is presented as the opposite of the factual discourse Woolf had challenged in the Edwardian materialists Wells and Bennett. The nurses spoke "not shaping pellets of information or handing ideas from one to another, but rolling words, like sweets on their tongue; which, as they thinned to transparency, gave off pink, green, and sweetness" (10). The sweets they savored concerned the cook, and fashions, and a "feller," who becomes a last "sweet swallowed," as the nurse turns on little toddling George a "sharp" command to "leave off grubbing" (11).

George's "grubbing" is an aesthetic discovery very like Woolf's childhood moment of seeing the flower whole in "A Sketch of the Past," as Mitchell Leaska has noted (*PH* 197):

> The flower blazed between the angles of the roots. Membrane after membrane was torn. It blazed a soft yellow, a lambent light under a film of velvet; it filled the caverns behind the eyes with light. All

that inner darkness became a hall, leaf smelling, earth smelling, of yellow light. And the tree was beyond the flower; the grass, the flower and the tree were entire. Down on his knees grubbing he held the flower complete. (*BA* 11)

George achieves a sense of unity "complete" of the flower in its setting, but also behind the eye, in his mind. This is Woolf's language of rapture, typical of other moments of being, such as Mrs. Dalloway's experience of Sally's kiss. The bodily sensation of burning and the torn membranes, suggestive of painful genital initiation, is followed by the pleasing and alleviating "film of velvet," flow of light, earthy smell, and possession. How different from the genital initiation of "A Sketch of the Past"! Yet in her own experience of the flower made whole and real through words, young Virginia has protection from harm, as well as a thought that is "likely to be useful later" (71–72).

Little George is oblivious to the nurse, but he is terrorized out of his reverie by his grandfather, who springs from behind the tree like an invasive bird, his phallic newspaper "cocked into a snout" (12). The rupture was a "game" to old Oliver. Traditionally, culture offers games for boys as training for masculine success in the world. The choice of instrument is deliberate on Woolf's part. The paper is the property of a fierce patriarch, who reads it to peg down world economics. The narrator tells us further that the newspaper is the book of the current generation, who are otherwise book-shy and gun-shy. They may be book-shy because traditional literature does not help with present violence. An article on rape will strike Isa's eye; its reports of war will preoccupy Giles. The challenge to improve their relationship is dependent upon relating their reading. Woolf relied heavily on the newspaper for factual evidence of male violence in *Three Guineas.* As early as *The Voyage Out,* the newspaper (in the form of the *Times,* read by the residents of a British hotel in Santa Marina) had allowed Woolf to break with traditional writing. Journalism invades the cultural autonomy and serenity of high art, with Woolf no longer maintaining what Andreas Huyssen has termed "the great divide."

His own fantasies contribute to a postcolonial reading of the family patriarch, Bartholomew Oliver, "of the Indian Civil Service, retired" (4). He has a reverie of his youthful self, helmeted and heroic, prepared for anyone who might pounce upon him in the wasteland: "in the sand a hoop of ribs; a bullock maggot-eaten in the sun; and in the shadow of the rock, savages; and in his hand a gun" (17). Bart is also a country gentleman, with ideas about art and literature. The narrator, with light mocking, poses him before his "country gentleman's library." He consults the authority of the dictionary over a question of origins, using the answer to condemn his sister's superstition. Bart was given a copy of Byron by his mother, in this very library, which he can still quote from. He also contributes to "PH Poetry" when verses from Swinburne run through his mind.

> O sister swallow, O sister swallow,
> How can thy heart be full of the spring? (115)

Old Oliver cannot understand his sister Lucy Swithin's joy in God, nor can he use poetry to unlock the sources of his son's misery, but he does attempt this.

However important his library, "the picture" is Oliver's primary art form. After the disastrous incident with his grandson, over the edge of his newspaper blown in the breeze, "he surveyed the landscape—flowing fields, heath and woods. Framed, they became a picture. Had he been a painter, he would have fixed his easel here, where the country, barred by trees, looked like a picture." Rather than transforming the world, Bart as artist selects a view that conforms to the expectations of the picture genre, and fixes himself there. The view is further contained in a frame and in bars made by trees. Even the artistic fantasy is contained. Once the breeze falls, Oliver's newspaper comes back into view, and he resumes reading financial accounts.

Oliver's love of pictures is expressed further in his purchase of "a picture he liked" of "a long lady." This is a more complicated picture, partly because of the way it plays in the novel. The description is made while no one is in the room. "In her yellow robe, leaning, with a pillar to support her, a silver arrow in her hand, and a feather in her hair, she led the eye up, down, from the curve to the straight, through glades of greenery and shades of silver, dun and rose into silence" (36). This silence is opposed to the picture of a "talk-producing" male ancestor, who has given instructions as to what it should contain. The description of the woman's picture lists a series of her accoutrements, which balance hard and soft items, much as Lily Briscoe set feathery and iron elements into her painting. She leads the gaze off into remote obscurity, frustrating language. Oliver's complaint that his race is inarticulate with pictures, as opposed to literature, may relate to this silencing, but he never completes an anecdote about an expert (identified as Roger Fry) who has come to see it. During the luncheon scene, William Dodge is transfixed by the picture, but beyond denying a misidentification of the painter, he says only that he likes it. The narrator composes and repeats several times the poetic phrases: "But she looked over their heads, looking at nothing. She led them down green glades into the heart of silence" (49).

Lucy Swithin, Bart Oliver's younger sister by three years, attracts his teasing jibes, yet he is fascinated by her having a mind so different from his. He muses, "She belonged to the unifiers; he to the separatists" (118).[45] Lucy's gaze is equal to the range offered by the lady of Bart's purchased painting. She is less distressed than her brother by reactions of silence. " 'We haven't the words—we haven't the words,' Mrs. Swithin protested. 'Behind the eyes; not on the lips; that's all' " (55). The comment unites her with little George, gathering his flower behind the eye. In this novel, the unifying vision is restricted to a very old woman and a young child—Lucy and George. This is a change from *Mrs. Dalloway* and *To the Lighthouse*—a condition, perhaps, of living in history during a tumultuous era.

Lucy greets the new day, opening her window (as Mrs. Dalloway opened her door) already having done several hours of reading in H. G. Wells's *Outline of History*. Her interest is really in prehistory, when no channel separated Britain from the Continent and rhododendrons thrived everywhere. In an early draft, William Dodge suggested that Lucy's sense of human sameness through time implies that she does not believe in history (*PH* 399). Lucy still experiences rapturous moments of being, expanding on them in rich though disorganized memory: "She was given to increasing the bounds of the moment by flights into past or future; or sidelong down corridors and alleys" (*BA* 9). Her mother had admonished her for "gaping," much as the nurse admonished George for "grubbing," but in both cases we suspect an active undermind. Lucy makes the proclamation to Miss La Trobe that she "could have played—Cleopatra"—a wild extension of the usual roles assigned to her. To her brother, for example, she remains virginal, despite marriage and two children. A tour of Lucy's imagination during a pause in the pageant reveals that her religion is "one-making." She reaches "a conclusion that *all* is harmony" (175). William and Isa know what she is thinking, as, smiling to each other, they consent that she should have comfort denied to them as moderns. Lucy's sense of faith suggests that the same swallows return from Africa to the great barn each year. Though her faith requires hours of prayer, her eye is readily seduced by light, or the contours of leaves in the lily pond. Her hope that the great carp will appear is satisfied, but what that fish represents is not clear. Lucy sees "ourselves" in the fish. William, who may nurture a theory of incest about Lucy and Bart, theorizes that her brother always rises from the depths of her pool.[46] Lucy does think of the rational explanation of greed for her crumbs that Bart would offer for the coming of the fish. The fish episode is further confused with Lucy's desire to reward the author and actors in the pageant with crumbs of praise. Much of the unity Lucy feels can be reduced to symptoms of confusion, bred by advanced age—an attribute that has won her the nicknames "old flimsy" and "batty" with the servants.

Lucy has a surprisingly negative effect on her nephew Giles. Though she doesn't so much as think a critical word of him during the day, Giles continues to feel mocked by her careless remark, made ten years previously, of "amazement, amusement, at men who spent their lives, buying and selling—ploughs? glass beads was it? or stocks and shares?—to savages who wished most oddly—for were they not beautiful naked?—to dress and live like the English" (47).[47] A weekend visitor, he cultivates a superior attitude. He has "strained" relations with his wife, and is scornful of the local "fogeys" for their immersion in the view and implicit insensitivity to the oncoming war. William Dodge becomes a new target for resentment because of his homosexuality—an affront Giles cannot put in words, but can act out by stamping on the "monstrous inversion" of a snake choked by the toad it has tried to consume. Giles is a hero only to his father, who is equally intolerant of sissies, and the self-styled "child of nature" Mrs. Manresa, who quickly forgets Dodge (who was her guest) when presented to Giles.

Lucy Swithin and William Dodge do much better together. He attributes the private house tour she gives him to her sensing of his trouble and her desire to help. But she reveals her own needs: " 'I felt wound tight here . . . ' She touched her bony forehead upon which a blue vein wriggled like a blue worm" (73). William thinks through a series of troubles related to his homosexuality. Though he never discloses them, William does feel healed by her. What he does say, "I'm William," revives Lucy, who shows "a ravishing girl's smile." William is persistent with his gaze in *Between the Acts*, but only Lucy returns the look. In an early version "their eyes met in the glass. They smiled, cut off from their bodies. They liked each other without waiting for their bodies to confirm it. It would take some time for their bodies to catch up. Perhaps they never would" (PH 305).[48] In the final version, the spell of their mutual truancy is broken when the sun strikes the gold cross Lucy wears. William belongs to a younger generation that distrusts the powers of the symbolic: "How could she weight herself down by that sleek symbol? How stamp herself so volatile, so vagrant, with that image?" (BA 73).

Miss La Trobe, the only openly practicing artist of the group, stands between the generations of elders, Lucy and Bart, and the young adults, William, Giles, and Isa—a notable position in a novel titled *Between the Acts*. As an autonomous, self-assured, productive person, a lesbian, and an outsider, Miss La Trobe has provided a lot of what recent feminists have sought from a female figure of the artist, though she expresses questionable authoritarian attitudes as well. "Outwardly she was swarthy, sturdy and thick set; strode about the fields in a smock frock; sometimes with a cigarette in her mouth; often with a whip in her hand; and used rather strong language—perhaps, then, she wasn't altogether a lady? At any rate, she had a passion for getting things up" (58). Miss La Trobe's identification with Woolf's friend Lilian Baylis (PH 209n), founder and manager of the Old Vic, lends biographical substance to her worldly appeal. Jane Marcus locates the Radclyffe Hall/Una Troubridge relationship, treated in volume 1, in her failed liaison with an actress. Aspects of her past, such as the raising of spaniels, are reminiscent of Vita Sackville-West.

As outsider to the family, and indeed the village, Miss La Trobe exists for them in fragmentary rumors that hint of exotic Russian ancestry and a variety of former occupations. The early typescript suggested that La Trobe had "expunged" her own biography. As in *Orlando* and *The Waves*, Woolf facetiously provides a biographer, whose goddess is truth, to fill in the gaps: a "father, who had fallen and been in prison," a baby at age eighteen "through no fault of her own," an assumed name, proprietorship of a tea shop, and the breeding of prize-winning spaniels (PH 78). In the published novel, there is a telling revelation about her problems in private life: "Since the row with the actress who had shared her bed and her purse the need of drink had grown on her. And the horror and the terror of being alone" (BA 211; see also PH 175). This situation has resonances with Djuna Barnes's *Nightwood*, which shows more extensively the anguish of Nora Flood over her failed lesbian relationship with Robin Vote.

La Trobe's pageant is a work of incongruities, pieced together from both sides of the cultural divide: the performers are villagers, got up as national entities in costumes made from common domestic products such as dish cloths and scouring pads. Poetry, consisting substantially of popular ballads, nursery rhymes, and music-hall songs, is mechanically reproduced by an invisible gramophone, which at times chuffs along wordlessly, like a grim reaper. Natural elements such as cows, swallows, and rain, as well as the village idiot, have access to the action in the open performance space. The program, produced in blurred carbon copies, is supplement, guide, and filler for the pageant, and an important bridge to the audience. Each act features a parodic play within the play, works La Trobe has fused from numerous identifiable Elizabethan, Restoration, and Victorian originals. These materials make us aware of the limited number of plots and themes recycled in the history of literature—the lost prince, the marriage arranged for financial motives, and the white man's burden of authority that governs numerous institutions, from empire to family. All of literary history returns in the modern finale, where the audience itself is incorporated in multiple, fragmented mirrors. Miss La Trobe's final caricature is self-parody—the "megaphonic, anonymous, loud-speaking affirmation," in effect a postmodern voice: "let's talk in words of one syllable, without larding, stuffing or cant. And calmly consider ourselves" (BA 187).

Old Bart Oliver identifies his role as an excuse for not helping set up the pageant: "We are the audience" (59). Throughout her play, no actors are more closely scrutinized by Miss La Trobe than these players of the audience. She runs through various states of mind, ranging from delicate comprehension of Lucy Swithin to a lust for control that flirts with fascism. Lucy violates her brother's taboo of leaving the artist aloof from the crowd. With halting indirection she suggests that Miss La Trobe has given her an enabling self-image—that of playing Cleopatra. Miss La Trobe interprets her unlikely statement as "You've stirred in me my unacted part" (153). This tribute stays in her mind, to be transformed into ever more troubling images:

> "You've twitched the invisible strings," was what the old lady meant; and revealed—of all people—Cleopatra! Glory possessed her. Ah, but she was not merely a twitcher of individual strings; she was one who seethes wandering bodies and floating voices in a cauldron, and makes rise up from its amorphous mass a re-created world. Her moment was on her—her glory. (153)

Thus she goes from a portrait of the artist as a puppeteer to a horrific cook—at first suggestive of a witch at her cauldron, but in her capturing and cooking of wandering beings, she anticipates the death-works of ovens, tended by the Nazis, with their own goal of a re-created world.

La Trobe collects audience reactions from her position behind a tree. Most are less assuring than Lucy. There is an initial "glare as if they were exposed to a frost." The villagers' words fail to reach the audience, and the gramophone at first produces nothing but its chuffing noise. Finally a "pompous popular tune brayed and blared," and Mrs. Manresa, humming and taken in, becomes a part of it, "Queen of the festival" (77–79). Miss La Trobe's attempts to brew emotion are frustrated by the interval imposed by the planners. Having caused the audience to exit the first act on the strains of "Dispersed are we," she takes stock: "Hadn't she, for twenty-five minutes, made them see? A vision imparted was relief from agony . . . for one moment . . . one moment. Then the music petered out on the last word *we*. She heard the breeze rustle in the branches. She saw Giles Oliver with his back to the audience. Also Cobbet of Cobbs Corner. She hadn't made them see. It was another damned failure" (98). When the audience reassembles, she hears scraps of their conversation and gnashes her teeth over her actors' delay: "Every moment the audience slipped the noose; split up into scraps and fragments" (122). In the midst of the second act, she agonizes over losing the emotion she has built. Like history, the wind carries most of the words of a song away, leaving "only a few great names—Babylon, Ninevah, Clytemnestra, Agamemnon, Troy." Just as she is declaring the "death" of her efforts, the "primeval voice" of the cows "took up the burden" and "continued the emotion" so that even she thanks heaven (139–41). A comparable moment of deadly failure of illusion comes just before the present portion of the final act, when Miss La Trobe's "experiment" has been to douche her audience with ten minutes of present-time reality. That failing, a douche of rain suggests the people of the world weeping (180), supplying "the voice that was no one's voice," needed at this point. On the one hand, it seems reassuring that nature supplements art, accomplishing a unified effect in these emergencies. Less reassuring is the susceptibility to the primitive. Woolf had been reading Freud on the herd instinct, appealed to with horrendous effect in the fascist politics of the 1930s. Likewise, "the voice that was no one's voice" may be as menacing as it is mystical.

Brief mention should go to Rev. Streatfield as official interpreter and spokesperson for the audience. His remarks add yet another genre to the pageant—the sermon. Again displaying herd-like compliance, members of the audience fold their hands as if in church. The narrator mocks him mercilessly, beginning by attributing to him a negative attitude toward words: "O Lord, protect and preserve us from words the defilers, from words the impure! What need have we of words to remind us?" (190). His opening words are blown away, as had been many of the words of the villagers, and it is some time before a whole sentence can emerge, let alone take on meaning. His response to "scraps, orts and fragments" is to suggest that "each is part of the whole," and that "we should unite" (192). Lucy Swithin would recall his "We act different parts; but are the same" as appropriate to her unifying spirituality. Streatfield does not have an easy time as a preacher in these circumstances. In the midst of his appeal for money, he is interrupted not by nature but by an apostolic twelve airplanes taking on the flight formation of the wild duck. He also loses his command of words and his sense of how to make an ending. Here he is assisted by the gramophone, with what is probably Miss La Trobe's ironic selection of music, the patriotic unifier "God Save the King."

The pageant is not a clear triumph, and Miss La Trobe hides rather than receive a vote of thanks from Rev. Streatfield. "Glory had been momentary; triumph was in having made a gift. But her last word on her play is 'a failure' " (209). As an afterthought on the play, she has scribbled in the margin "I am the slave of my audience" (211). This qualifies the power of the author, though it does not necessarily overthrow the system that produces authoritarianism.

After the acts, Miss La Trobe gives greater range to what Woolf would term her "undermind," retreating to the unlikely setting of the village pub. Even before her performance, as she surveyed the scene, she had muttered, "It has the makings . . . ," and we were told that "another play always lay behind the play she had just written." The vision that prepares the words for her next play is unaccountably composed of the undisclosed artistic fantasies of a host of characters—a loose gesture toward unity on Woolf's part. It partakes of the pool at Pointz Hall that yields up its fish to Lucy, the savages about to spring from behind the rock in the desert in Bart's reverie, and a beast of burden Isa identifies with. Miss La Trobe sees at first a rock and figures, but no words: "It would be midnight; there would be two figures, half concealed by a rock. The curtain would rise. What would the first words be? The words escaped her" (210). The "two figures" have suggested a new creation myth to some; they may anticipate Giles and Isa, faded into "the night that dwellers in caves had watched from some high place among the rocks," as described in the second ending to the novel (219). Yet, since word generation is at stake, the "figures" could even be figures of language, the speech that must be produced if the world is to move on and mend. When words come, they are preceded by Miss La Trobe's becoming unconscious. She waters words; they spring from the place where they were planted, the primordial mud, and are associated with dumb animals:

> She raised her glass to her lips. And drank. And listened. Words of one syllable sank down into the mud. She drowsed; she nodded. The mud became fertile. Words rose above the intolerably laden dumb oxen plodding through the mud. Words without meaning—wonderful words. (212)[49]

A final fertilizing moment comes in a typical distraction (or inspiration) from nature. The tree outside is suddenly "pelted with starlings," an unsentimentalized event in nature first experienced when La Trobe departed her pageant, declaring it a "failure." The birds then "pelted" the tree "like so many winged stones," a description that echoes the cast seed metaphor and commences their devouring of seeds. They also have a semiotic language; they made the tree "a rhapsody, a quivering cacophony, a whizz and vibrant rapture, branches, leaves, birds syllabling discordantly life, life, life, without measure, without stop devouring the tree. Then up! Then off!" (209). They reappear in the final scene, setting off Miss La Trobe's final vision in words: "She set down her glass. She heard the first words" (212).[50] There is no show of words. We must imagine them. And Miss La Trobe must yield the stage to Isa and Giles for the final scene in Pointz Hall.[51] This turn to the visual, the inarticulate, and the word of one syllable planted in dirt or water is a major change in Miss La Trobe's attitude toward authority.

Though Miss La Trobe is the most obvious artist figure of *Between the Acts*, it is well to remember that the work has two writers and two endings. Isa has been written off too easily in accounts of *Between the Acts*. She is indicted in patterns of child neglect by DeSalvo (199–200), while Mitchell Leaska finds the novel a "long suicide note" for both Isa and Woolf. It is Isa who is assigned the preponderance of the "PH Poetry" so important to the consistency of the novel. The double ending of this work was anticipated in both *Mrs. Dalloway,* with its insane and sane outcomes, and *To the Lighthouse,* with Mrs. Ramsay's death in mid-novel, shifting interest to Lily, whose painting alternates with the family's sailing. It is clear from surviving drafts of *Between the Acts* that it was Isa's second ending, rather than Miss La Trobe's working words from mud, that gave the greater challenge to Woolf. Their double and converging women's art may be her final contribution to late modernism. Isa rarely completes poems, and though she mutters verses, she does not deliberately share them. The possibility that her poetry and other expressive efforts are "abortive" is one of the first opinions expressed in the work. Isa gave up fishing—a metaphor of grasping literary ideas for Woolf—having tangled with Giles's line. Watching Giles land a salmon, she had been landed herself. Now she hides her verses in an account book so that he won't discover them. Indeed, Isa may be just another of Woolf's period studies of how difficult it is for women to be writers. Whereas the late 1920s could produce a promising writer in Mary Carmichael of *A Room of One's Own*, conditions have worsened a decade later, with war again demanding babies of the younger generation of women. Abortive poetry may actually be appropriate, where life is only to be sacrificed. *Jacob's Room* returns as an intertext to this plot. Jacob Flanders begins enraptured by his encounters with life, as does little George. He ends apparently as cannon fodder, leaving his mother to find a use for his empty shoes.[52] Isa is troubled repeatedly by her husband's masculine boots, and the cultural attitudes they represent. Blood on his boots makes Giles childish, not heroic, though he assumes the pose of taking on the world's woes for her. She detests the patent leather pumps of his urban professional class. One of the final images Isa contemplates is a derelict boot upon a shore, companion perhaps of the demolished sand castles which are all that remains of defensive male modernism after Woolf.[53]

Early in the novel, Isa sits at a three-fold mirror, where we get a sense of her postmodern crisis of the self. Isa plays several selves in rapid succession. William Dodge will suggest that she dons a different "dress" for successive encounters with him, her son, and her husband. Isa can conjure up love for Giles through what she identifies as a "cliché conveniently provided by fiction" (14): He is "the father of my children." In a second aspect, she tries imaginatively to place her children on an innocent "green island, hedged about with snowdrops." Her children do claim her. She has sat up with little George during his illness the night before, knows how much he has had for breakfast, and notes that he is lagging behind the nurses, troubling her fantasy of islanded bliss (14). She detects George struggling toward her through the large crowd in the barn, and finds him milk and cake before a nurse interrupts.[54] Thirdly, Isa feels "in love" with a gentleman farmer, and tries to get her sense of their connection into verse. Although Isa performs the domestic functions of Pointz Hall, ordering lunch and supervising its preparation, and plays the role of a genial daughter-in-law with Bart, she mentally bristles at his teasing about George's supposed cowardice. Bart is a "brute" to place her in the double bind of wanting to defend her child while she maintains her loathing for "the domestic, the possessive; the maternal." No feminine essentialist here!

I think that Isa has been dismissed too quickly as a woman writer of her generation. In "The Narrow Bridge of Art," Woolf calls for a new form of novel:

> It will express the feeling and ideas of the character closely and vividly, but from a different angle. It will resemble poetry in this that it will give not only or mainly people's relations to each other and their activities together, as the novel has hitherto done, but it will give the relation of the mind to general ideas and its soliloquy in solitude. . . . We have come to forget that a large and important part of life consists in our emotions toward such things as roses and nightingales, the dawn, the sunset, life, death, and fate. . . . We long sometimes to escape from the incessant, the remorseless analysis of falling into love and falling out of love. . . . We long for some more impersonal relationship. We long for ideas, for dreams, for imaginations, for poetry. (2 CE 225)

Early in the novel Isa seeks poetic expression for her "falling in love" with Rupert Haines, the gentleman farmer in whose "ravaged face she always felt mystery; and in his silence, passion." On the rings of words quoted from Byron, Isa imagines herself and Haines "floated . . . like two swans down stream" (5). But it is a troubled vision, the swans burdened already in her imagination with duckweed, and Mrs. Haines alerted to the emotion between them, and set to destroy it with a bird's beak (6). Byron is the poet of Bart's generation, not Isa's. She struggles with words, metaphors, and rhymes to express the feeling of being "in love" excited by her limited interactions with Haines. His few words "could so attach themselves to a certain spot in her; and thus lie between them like a wire, tingling, tangling, vibrating." She reaches to the technological image of an airplane propeller, spinning so fast that "the flails became one flail and up soared the plane." But Isa loses her momentum over rhyme and turns her attention to ordering fish on the telephone—a poor substitute for catching them fresh herself. Isa fails to come up with verses worthy of recording in her secret book of poetry (15).

In the early typescript, Haines was cast in a Byronic mold, and was rumored to have fathered various children out of wedlock, including Dodge's. Both he and Isa admire Edward Thomas (PH 38), one of the soldier poets who died in World War I. In the final version, Thomas's poem "Old Man" continues to be referred to in Isa's fingering of the plant "old man's beard" (see Leaska's notes, PH 191–93).[55] Under the influence of Elizabethan verses from the pageant, she picks a shred of the plant, which grows "outside the nursery window." Significant to her own art, Isa sees herself "shrivelling the shreds in lieu of words, for no words grow there, nor roses either" (BA 208). The Haines poetry and the fantasy of having a child by him are abortive. But they do not cancel her potential as a poet. From her shreds of leaves may rise words, as from Miss La Trobe's mud, or the ancient syllables of the woman by the station in *Mrs. Dalloway*.

Love is clearly not at stake in Isa's relationship to William Dodge. Her interactions with this uninvited guest are more deliberate and productive in terms of positioning herself as a poet than her longing after Haines. Isa identifies William as "her semblable, her conspirator" (207). Their common facility with recollecting lines of poetry is evident in the discussion after lunch, when Isa supplies some lines for the unexpressive Giles, and William quickly follows suit. Once William speaks of deriving his love of painting from his father, Isa makes a flurried disclosure that her penchant for poetry came from an eccentric and unproductive uncle, a clergyman people thought mad, who made up and recited poems in his garden (51). In the earlier typescript, Isa had imagined of William that "probably he had an old mother. She was devoted to him; he to her" (PH 81), as was the case with E. M. Forster. Leaska compares Dodge's homosexual confessions to ones Hugh Walpole made to Woolf (PH). William observes Isa's habit of murmuring verses, to the point of her discomfiture. At one point, catching her at it, he invokes this strange uncle as he puts her chair back into its proper slot. He is the implicit expert on marginal sexuality. Isa in turn is aware of Giles's suppressed rage over William's homosexuality—a word both of them ban from their vocabulary. Unlike Miss La Trobe, she considers this a subject of art. She attempts verses on a future world beyond judgment "somewhere, this cloud, this crust, this doubt, this dust—She waited for a rhyme, it failed her; but somewhere surely one sun would shine and all without a doubt, would be clear" (BA 61). The product is reminiscent of Blake's poem of difference, "Little Black Boy." As with her Haines verses, she stumbles over rhyme. When the actual sun gets hotter, as they sit watching the view, Isa feels prisoned, and longs for "a beaker of cold water" (66).

William had hoped to tour the greenhouse with Isa because he wanted an aesthetic experience of her in that setting, comparable to his gaze at the woman in Bart's painting. In an early typescript version William also looked forward to talking "as [very clever] people talk in books, [about] the play" (PH 489). But an encounter with Giles diverts these wishes: "the muscular, the hirsute, the virile plunged him into emotions in which the mind had no share. He forgot how she would have looked against vine leaf in a greenhouse. Only at Giles he looked; and looked and looked" (BA 106). But when Isa invites him, William must follow, as earlier he had followed the elderly Lucy. He finds unwittingly that he fulfills some of Isa's needs, just as he had Lucy's. With William as audience, Isa performs dramatic poetry. While she makes the excuse that the play runs in her mind, she is really enacting the more personal drama to her own poetry: "Fly then, follow . . . the dappled herds in the cedar grove, who, sporting, play . . . I pluck the bitter herb." Isa poses before the plants, but she does so much more dramatically than William might have wished, clutching a suicidal knife to her throat and reciting, "And from her bosom's snowy antre drew the gleaming blade" (112–13). This is a rewrite of her previous muttering from Swinburne's Persephone, "To what dark antre of the unvisited earth, or wind-brushed forest, shall we go now?" (51). Acknowledging that this all has been a performance, Isa greets William with an ironic smile.

Their actual conversation in the greenhouse is reported only in a few initial scraps related to their families. In William's mind, however, the interview falls into a pattern of what "always" happens with women such as Isa: "From her tone he knew she guessed, as women always guessed, everything. They knew at once they had nothing to fear, nothing to hope. At first they resented—serving as statues in a greenhouse. Then they liked it. For then they could say—as she did—whatever came into their heads" (114). A young grape leaf hanging above them is repeated as an image: "The future shadowed their present, like the sun coming through the many-veined transparent vine leaf; a criss-cross of lines making no pattern" (114). Or perhaps this passionless unconnected criss-cross was the pattern of their generation's art, of Woolf's experience of Forster, Walpole, and Lytton Strachey, whose first name, Giles, she incorporated into the text. William is wrong about Isa's accommodation, however. She has more important things to do.

I should like to argue that Isa is capable of a new form of writing, reacting to the current crisis of culture, and partaking of mixed genres and diverse levels of culture. Her most important creative work of the day emerges from her glimpse at the newspaper. She sees the account of rape in several phases or reactions—first in fragments that she gives traditional labels: "fantastic," then "romantic," and then "word upon word" as "real":

> The troopers told her the horse had a green tail; but she found it was just an ordinary horse. And they dragged her up to the barrack room where she was thrown upon a bed. Then one of the troopers removed part of her clothing, and she screamed and hit him about the face. . . .

Isa reconstitutes the "real" palimpsestically in her own space: "on the mahogany door panels she saw the Arch in Whitehall; through the Arch the barrack room; in the barrack room the bed, and on the bed the girl was screaming and hitting him about the face, when the door, (for in fact it was a door) opened and in came Mrs. Swithin carrying a hammer" (20). The final element is of course Woolf's textual intervention, making an unexpected comment on the sexuality of Lucy with Bart. The palimpsest remains important to Isa's later artistic conceptions. Isa is prepared to fit Lucy Swithin into the predictable routine that has caught both of the women of this household. Lucy's words "were like the first peal of a chime of bells. As the first peals, you hear the second; as the second peals, you hear the third." But now "the same chime followed the same chime, only this year beneath the chime she heard: 'The girl screamed and hit him about the face with a hammer.' " She can also see the blows as they fall between Lucy and Bart: "He had struck her faith" (23), and "What an angel she was—the old woman! Thus to salute the children; to beat up against those immensities and the old man's irreverences her skinny hands, her laughing eyes!" (24).

The newspaper account also runs under what has apparently become a self-identified poetic fantasy for Isa. Wandering alone during the second interval, Isa picks a flower to "press it so, twixt thumb and finger"—romantic language suitable to being "in love" with Haines, but she drops it when he proves inaccessible. Mimicking Swinburne's Persephone (PH 445), she considers death—wandering down "draughty tunnels" to "some harvestless dim field where no evening lets fall her mantle." But Swinburne is also a poet of the past generation. Isa has a different conception. She stops finally in the stable yard near "the great pear tree," and takes up "the burden that the past laid on me, last little donkey in the long caravanserai crossing the desert." The prospect of the clock striking and the voices of people passing the stable yard complicate the fantasy, insinuating elements of Christ's birth in the stable of the inn, of the last judgment, "the day we are stripped naked," and even Freudian psychology of the herd. She may be able to do something about her burden when the lightning strikes and "the thongs are burst that the dead tied." There are no authorities: "None speaks with a single voice. None with a voice free from the old vibrations. Always I hear corrupt murmurs; the chink of gold and metal" (BA 156)—capitalist corruption of the temple. She bids, "On, little donkey, patiently stumble. Hear not the frantic cries of the leaders who in that they seek to lead desert us." She will hear "the brawl in the barrack room when they stripped her naked; or the cry which in London when I thrust the window open someone cries" (156). In an earlier draft, Woolf did not refer back to the rape in the barrack, but had other cries, in "sirens that blow up the river" (PH 505) from the conflict of commercial vessels, but also suggestive of the noises of war. In ending this sequence, Woolf again makes a palimpsest of Isa's poetic fantasy and present events. Giles and Mrs. Manresa burst from the greenhouse door together, and Isa brings up the end of the caravan, unseen, as she returns to the pageant. When she feels unhappy toward the start of the last act, Isa murmurs upon her donkey lines (BA 156). This time, however, she brushes off William's knowing eye, suffering him no longer. To replace the confusion of voices she experiences between the acts, Isa seems to find a healing voice in the rain that joins the pageant in the final act (181).

Although Miss La Trobe is never aware of her as a member of her audience, Isa has significant reactions to the pageant. Unable to sort out the plot of the Elizabethan segment, Isa questions whether plot matters. "The plot is only there to beget emotion. There were only two emotions: love; and hate. . . . Perhaps Miss La Trobe meant that when she cut this knot in the centre?" (90–91). After this, there is one more event, the coming of "sweet Carinthia" to the prince, "My love! My Lord!" Isa asks, "Who came? . . . The nightingale's song? The pearl in night's black ear? Love embodied." The Procne/Philomela myth, with its hideous blend of love and hate and its recourse to nightingale and sparrow, is richly embedded into *Between the Acts,* and more productively worked than it was in Eliot's *The Waste Land.* " 'It was enough. Enough. Enough,' Isa repeated. All else was verbiage, repetition" (91). Isa is preoccupied with the love/hate emotions she feels for Giles throughout the play. But an anonymous commentator on the end of the Elizabethan play tells us, "Peace was the third emotion. Love. Hate. Peace. Three emotions made the ply 'of human life" (92).

After the play, Isa and Lucy discuss its meaning. Perhaps wanting assurance for her own sense of unity, Lucy asks whether Isa agrees with the minister's summary: "We act different parts but are the same." Isa both agrees and disagrees:

> "Yes, Isa answered. "No," she added. It was Yes, No. Yes, yes, yes, the tide rushed out embracing. No, no, no, it contracted. The old boot appeared on the shingle.
>
> "Orts, scraps and fragments," she quoted what she remembered of the vanishing play. (215)

In these "Yes, No" lines, Isa no longer murmurs received verses, or worries over rhyme. She has taken up a tidal rhythm. The old boot was a figure for Rev. Streatfield as he began his summary of the meaning of the pageant, but it is also Giles's bloody boot—hopefully derelict at last. A few moments later, she sees Giles again, clad down to the shoes in the dress of the professional classes; he is loved as handsome but still hated. In what is probably her thought, we learn, "Love and hate—how they tore her asunder! Surely it was time someone invented a new plot, or that the author came out of the bushes [*sic*]" (215).[56] Isa rebels in one sentence against the antagonistic binary that has torn her, and against the authoritarianism of the pageant of literature she has witnessed. Isa has one more murmur, in response to Lucy's routine remarks, " 'This year, last year, next year, never,' Isa murmured." Her text may be an ending to it all, or a protest that finally changes the authorized love/hate plot. Instead of echoing Byron, Isa has moved into rhythms, without rhyme, suggestive of the revolutionary poetics of Gertrude Stein. Woolf leaves us, as her reading audience, to determine what Giles and Isa spoke.

Webbing, networking, tunneling, caricature, saturation, and mobile, dramatic positioning all contribute to Woolf's formal process, leading to obligations handed on to her audience. Ever cautious that words are fabrications that too often satisfy the individual ego, restricting vision, and eager to have a "whole" sense of the interdependencies, Woolf cultivates diverse but fairly consistent elements in her art. She repeatedly offers a set of characters whose different dispositions and views are comprehended on conscious and unconscious levels. Woolf is interested in ways that minds are shaped both by external cultural norms, susceptible to her critique, and by internal forces of psychology and memory, so elusive as to require inventive fictional strategies for apprehension. These varied, layered views intersect and connect, saturating the reader. Woolf apprehends the reader's mind as a matrix for collecting and patterning experience: "some design that has been traced upon our minds which reading brings to light. Desires, appetites . . . fill it in, scoring now in this direction now in that" ("Phases of Fiction" 93). Individuals have momentary visions of incandescent power, transparent clarity, or wholeness. With her summoning back of the lost woman writer Judith Shakespeare, and demanding her reception by her audience in *A Room of One's Own,* Woolf dramatizes the need to read from and into neglected positions, and to network across literary generations. Postmodern readers and critics can hope not just to capture a fragment of present life, or a written treasure from the past. Having created historic new conditions for art, they can experience rapture in connection, saturation, and re-vision.

# 2 Barnes's Beasts Turning Human

"There was in her every movement a slight drag, as if the past were a web about her, as there is a web of time about a very old building. There is a sensible weight in the air around a thirteenth-century edifice," he said with a touch of pomposity, "that is unlike the light air about a new structure; the new building seems to repulse it, the old to gather it in."

— *Nightwood* 119

I pushed four children from my list and yet
One stayed in the web to pull it down—

— *The Antiphon* 117

It is not difficult to locate the figure of the web in Djuna Barnes's writing. To add to their interest, Barnes's webs are usually inhabited by at least one beast. The web I begin with is a tapestry. Barnes's short story "Smoke" introduces a "poor little rich girl" who "made the mistake of loving tapestries best and nature second best.[1] Somehow she had gotten the two things mixed" (*Smoke and Other Early Stories* 126). Like many of Barnes's aphorisms and figures of speech, this anecdote of mixing nature with craft arrests the reader's progress through the narrative; it reverses our expectations, demanding complex consideration.[2] What we find out can be applied toward an understanding of gender, nature, culture, craft, and representation in several of Barnes's most confusing and compelling works— *Ryder* (published 1928), *Nightwood* (published 1936), and *The Antiphon* (published 1954). Barnes helps us refigure the category of the "primitive" constructed by modern ethnographers and widely dispersed in modernist texts.

To postmoderns, the girl who loved tapestry raises questions about representation. She has a preference for nature as fabricated and deployed by culture. In confronting essentialism, postmoderns have come to question whether we can have nature any other way.[3] The little lover of tapestry encourages other questions. Barnes forces us to think about economic class. The tapestry is on show to the "rich," but paradoxically her privilege makes this consumer "poor." We might inquire further into her idea or experience of nature, that she likes it less than an artifact. Is nature spiritually debasing, or physically threatening? A concern with his mortality in nature led Yeats to pursue the artifact in his Byzantium poems. But for Philomela, her craft was a response to violence, an access to power. Reading as feminists, we might say that the girl who loved tapestry has proven susceptible to a form of art associated with women. Women's needlecraft, from the tapestry of the mythic Philomela to the real artisanal products of our foremothers, was cited in the introduction to volume 1 as a force in feminist theory. Barnes has chosen a self-reflexive metaphor.

"Have you seen the divine unicorn tapestries at the Cluny?" Barnes wrote to Charles Henri Ford (Barnes letter to Ford, 10 Apr. 1934, Texas). She had a liking for tapestries and their extraordinary animal subjects and often took her metaphors from needlecraft and its favored images.[4] These include Barnes's much-used trope of the hunt and common references to flowers, woods, fields of grain, and animals led to ritual slaughter. Many of her stylistic devices are comparable to the rhetoric of needlework—knotty aphorism, raveling machine-sewn chain stitch, parallel filling, repetitive reinforcing, parodic jabs, and ruthless ripping out. Puzzles and secrets, as well as worn maxims, and traditional ecclesiastical emblems are typically stitched into fabric, to be worn or displayed on a wall or cushion. Barnes reported to Natalie Barney a plan to "appropriate your idea of embroidered Sentiment" in the decor of her Paris apartment (Barnes letter to Barney, [10 Sept. 1927], Jacques Doucet). The archaic craft of tapestry matches Barnes's fondness for various period styles of language.

The embroidered nature of beasts, woods, and fields throughout Djuna Barnes's art illuminates the ongoing feminist discussion of binaries and essentialism. We currently struggle about the ways that woman has been essentialized as nature, or in procreative, maternal, and heterosexual functions, even in supposed feminist texts.[5] As noted in the Introduction to volume 1, binary division of nature (construed as feminine) vs. culture (construed as masculine) has been challenged in poststructuralist theory since the 1970s. But this has only slowly crept into Barnes studies. Louis Kannenstine patterned his 1977 study of Barnes upon the concept of duality, offering a list of binaries that includes animal vs. saint (xv) and nature vs. civilization (6). According to this traditional handling of binaries, to occupy a middle state is to be tormented and damned, and hence undesirable.[6] Barnes encourages us to see this territory as a place of discovery. Donna Gerstenberger suggests that *Nightwood* demands, in a way that *The Waste Land* does not, a reading against the dominant text of binary oppositions (130).[7] Barnes's beasts can also enter and revise what Margot Norris has identified as a "biocentric" tradition of modern literature, prepared by Darwin and Nietzsche, and practiced by Kafka, Lawrence, and Hemingway.[8] Eventually, Barnes's work should be placed in some relation to the careful imaging of nature by her friends H. D. and Marianne Moore.

It seems to me that Barnes breaks with binary tradition by calling attention to impositions of culture, including its rules of gender, upon nature. Barnes alerts us to the process of fabrication by dispersing throughout her works tapestries such as the ones cited in "Smoke," and other crafts that take natural images or the hunt as their subject matter. She brings beasts and plants indoors, and she goes to the circus, as young journalist, mature novelist, and finally the aged poet who wrote *Creatures in an Alphabet*. By these means, Barnes suggests that we have always had nature only as fabricated and deployed by culture, and as recorded in the word. She insists further that nature does not stay conveniently separate or "other" from culture, and that evolution has not safely or permanently delivered human beings to civilization. She constructs a blurred middle ground between the bestial and the human, disrupting these categories and the very practice of categorization. This blurring of distinctions between the animal and the human is part of her general tendency to focus on intermediate grounds that lie between accepted, overdetermined categories, and interfere with neat progressions. Similarly, she develops a vast intermediate ground of gender, diversified by racial, homosexual, lesbian, and bisexual identifications, and—as pursued in this chapter—by species and mythic composite animals. In a repeated Barnes plot, we find girls hunted in the field and brought down to earth, to childbed and even death. As the animal gazes at the human, or even turns to a woman in her texts, we escape both otherness and essentialism. Barnes places into question the whole system of male mastery of the physical world, from Hegel through Nietzsche, and opens new visions and enactments of desire.

## Posed, Sketched, and Stitched

Though male modernists should not be lumped together for their treatment of women in relation to nature and culture, they did leave a heritage of woman characters now famous for their primitive, unconscious manifestations of nature: Conrad's "savage and superb" woman of

*Heart of Darkness*, Joyce's bird girl of *A Portrait of the Artist as a Young Man*, or his "huge earth ball" Molly Bloom from *Ulysses* (1 *Letters of James Joyce* 170), and Lawrence's Lady Chatterley, and March of *The Fox*, both brought to phallic satisfaction by a man in control of nature. As Susan Griffin has suggested, women, like exotic birds, and often fetishistically clad in their plumage or in fur, were to be looked upon as "other" by the male hunter/gazer, master, and cultural creator (104). Laura Mulvey has given us the term "fetishistic scopophilia" for this staple of male art (438). As demonstrated in volume 1, Conrad, Joyce, and Lawrence all received gender-related critiques from Woolf, West, and Barnes on this score. Barnes offers another version.

Djuna Barnes was the subject as well as the producer of visual art, as were many of her female contemporaries. Carolyn Burke, in reviewing the New York history of Barnes and Mina Loy, quotes photographer Man Ray's impression of them as "stunning subjects" (68). Burke comments that "female artists could not help seeing themselves as signs or counters within a symbolic system not of their own making" (69). They are arrested in the specular economy of the male gaze, as we have come to understand it in Luce Irigaray's resistance to the symbolic systems outlined by Jacques Lacan. Barnes dressed the part of visual object in a second-hand cape, stylish turbans, and cloche hats set low on the brow. In a 1922 article significantly titled "Against Nature: In Which Everything That Is Young, Inadequate and Tiresome Is Included in the Term Natural," Barnes (using her pen name Lydia Steptoe) offers a self-mocking persona. This character recalls herself in nature at twenty-three, taking a pre-Raphaelite pose: "I was wearing Burne Jones gowns and stretching my throat till it ached" (60). She was well understood only by a cultivator of orchids—a significant mentor. Fungi (plants, such as orchids, living off of rotting vegetation) would continue to fascinate Barnes, perhaps as an intermediate species, in *Ryder* and *Nightwood*. Furthermore, orchids are grown as exotics, for display.

In photographs, Barnes is often captured in profile. Though a fashionable pose requested by photographers, Barnes's typical profiles have suggested a strategy of evasion to both Shari Benstock (234) and Joan Retallack. Retallack describes one youthful portrait: "She turns with wounded equine pride at a ninety-degree angle from the overly inquisitive camera" (46). The photo was taken in 1906, when Barnes was involved in the puzzling correspondence that hints at incest with her paternal grandmother,

Zadel, and a forced marriage. Barnes is averted, downcast, and sad in this photo, which she inscribed "For Mother from Djuna" (see Plate 1). But the evasion is not limited to women. In *Nightwood,* the homosexual storyteller and philosopher of sex Dr. O'Connor sees the profile as the best view of what he considers the "unnatural" third sex, hiding its "conjunction of identical cleaved halves of sexual misgiving" (148). As noted in volume 1, Barnes described "the most characteristic pose of James Joyce" as "that of the head, turned farther away than disgust and not so far as death" ("James Joyce" 293–94).

Animals become subjects in the art and writing of Barnes and women associated with her. Barnes may well have known her grandmother's "The Children's Night," a Christmas verse fantasy published in *Harper's New Monthly Magazine* in 1875, and later included in Zadel Barnes Gustafson's major collection, *Meg: A Pastoral.* As a mother sits sewing by the fire, she sees a succession of primarily female figures from children's stories and Victorian romance, often in the company of animals: Cinderella, Hugo's Cosette from *Les Misérables,* the little doll's dressmaker from Dickens, Bo-peep with her sheep, Beauty and her "old Bruin" beast, the sea maid Undine singing among the reeds, Bonny Kilmeny escorting Alice Learmont, a child saved from changeling status when her mother embraced her in a series of animal forms, and Thackeray's Betsina, who arrives astride a "hungry lion, lean and wild." The beast is calmed by his gaze on Kilmeny. The original *Harper's* version was lavishly illustrated by a leading artist, Edwin Austin Abbey, and his lion resembles one that appeared in Barnes's illustrations for *Ladies Almanack* (see Plates 2 and 3). The story "Children's Night" becomes the mother's gift to her young daughter—an arrangement that anticipates Zadel's mentorship of Djuna, described in volume 1. Zadel took Djuna to the circus.

Thelma Wood—Barnes's lover of the Paris years, to whom *Ryder* is dedicated, and on whom Robin Vote of *Nightwood* is patterned—took images from nature as the subjects for many of her silverpoint etchings. Technically, this art is another form of needlework.[9] Her subjects included deeply cupped flowers, leaves, and a frog encroaching on a ladies' high-button boot, sea creatures relating to one another in various, sometimes threatening ways beneath an antique sailing ship, skeletal apes in trees, a tiger in a jungle setting, and oxen comparable to ones in Barnes's own drawings for *Ryder* (see Plates 4–8).

Barnes uses "Dear Dark Horse" as a salutation in correspondence to

Plate 1. Djuna Barnes, 1906.

Papers of Djuna Barnes, Special Collections,
University of Maryland at College Park Libraries.

Plate 2. Edwin Austin Abbey illustration of "hungry lion."

From Zadel Barnes Gustafson,

"The Children's Night."

Plate 3. Barnes's front illustration, including lion.

From Barnes, *Ladies Almanack.*

Papers of Djuna Barnes, Special Collections,

University of Maryland at College Park Libraries.

Plate 4. Thelma Wood drawing of "Cattle."

Plate 5. Thelma Wood drawing of boot and frog.

Plate 6. Thelma Wood drawing of sea creatures and ship. 1919.

Papers of Djuna Barnes, Special Collections,

University of Maryland at College Park Libraries.

Plate 7. Thelma Wood drawing of apes.

Papers of Saxon Barnes, Special Collections,
University of Maryland at College Park Libraries.

Plate 8. Thelma Wood drawing of tiger.

Papers of Saxon Barnes, Special Collections,
University of Maryland at College Park Libraries.

Natalie Barney. As the steed of the Amazon, this may serve as a lesbian code name. Barney's long-term lover, Romaine Brooks, included a statuette of a dark horse in her 1920 portrait of Barney (see Plate 10 in vol. 1).

Barnes provided sketches for many of her early journalistic articles; simple line portraits accompanied interviews of workers, Eastern European immigrants, the people of Chinatown, and the Greenwich Village crowd. Pen and ink drawings in the manner of Beardsley caught more eccentric human figures. Barnes's sketches of couples dancing and marionettes carried a sense of line and gendered power relations (see plates in Field 47, and Broe, ed. 114). Four of the five drawings of Barnes's 1915 pamphlet, *The Book of Repulsive Women,* present peculiar human forms in relation to nature—a mound of fruit, stars over a hillside, plunging roots, and chickens in the same pose as a stylized walking figure. In the most complicated drawing, I at first mistook disembodied, elongated arms and hands that enter the picture from the right for animal forms (see Plate 9). These limbs also have a phallic quality, penetrating into the picture.[10] The animal and the human merge in Barnes's intricately posed female nude, represented kneeling on one leg with the back leg extended on a fragmentary brick wall, clutching two four-petaled flowers on straggling stems (see Plate 10). The woman/creature's back leg dwindles without achieving a foot, an erect tail rises in a dotted line above her buttocks, and two feathers or ears top her head. Her facial features are masked or made up so that a larger-than-human grimace and a small horn appear. Bizarre makeup of this sort was carried to the extreme by Barnes's friend Elsa, Baroness Von Freytag-Loringhoven.[11] Barnes's female figure is ritualistically oriented toward the side of the picture where the dark background is cut away below by white vertical marks resembling sprouts, and above by a crescent shape. This figure anticipates Robin Vote of *Nightwood,* perceived by a spectator narrator as the "beast turning human" (37), with "temples like those of young beasts cutting horns" (134), as the doctor represents her. She also suggests the lost lover giving a "hyena" smile, one of the lonely Doctor's observations to Robin's deserted lover, Nora Flood (87). This creature is entranced, like Robin when she is engaged in rituals in various chapels, and when she lifted her baby aloft.

Animals regularly appear in relation to humans in Barnes's illustrations for *Ryder,* as they had in her acknowledged source, *L'imagerie populaire,* a 1926 collection of images dating back to the fifteenth century. Barnes's favorite set of images from the French source seem to have been ones that reversed power relations among animals and humans, such that

Plate 9. Barnes drawing of hands.

*The Book of Repulsive Women.*

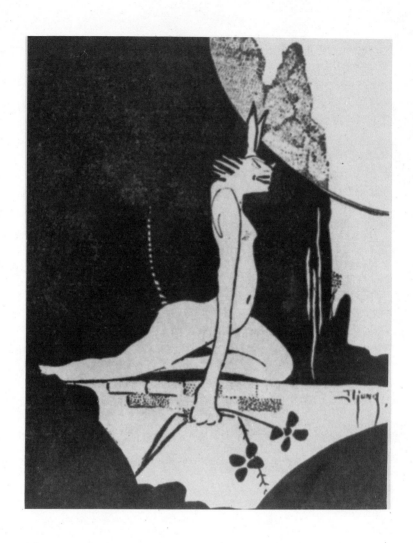

Plate 10. Barnes drawing of female nude.

*The Book of Repulsive Women.*

Plate 11. Animal reversals from *L'imagerie populaire.*

mice chase cats, and animals flog or even butcher humans (see Plate 11).[12] Many of her drawings for *Ryder* were not included in the first edition, falling victim to the publisher's fears that the work would be censored. A great deal was lost by this. Both form and content were violated in their exclusion. They are a subversive part of her intended text, remarkably connecting her modernism to popular culture. Among the fatalities to the censor were Barnes's drawings of a gigantic Pennyfinder the Bull, urinating in the cobbled main street of his home town (R, 1990 ed. 63), and the composite Beast Thingumbob, hunched over the hoofed, many-breasted, nearly faceless woman he loved (see Plate 12). A menagerie of farm animals did survive beneath the family tree that prefaces the work. *Ladies Almanack* abounds in equestrian poses, and an illustration of Wendell posed on his horse precedes the first chapter of *Ryder* (see Plate 13).

Despite many resemblances to popular French imagery, the *Ryder* drawings also have the flat, hatched, stitched-over texture, and in some cases the palette of tapestry or needlework.[13] *Ryder*'s fifty short chapters, in diverse styles, are like samplers, or blocks to be pieced into a quilt, stitched through its numerous layers. As I have suggested in the opening example, needlework as a trope and an activity bears critical messages about the confusions of culture and nature in Barnes. Women of *Ryder* and *The Antiphon* are pacified by the activity, which we have traced back to Zadel Barnes Gustafsen's writing. Augusta, the mother figure in *The Antiphon,* carries a spool for lacemaking—an occupation that kept her "from sulking over worser matters" (126). These included a mother-in-law who knit little things for the Swahili; her husband Titus's first paramour, who cried as she stitched, "We'll sew us out of bondage yet!" (144); and his mistress, who regularly packs a sewing machine. Miranda, the daughter figure of *The Antiphon,* is clad in a richly embroidered theatrical costume. As she enters, she declares, "Here's a rip in nature." In 1939, the family home near Dover in England has sustained the ravages of war—among these a broken wall where another fabrication of nature, a grey baize donkey, is visible. The play also brings a break with domestic fabrications, notably Augusta's toleration of the abusive and incestuous behaviors of Titus, her deceased husband (182). With her daughter Miranda apparently in mind, Augusta says, "I pushed four children from my list and yet / One stayed in the web to pull it down" (117).[14]

For *Ryder,* Barnes provided another illustration not used in the first edition, of two women all too serenely knitting. They sit on either side of a blazing fireplace, their feet upon another female craft, a braided rag

Plate 12. Djuna Barnes illustration

from *Ryder*: Beast Thingumbob.

Papers of Djuna Barnes, Special Collections,

University of Maryland at College Park Libraries.

Plate 13. Djuna Barnes illustration
from *Ryder*: Wendell on horseback.
Papers of Djuna Barnes, Special Collections,
University of Maryland at College Park Libraries.

rug.[15] The illustration is captioned in a red tasseled hanging copied from *L'imagerie populaire*: "Ye olde Wives Tail [*sic*]—or how Wendell was Comforted" (see Plate 14). The women are Amelia and Kate Careless, two wives of the prolific Wendell, who together with their broods of children share the same home. The product of their labors carries phallocentrism to the extreme. They are knitting codpieces for Wendell's busy genitals.

In chapter 8 of *Ryder*, the cultured, talented, and witty sisters Louise play piano duets in a room filled with tokens of male art, "their backs to a goodly collection of Fielding and Smollett, Daudet and Mallarmé, facing two heavy busts of Chopin" (48). One sets to embroidering Biblical scenes, while the other describes the "nature" (meaning the reproductive facility) of the central male figure of the novel, Wendell Ryder. The embroidery of the first Louise textualizes female suffering, though this is humorously undercut with her overspecification of thread. The subjects are "a bulrush, and a Moses, a Hagar, symbolically crying in the wilderness in white, three-ply floss tears" (49).[16]

The tale of the second Louise introduces tapestry as a trope. She briefly constructs a positive vision of female community. Her landscape features "undulating ground, bursting with pea-pod, bean-pod and chicory, melon plant and gourd plant and rutabaga; here the eyes of the potatoes looking forth, and there the deep-banked fires of many a mound of manure, a perfect prostrate tapestry of fecundity." Notable features are the gaze of potatoes and the positive reading of excrement as a fertilizer. In this field six mistresses are "sewing, washing, swelling," and finally engaging in play that becomes distinctly erotic: "hot with leaping heart and pelvis, and fell over upon each other, laughing and limp" (50).[17] However, the "perfect prostrate tapestry of fecundity" and feminine play is violated by Wendell, as he penetrates the fancies of the women. Indeed, he always was potential as an intervention in the narrative, which is premised on his sexual prowess as "nature" and the already existing designation, mistresses.

Figuratively, Wendell takes on aspects of Milton's Satan, or the beasts of Biblical apocalypse: "setting forth from the earth with stupendous great wings, outstripping the cornfields and the mountains, and rising into the clouds, like an enormous and beloved insect, with strong hands upward and arched feet downward, and thundering male parts hung like a terrible anvil, whereon one beats out the resurrection and the death" (50–51). The similes of the second sister Louise undo themselves in well-wrought absurdity, starting with the "enormous and beloved insect," sur-

Plate 14. Djuna Barnes illustration

from *Ryder*: Wives knitting codpieces.

Papers of Djuna Barnes, Special Collections,

University of Maryland at College Park Libraries.

mounting nature like an angel, only to have his genitals exposed. He is perhaps the masculine equivalent of the furies, which appear in an intimate scene of Woolf's *Orlando,* or another version of Dedalus in flight, haunting Joyce's imagination in *A Portrait of the Artist as a Young Man.* The second simile, the "terrible anvil," evokes Blake's alternate creation story in "The Tyger." The offering of "the resurrection and the death" is ominous to Wendell's female audience. Old fertility rites have been replaced by the deadly effects of male penetration. But the hammering on male genitals has absurd and painful implications to the male. Barnes could well be jesting about the masculine hardness, seen as an aesthetic ideal in Poundian modernism.

Barnes also uses stitchery to comment upon sexuality, as altered from a "natural" state. The trapeze artist Fra Mann of *Nightwood* is altered by stitchery, offering a knotty problem for interpretation: "The span of the tightly stitched crotch was so much her own flesh that she was as unsexed as a doll. The needle that had made one the property of the child made the other the property of no man" (13). The doll becomes emotional property between the lesbian lovers Nora Flood and Robin Vote, and the object of commentary by Dr. O'Connor as he takes on the cultural message that homosexuality is unnatural and immature.[18] Fra Mann's tight, self-possessing stitchery is the opposite of the garment of a "chain-stitched" prostitute "ravelling grandly into vice in 'Seen from the "L" ' " (*The Book of Repulsive Women* 95). Cast from the hands of a puritanical mother, the stitch aims at prevention. In "Run Girls Run," a mother attempts to reinforce her daughter's morality by "darning maxims as fast as she could stitch them into the hosen, and thou-shalt-nots in crotch work" of her daughter's clothes.[19]

Nikka the nigger, a carnivalesque character from *Nightwood* "who used to fight the bear in *Cirque de Paris,*" has undergone needlework in the form of tattoos that cover most of his body. Jane Marcus uses the "endless play" of his tattooed text as a figure for Barnes's self-contradictory prose style ("Laughing at Leviticus" 224–25). Dr. O'Connor, who considers the adornment barbarous and depraved, quotes Nikka saying that he "loved beauty and would have it about him" (*NW* 17). There is considerable irony in the content of these tattoos—irony which could be deliberately placed by Nikka, by his employers, by the Doctor as narrator, or at another level of the complex narrative. The text mixes in other reports, and is further complicated by the presence of the masquerading Jew, Felix Volkbein, as O'Connor's audience. Nikka's chest, adorned by "a beautiful caravel in full sail" combined with a small loin cloth "abulge as if with a deep sea catch" (16–17), replicates one of Thelma Wood's silver-point works (see Plate 11). But the ship could be a slave ship, and the bulge emphasizes his sexual being. His penis is rumored by those who have seen it "at a stretch" to be lettered with the name Desdemona. O'Connor's re-action to this plays around racist stereotypes—as did the original Shake-spearean drama. He reports that, despite this apparent sexual prowess, Nikka "couldn't have done a thing (and I know what I am talking about in spite of all that has been said about the black boys) if you had stood him in a gig-mill for a week" (16). Nikka is covered with a semiotics of privilege—the Shakespearean text, lace cuffs, and floral designs from homes of the Rothschilds—wealthy Jews who, like Felix, collect classic artifacts, and could be patrons of the arts. But Nikka possesses none of these things, and (in awful anticipation of the Holocaust) perhaps not even his own skin.[20]

## Perils of Field and Wood

As noted above, the second sister Louise begins her narrative in a fertile and feminine field, only to have it invaded by an apocalyptic male claim, thundered on a phallic anvil. In Barnes the field is often the site for girls' sexual initiation; the wood becomes a place of recovery for women worn from patriarchy. "From Fifth Avenue Up," the first poem in Barnes's *Book of Repulsive Women,* is typically cited for its suggestions of lesbian orgy. A woman is seen

> Sagging down with bulging
>     Hair to sip,
> The dappled damp from some vague
>     Under lip.
> Your soft saliva loosed.

Despite the urban address of its title, the poem is situated in a field, set beneath the stars. It is stated in the conditional mood, as if presenting a potential rather than an actual being. The woman who is to be known "for what you are" emerges from a past worthy of a drawing by Max Ernst. Culture has dealt her the surrealist flight of madness, with legs "half strangled in your lace." As if in reverse to the situation of Robin in *Nightwood,* the woman turns beast, or more specifically, serpent. This beast reacts in mixed fear and defiance:

We'd see your body in the grass
 . . . And hear your short sharp modern
Babylonic cries . . .
We'd feel you
Coil in fear
Leaning across the fertile
Fields to leer. (91)

Barnes borrows from Eden as well as Babylon in this poem, superimposing lesbian orgy and heterosexual innocence, ejection from the garden, and vision of a more fertile field as possibilities.

"Love and the Beast" is a poem Barnes composed in 1924 for Romaine Brooks. It presents a beast with "icy mane," "arctic head," and "wint'ry eye" which is doubly fantastic, being "a phantom's dream." It was born "as the forest tears" and "Marks the shadow come and go / Pacing down mortality / with a last immortal cry." This beast bears above its head a pyre, presumably of lesbian love: "Echoless by same on same / But kind to kind."

Amelia of *Ryder* has a vision of a jungle made fertile by dung, returning to the earth; this natural cycle is interrupted by Wendell's interventions. Amelia notes that, unlike him, dunging needs no recourse to words. Amelia has a special affinity to a dark side of nature found in the wood: "She had a marked partiality for the canker in the family tree. Tramping about in the woods she turned up the leaves for moss and bugs with a high pleasure," but she detested housework (R 38). After fifteen years of confinement by Wendell, she is "well pleased" to ride away on his horse: "She dreamed to such purpose that she rode into a bog, unseeing, where skunk cabbages flourished fitly. She hummed to herself (a bar of the 'Spring Song' as it had been sung in the Conservatory), trampling down the jack-in-the-pulpits, jogging over the green moss, and the grey moss, all under the boughs" (186). The wood, made fertile by decay, experienced in a dreamlike state suggestive of Robin's in *Nightwood* and carelessly traversed, provides brief respite from patriarchal demands.

"Rape and Repining," the fifth chapter of *Ryder*, provides the most memorable text for studying the fate of the young woman in the field. The season is spring. The place is Tittencote, the English village where Wendell's wife Amelia originated. Its name suggests both a small English bird and, if we indulge in slang and puns, the female breast—the tit in coat. Tits, referred to as "pink tops" or PT's, were a standard reference in the erotic correspondence between Djuna and her grandmother Zadel Barnes. "Rape and Repining" opens harmlessly enough in the style of a light, pastoral Elizabethan song:

> What ho! Spring again! Rape again, and the Cock not yet at his Crowing! Fie, alack! 'Tis Rape, yea, Rape it is, and the Hay-shock left a-leaning! Ah, dilly, dilly, dilly. . . . (26)

This song is reminiscent of the lyric sung in Shakespeare's *As You Like It*, "It Was a Lover and His Lass," set in "the green corn field," and "in the spring time, the spring time, the only pretty ring time; When birds do sing, hey ding-a-ding-a-ding" and "lovers love the spring." The stylistic veneer of traditional Elizabethan lyrical elements—"dilly dillys" and the celebration of the emergence of spring—is violated by the horrific word "rape." Rape usurps the position of love amid spring and the traditional "dilly, dillys." In Elizabethan-style verses such as "Bid Adieu" from *Chamber Music*, James Joyce's basic message is that the maiden should "unzone [her] girlish bosom" to love who "has come to woo thee and woo thy girlish ways." Barnes's insertion of rape into traditional lyric invites us to read beneath the decorative surface, detecting a subtext of male opportunism and violation. As Eliot has it in his own revising of Chaucer, April is the cruelest month—but for unexpected reasons.

Repining by acculturated women, however, constitutes the central, major part of the chapter. The textuality thickens with a series of puritanical, legal, and civic assaults on the girl of lost innocence. Parodying various period styles, Barnes accumulates numerous versions of the event, and the reactions of a society of women bound by puritanical traditions and patriarchal law. We move from an Elizabethan song, to a vituperative catalogue worthy of an Irish street vendor, to a survey of all creatures great and small, typical of the eighteenth century. One female voice cites the neglect of themes of female destruction by male "Wits" (36). There is a "Beast of Time" suggestive of the early romantic Blake, or the early modernist Yeats (35). Metaphors of moral tailoring that once served Carlyle now offer girls a " 'No' with 'No' enough [know enough] in the Weave." There are more modern ruptures: "The Bobbin fats with Knotted Thread, and when it comes to sewing, what Garment shall be stitched of it, that shall not rip in Open Places and shame the Leg?" (32).

The moral attitudes expressed in the course of the chapter invite feminist cultural critique. In an early paragraph we have the doctrine of original sin and the forces of law, the church and the rabble literally brought into question as they seek to undo rape:

> Can Hounds track her down to Original Approval: the Law frame her Maidenly again; the not-oft-occurring-particular-Popish dispensation reset her Virginal? Can Conclaves and Hosts, Mob and Rabble, Stone her back into that sweet and lost condition? Nay, nor one Nun going down before the down going Candle, pray her neat. (26)

In a later passage, history repeats the night fears of the individual. Barnes's juxtaposition of flowering and ruins of civilizations resonates with Joyce's repeated use of a motif from Edgar Quinet, of flowers dancing on ruins in *Finnegans Wake*:

> Great things by Little are thus brought to Dust. Fair Rome sees Men come buttoning up her Appian Way, and an Ass brays over Babylon. Strong Nations rise and come to Flower under the Hee of one Emperor, and are brought low under the Haw of the next. And here, in the Heart of excellent small things, a County over which no Blood has been shed, save once in a Slip of History, a Girl has brought the very Rafters and Pinnacles of her House about her Ears, her one Nocturnal Tear bringing down many in the Morning. (R 28–29)[21]

The women gossip and listen to faint sounds carried through the earth. The female figure prone on the earth is a regular trope for Barnes. For this chapter, she supplied an illustration of five women littered on an arid landscape, wearing voluminous and elaborately confining old-fashioned dresses that ignore human contours, their limbs contorted for listening with ears to the ground.[22] The women next assemble as a pack of hunting dogs to track the "deer" girl. In mob mentality, they resemble a fascist military machine, or the Ku Klux Klan, whipped into mass hatred:

> Ear to the Ground, my Gossips! Hear you not a Sound of it, though you touch Dirt a thousand miles from Home? This way, good Wives! Muzzles to Windward! Is there not a Stench of the matter in every Breeze, blow it East, West, North or South? . . . Lift up your Hundred Feet, and let down your Hundred, have you not, at your Beck and Call, twice your Numerical Hate, with which to

make a catch of her and an Example? Now, now! She falls at yonder Ditch, and, like a Deer, turns face on, weeping for clemency. Now have at her! (29–30)

Their physical punishment, fishy and filthy epithets, and interrogation of the overtaken girl take on prurient, sadistic tones. She is belabored for details and suspected of failure to resist.

> Box her Ears, the Dirty Wanton!—and was it coming over the Stile, or was it this side of the Fence or the other? How went he about it? Did he lie to you, Frowsy Smelt? . . . Were you easily bedabbled, or came you reluctant to the Filthing? Backward looking, or leaping at the Bait? Leaping it was, I warrant me, and I'll give my Neighbour here my second Best rolling Pin, an I'm not in the Right of it! (30)

The second-best rolling pin is reminiscent of Ann Hathaway's punitive second-best bed, a piece of evidence that preoccupies Joyce's Stephen Dedalus in a critical performance that makes much of the impact of cuckoldry on Shakespeare ("Scylla and Charybdis," *Ulysses*). The language is playful. Lie is a sexual pun. It is used earlier in the novel for Sophia, Wendell's mother, who learned to "lie" as a girl when she herself was laid by an opportunistic Latin teacher. There is a double concept of "right," the value-laden coinage for coitus, "filthing." Pubic hair rises like the fur on the back of a combative dog, registering public indignation over future liabilities of the expected child: " 'Tis such who Poison Wells, and make the Hackle rise on every Pubic Inch" (31). Women are the most avid fault-finders in *Ryder*, though they may call upon men to enforce the cultural norms that Wendell violates, such as compulsory school attendance and monogamy. The raped maiden has committed cultural sins against value and time, as realized in female domestic labor: "Time made stout by Good Wives stitching, and washing, baking and praying" (33).

There are additional speculations on the dangers of a dazed or somnolent state in women:

> Or were you, Little Cabbage, in a State of Coma, wherein a Man may step, the Beggar, and find you all he would, though nowhere Yourself! 'Tis a Pox of a Pity that a Woman's Wits may be as scattered as Chaff, yet her Chastity well enough in one Place to bring her to Damnation! (30)

Somnolent and entranced states may provide peace for Robin Vote of *Nightwood,* but they also make her vulnerable to lovers who claim her to consciousness and culture. Barnes continued reworking the rape text for *Nightwood,* though it disappeared in the enormous cuts made to secure publication through Eliot at Faber and Faber. The drafts contain the speculation "Culled she a plover's egg . . . did she unthinking come a thought nearer God and the mystery of his manner, or was it in ignorance (the very fountain of trouble) that she reaped eye sockets of late tears" ("Run Girls Run").[23]

The theme of rape received unusual treatment for its day in Barnes's chapter from *Ryder.* Barnes encourages an awareness of acquaintance rape. The rapist seems to be a fourteen-year old country bumpkin, met in a haystack or the ditch of a field, an event to "make some Pimpish Fellow a Braggart and a Nuisance" (31). The most shocking finding in Barnes's rape chapter is that, though there is an excess of verbiage to protect church, family, and economy, consolation of the girl is lacking. The victim of rape, especially acquaintance rape, is frequently on trial, as Barnes makes clear.

In Joyce's *Finnegans Wake,* the setting for ALP's first sexual encounter is slightly reminiscent of the fields of sexual experience in Barnes—"barley fields and penny lotts at Humphrey's ford of hurdles town" (203.06). But unlike the female figures of *Ryder,* ALP has few regrets. This is a part of her happy youth, as opposed to the lamentable time when she faces the fall and presumed death of her husband, HCE. Her rape in nature becomes a "happy fault" (292.34). It is worth noting that paternal incest is a concern of both Joyce and Barnes. HCE's complex sexual guilt may spring from desire for his daughter. The victim in Barnes's "Run Girls Run" gives the following account: "A Breeze flung up my kirtle and browsed at my thigh, a gale drenched my withers, ah me. A storm is a story, yet it appears a tempest's a father? They say it is good for the barley, but what of me!" Paternal rape, sketched in barnyard terms, would take on great force in drafts for the second act of Barnes's *Antiphon.* Although critics have wanted to compare Barnes's works to Eliot's *The Waste Land,* the comparison falls down with the landscape, which unlike the dry red rocks of Eliot's scenes remains fertile and productive, though at considerable cost to the young female.

The final voice of matronly female repining in "Rape and Repining" suggests a more constructive future course for the survivor of rape. Lying in a field of exile, the maiden must repair herself through her own wits and a cultivated sense of women's reasoning.

> So lay about you, so scratch, slap, pinch, pull, that you turn to Honest Flesh. Thus to come to the very Pip and Core of Truth, through Good Woman's reasoning—though to that Faculty no Credence has been given by Philosopher or Scribe adown the very ageless ages—to make of a Point no Point at all on which to haggle. . . .
> And I myself ask no Better Portion than that you fall to me, for then should all Eyes behold the Bone of Truth, the Marrow of Justice! For I'd have all Destruction in you well destroyed before the Striking of another Midnight Bell! (R 36)

An experienced woman here reconstitutes a damaged young one with bone and marrow of her self. The going down to the human core is reminiscent of Yeats's "rag and bone shop of the heart" ("The Circus Animals' Desertion"). As noted earlier, bowing down is a favorite gesture of recovery for Barnes. In this case, the action suggests the scratching and pecking of a hen scavenging for grain, or a radical encounter with the very frame of the female body in the purging rituals of mysticism, or even witchcraft. "Good woman's reasoning" is shown throughout the chapter to be flawed by cultural notions of "good," but still potentially distinct in process and content from male reasoning. Woman defines and resists her place in society and also in the cycles of nature. Rape is gone from the final Elizabethan song. The maiden is addressed in a mildly affectionate phrase, "O Little One," and there are signs of emerging growth: "The Earth divides, and the Leaves put forth, and the Heart sings dilly, dilly, dilly!" We close with a tough philosophy of coping with difference that, unlike Joyce's typical feminine codas, avoids sentimentality, and aims at an end to destruction. "It is Girls' Weather, and Boys' Luck!" Barnes finds that girls are trapped in a rapacious sequence of nature. They need not accept guilt, and in bowing down to earth, they may find a reason of their own.

This rape scenario merits comparison to Victorian accounts of temptations, such as the brookside lure of Christina Rossetti's "Goblin Market," in which the Christian sacrifice of Lizzy redeems the folly of her more curious sister, Laura, reclaiming them both for marriage and maternity. Barnes had a model closer to home. In "Meg: A Pastoral," published in 1979 by Zadel Barnes, a maiden preserves her virtue for a worthy lover, John, who is serving as a Union soldier. John has demonstrated compassion, both for his mother in childhood and for his rival, Hugh, in war. Hugh had come to Meg bearing the gift of a willow wand, destructively taken from a bird's nest, and demanding a sprig of her jasmine in return. Later, when he tried to touch her in the garden, she evaded him. Hearing of this resistance, Meg's father is sure "his darling is pure and true / No vision of scythe and ripe-bending grain!" Like John, he is moved by "mothers, lovingest martyrs of earth," who "sink into swift sleep betwixt pangs of birth" (26). Meg is eventually united with the war-wounded John, and is last seen crossing the field with him, spared of a faithless lover by her virtue. Barnes had complicated materials for appropriation and parody in this grandmotherly text. The field was consistently the scene of feminine initiation. Unlike the yielding maiden of "Rape and Repining," the prudent Meg retains her family's approval, and presumably that of the *Harper's* audience. The idealization of maternal sacrifice by lover and father and the importance of the father-daughter bond anticipate values of Wendell Wald, the son to whom Sophia/Zadel was lastingly bonded.

Robin Vote begins *Nightwood* lying in a Gauguin-like jungle of her own making, and concludes it in the wood.[24] But both positionings are knotted in narrative. Robin's entry into the text comes in a series of narrative representations—the "night beast" of one rejected book title, "La Somnambule" of the chapter title, she has "fainted" according to a hotel employee, whose designation as a "chasseur" evokes the hunt. It is an anonymous but far from culturally neutral narrator who notes that Robin is surrounded by "a confusion of potted plants, exotic palms, and cut flowers, faintly over-sung by the notes of unseen birds," which are not silenced by the "good housewife's cover." The narrator also compares her exhalations to fungi, and her flesh to plant life (34). An allusion to the paintings of Rousseau and an analogy to a promoter's stage set remind us that nature is constructed and performative when it reaches us through the arts. Robin's resurrection by men is neither desired nor unselfish on their parts. During his ministrations, Doctor O'Connor steals her perfume and her cash—possessions with cultural value, serving to confuse the natural image of her promoted by the narrator. Felix Volkbein, a wandering Jew and the son of a pretender to aristocracy, next co-opts her for marriage, intending that Robin perpetuate both his male line and the urban, gentile culture that obsesses him. At the end of the novel, Robin seeks out a ruined chapel in the woods, close to the American origin of Nora Flood. There she coerces a dog into ritual performance, as Nora watches.

## Bestiaries First and Last

As noted above, before settling on *Nightwood* as a title for her best-known novel, Barnes considered *Night Beast*. She told Emily Holmes Coleman that she regretted the "debased meaning now put on that nice word beast" (Barnes letter to Coleman, 1935, Delaware). This brief statement hints at the variable construction of "beast" in language. It unsettles essentialism, and challenges categories and their rank orders of privilege. *Nightwood* and several other Barnes texts are constructed amid representations of the bestial. As a word, "beast" carries a heavier emotional charge than "animal." Beast is the other of the human, threatens it, and provides it with a sense of origin. Beasts are a constant presence in Barnes's work. She feminizes the goats and heifers she tended as a child in Cornwall-on-Hudson and on Long Island. Horses are masterful extensions of Wendell in *Ryder* and Titus of *The Antiphon*. Titus is remembered riding his horse up the steps of the family mansion. In one of Barnes's best early stories, "A Night among the Horses," a man is trampled by the horses he has tended and wishes to return to. Ironically, this happens because he wears the alien garb of high society, demanded by a mistress he resents and evades. The association of horses with Natalie Barney and Romaine Brooks suits their amazonian associations. Barnes probes the human connections to the animal inmates of zoos and circuses, the latter often the colleagues of the marginalized humans of the sideshow.

As a Greenwich Village journalist, Barnes visited the Hippodrome Circus for a story that showed particular empathy for the elephants, bears, camels, and great cats: "Djuna Barnes Probes the Souls of the Jungle Folk at the Hippodrome Circus."[25] The visit has both public and private aspects, as it is her duty through interviews and observation of the show to record the ways that the animals have been made over into performers, or characterized for behaviors such as the bear hug, or the man-eating propensities of the tiger. Barnes was after something else when she "went down afterwards into the depths where the animals are kept," avoiding keepers as well as the public, "and finding myself quite alone with nothing but my iniquitous past, I slowly and softly raised my hand—in salute!" (197).[26]

"The Girl and the Gorilla" also breaks the species barrier, as Barnes characterizes the young female gorilla Dinah and New York women as merely "different kinds of femininity." Dinah's look, touch, and attitude are all important to Barnes, who is allowed to enter her cage with a keeper. "She has a cold sort of appraising stare that holds neither envy nor malice." Her hug is "at once impersonal and condescending and yet rather agreeable." Dinah places her head on Barnes's knee, and Barnes is "pleased that she had found something in me . . . to make her trustful." As in the Hippodrome article, Barnes plays with the assignment of human attitudes to animal beings. She undercuts her own humanizing by noting that Dinah spoils the effect of trustful union by placing an orange peel upon her head. Cultural politics enter the article at the end, as Dinah is hauled off by Engelholm her keeper, "Germany gaining upon Africa with difficulty." Engelholm can find no way to "symbolize Dinah's soul and personality," and is seen as a demonstration that "even here Kipling's remark about the female of the species holds true" (184)—an observation that puts Kipling at risk, as well as the imperial German keeper.[27] The deployment of pictures of Djuna and the young ape, gazing at each other on either side of a male authority figure isolated in a neat circle, enhances the subversive value of her prose (see Plate 15).

Barnes's fascination with animals held to her final, ninetieth year, when with help from Frances McCullough she assembled *Creatures in an Alphabet* for publication. She returns to favorite animals present in earlier work—asps and lynxes, camels and lions of her journalism, *Ryder*, and *Nightwood*. The verses are rewarding if they are read with respect for Barnes's abiding wit. Barnes is as much engaged by the process of selecting words from her precious OED as she is committed to the beasts she makes newly familiar. I know the donkey in a new way, because she has described its Heehaw as "solfeggio"—a term that would send most readers to the dictionary. Her brief but demanding verses are accompanied by illustrations from various art collections, including William Blake's own tyger that "won't keep its master's page." Andrew Field dismisses the volume as "a slight work," though he notes the presence of familiar Barnes themes (244). The gaze, popular opinions of animals, and issues of gender, mastery, and divinity permeate the poems. The opening poem suggests a nature ordered by God, and reassuring to children, who are the

Plate 15. Barnes, "The Girl and the Gorilla." *World Magazine.*

Papers of Djuna Barnes, Special Collections,

University of Maryland at College Park Libraries.

normal audience for bestiaries. But by the time we get to lynx kisses and otters holding otters' (others') hands, there are humanized discrepancies that cast the whole system in doubt, while fulfilling the human love of pun and rhyme:

> The adder in the grass can hiss
> The lynxes in the dark can kiss
> Each otter holds his otter's hand
> For this is how the Lord has planned

The camel overcomes human mastery:

> With cloven lip, with baleful eye
> The Camel wears the caliph high
> But though he do the master's will,
> He himself's his habit still

The peacock is popularly said to go "among itself," a notion Barnes turns to a metaphysical question:

> With all its thousand eyes ajar,
> Is it itself it's looking for?

Barnes unsettles conventional binary judgments of otherness by playing with "three" and "both":

> The kinkajou, the hanging sloth,
> Or any else that looks uncouth
> Aren't they somewhat upside down?
> Or are they merely three of both?

In the seal, Barnes sees an all too docile bride lounging like Mme Récamier.[28] She makes a flock of quail "an old man's titter, a young man's game." The final illustration, set to the folk verse "Round the mulberry we go," shows a circle made from two lizards, each latched to the other's tail, in an endless and savage natural cycle.

Death had been a favored theme for Barnes since her earliest journalism. In her final years, she confronted it as a common experience of beast and human in a long sequence of "spiritual" poems. Typescript variations, most of them heavily written over, survive from the early 1970s. Two lines, much varied, stand at the top of several pages:

> There is no gender in a fossil's eye,
> Pander, pass by.

Variations written in for "gender" include haven, sanctuary, shelter—alternatives that take the statement in metaphysical directions, doubly denying gender. The would-be Trojan assassin and the procurer of Cressida, Pandarus (whose name goes to the despicable verb "pander"), is alternatively "Rentier" (one who lives on the unearned income of stocks) and "*Voyeur*," as the one being instructed to "pass by."[29] The pages are peopled (and sometimes titled) with "parasites, predators, imagos, ghosts and specters." These haunt or feed upon a horizontal female form, whose profile is typically oriented down in the earth in the "bow down" gesture that we have noted in *Ryder* and *The Book of Repulsive Women*. This is the last of gender, before life itself is devoured. In one manifestation a female figure is a "cattle-faced Pucelle," Io—one of Zeus's loves transformed to a heifer by the envious Juno, and pursued by a gadfly into Egypt, where she is associated with Isis. Blood and knives also figure in these violent and despairing pages, as they did in *The Antiphon*. In Barnes's last published poem, "Rite of Spring," man's inability to "purge his body of its theme" is contrasted with the silkworm that can "spin a shroud to re-consider in" (quoted in Field 243). Resonant with H. D.'s "The Walls Do Not Fall," the craft of an insect suggests a mending strategy.

## Bull's Ease in *Ryder*

*Ryder* begins in a Biblical tone with a chapter titled "Jesus Mundane." An authoritative voice sets prohibitions that include human consideration of animals:

> Reach not beyond the image. For these idols and these lambrequins and these fluted candles, with their seven burnings and their seven times seven droppings, and the altar, and the chancel, and the nave, and the aisles, are not for thee in the spirit, but for thee only in the outward manifestation; nor are the Beasts for thee, with the eyes back and the eyes front, nor for thee the bleeding of the heart, with its fire and its ice. . . . For some is the image, and for some the Thing, and for others the Thing that even the Thing knows naught of; and for one only the meaning of That beyond That. (2)

The foregrounding of the image and insistence on "the thing" are reminiscent of Ezra Pound's description of imagism as a stylistic priority that seeks "the thing itself." Such images can be accomplished only by high moderns, if we accept the modernist program of Pound.[30] Likewise, the church saves its mysteries for the priestly anointed. Beasts, too, cited with particular attention to their eyes, are not to be pondered, being presumably the concern of the deity. Elsewhere in the chapter people are instructed not to feel superior to the fruits of the field or to animals, subverting a Darwinian hierarchy among the species, and the classical chain of being.[31] In both *Ryder* and *The Antiphon* the father figures assume the authority of the deity in relating to nature, assuming a special relationship with field, woman, and beast.

In *Ryder* Wendell has settled his two wives and many children at the accurately named farm "Bull's Ease." His first wife, Amelia, has given up life in England and a musical vocation to assume the burdens of childbirth, mothering, farming, and needlework.[32] Wendell is helped to his life of ease by his mother, Sophia, an enterprising woman who wins admiration and cash from men through the essentializing gesture of bidding them to "call me mother." Labor is typically assigned to women of "Bull's Ease."

Wendell makes claims to nature through his procreative habits and his relation to animals. He dresses in sheepskin, talks to farm animals, rides a remarkable horse named Hisodalgus, and casts his seed as widely and simultaneously as possible among the fertile females of the area. One indication of his preparedness is that he attaches a sponge for genital hygiene to the pommel of his saddle—a bit of equipment caught in the drawing placed as a preface to the novel (see Plate 13). Wendell's procreative prodigiousness was emphasized in contemporary advertising for the novel. It caught the imagination of *transition* editor Eugene Jolas, who predicted that "Ryder will go down in American literature as the archetype of the imaginative swashbuckling super-male" (326), a judgment that reigned on the original book-jacket flap.

Wendell is probably as close to animals such as Hisodalgus and the creatures in his field as he is to his lovers and members of his family. He reads the love look in the eye of a catalogue of animals—sheep, lynxes, weasels, hares, and cock-hens (77–78). Not surprisingly, animals have the key roles in the stories he tells to his children: The godlike Pennyfinder the Bull was "besainted" by a whole town, mourned accordingly, by man and beast, and eaten in the end, in a cycle willed by the Lord (78). More remarkable is the Beast Thingumbob, a fabulous creature compounded of raptor's wings, ram's horns, and lion's tail and paws, as shown in an illustration withheld from the first edition (Plate 12). In taking up this "thing" as a story for his children, Wendell ignores the restrictions of "Jesus Mundane." The beast mates with a more human dream creature shown stretched on her back, as he looms over her in a pose that mixes angelic mourning with bestial devouring. Her unusual features include soft hoofs and ten breasts, which in form and abundance are reminiscent of breasts sketched by Zadel in her erotic letters to young Djuna. The creature has no seam to her soul, "either on the one side or on the other side, as we do." She also has almost no face; her only features are eyebrows. She tells Thingumbob she was fathered and mothered by the underworld, but despite her ten hundred and ten years, he will outlive her. He must bury her quickly, and drag from her body ten sons. These things accomplished, the beast cries over them in his nest as "the useless gift of love" (149–53). Beast Thingumbob, like Jesus Mundane, is a version of Wendell. Like him Wendell has filled his small nest with offspring, numbering about ten, if stillbirths and mating outside the home are counted. He has lost at least one partner to childbirth, and seems to indulge himself in mourning women who die in childbirth, granting them sainthood in his private religion.[33]

Both Sophia and Amelia take the equation of Ryder with nature seriously, though not necessarily admiringly. It is nature of an unregulated sort that proves wasteful of life. The dying Sophia approves of her son and his several women, setting them in a pattern of defiance of culture: "You are a lover of women, you commit them to children, you lust openly and sweetly like . . . the beast of the field, because you are nature, all of you, all of you, and nature is terrible when law hunts it down" (317). Amelia is surprised to find him mortal. She concedes, "He is nature in its other shape. . . . He is a deed that must be committed" (321). "Committed" resonates with Sophia's statement on committing women to children. But Amelia orients the commitment differently, making Wendell the deed women commit, not because they wish to but because they must. While Sophia is a lofty manipulator of two generations, exerting bisexual power through her son, Amelia becomes a mere instrument.

In other estimates, Wendell does not come off so well. Amelia has problems living with a second wife and expresses her rage in a decadent bird metaphor: "He nests with vermin, that beneath the shadow of his wings, corruption breeds, that he moults bastards, and broods upon exceeding bad eggs!" (193). Wendell explains to one of his lovers that he will create a new race of Ryder, who will possess a long catalogue of bestial abilities and have knowledge of animals' physical attributes and animal "hearts within hearts" (278–79). The woman undercuts this vision by naming their child "Nothing and Never," and calling for an iced calf's head on a platter. The death's head instantly silences Wendell, who is much better able to accept the procreative aspects of nature than the mortal ones (see Plumb 76). Amelia, Sophia, and Julie (the daughter of Amelia and Wendell, usually taken as Barnes's persona) cope much better with dead babies, dead birds, and death as it occurs in the action of the novel.

Kate and Amelia record the waste of Wendell's use of nature as they clean his dovecote. In this enclosure, the pigeons "young are most gruesome, and die by the million!" as Kate observes. "To man is the vision, to his wife the droppings!" muses Amelia (145). Amelia has a vision or fantasy of the jungle before man: "There you had turds of some account, beasts paying back the earth in coin new minted," and she imagines vegetation from the smallest rushes to the greatest trees praising the lord for this "supplication" from the beasts. Now, in contrast, man has put a floor under everything, and the man's word, rather than the beast's turd, is what goes down into the earth: "And what is there in a word that is magnificent or of help to the land?" (146). Kate delights in Amelia's jungle. Amelia notes that as she "never had much education . . . the jungle was never scratched off my heart." With the "faulty fancies" of Wendell, the women are left to profitless dunging (146–47), and Wendell is the victim of his own misconceived schemes.[34]

Wendell equates women with nature, taking license with both. He gives women and children the same level of care that he gives to his animals, offering them similar food, and complaining that they pose the same problems. He wants to label both his cows and his wives as possessions with the use of ear staples.[35] He tries to teach animals to speak. Exploration of nature is like probing a woman's secret places to him. Wendell does mechanical and chemical experiments with the vagina of the bovinely passive Kate—work that offers a good parody of science, along the lines of Susan Griffin's critique. Though Kate is her rival as a live-in mistress, Wendell's wife, Amelia, disapproves of the project. Out fishing with his children, Wendell vivisects crabs "to unhook my-ladies' chamber from their insides." Julie's brother Tim blocks her view. While "my lady's chamber" would seem to originate in the nursery rhyme "Goosy Goosy Gander," Tim's voyeuristic description suggests viewing a woman on the toilet, with her pubic hair on display: "Oh! she is sitting on her throne and she has yellow hair!" (149).

*Barnes's Beasts Turning Human* 109

Paternal violation of a female beast is more directly conflated with the daughter in drafts of *The Antiphon*. In a second draft version of Act 2 it is recalled that, angered by her resistance to sexual rituals involving virgin sacrifice, Titus dangled Miranda by a hay-hook from the barn. His son recalls, "I've seen heifers dangling from an halter / Just like that, while he charged the rape-blade in" (quoted in Curry 291). Titus's ritual coring of a bitch as the moon rose has survived in the final draft (164), though the fact that he used Augusta's letters as shot "to kill two prides a throw" has not (quoted ibid. 294). Rape scenarios disappeared in both *Nightwood* and *The Antiphon* as they were prepared for publication, though not by any specific request by the editors that I have been able to find. Asked to edit down that particular act of the play, Barnes selected the material.

Barnes offers many hunters in her texts. In *Ryder*, Sophia's first husband was John Peel, a name shared with the hero of an English song who was cherished for his love of riding to the hounds. Amelia's father preferred rabbit hunting to being with his wife and used his whip on his daughter (38). It should be recalled, however, that the metaphorical hunt by matrons is one form of repining in the "Rape and Repining" chapter of *Ryder*. In *The Antiphon* Miranda eventually tells her mother that her sons have come to hunt her down (220), though ironically Augusta has hunted with her favorite son.

Women repeatedly make reference to beasts as allies, particularly in times of persecution and flight. The judgmental voice of "Rape and Repining" magnifies the girl's condition in the eyes of a catalogue of animals: "To the Oblong Eye of the Deer, is not your Condition lengthened? By the Owl, is there not purchased a Dreadful Rotundity? To the Shallow Eye of the Fish, you are but a little staled, but to the Bossy Eye of the Ox, you may ride as High and Damned as Jezebel" (31). Sophia calls upon all of nature to lament the infidelity of her second husband: "Lament, ye many waters, lament, ye mountains and trees, and the grass thereunder and the roots unseen! Lament, ye fishes of the sea and birds of the air, and cattle ever going over, and mole ever going under. Lament, ye dark cisterns and wells of well water, and gutters to the rain, and pitchers at the spring!" (102–103). While these call upon traditions of pathetic fallacy, neither is as convincing as human empathy for nature. The mother of five, Amelia always fears death from childbirth, and warns her daughter Julie (who like Barnes has witnessed her mother's labor) to avoid her lot.

Close to her own confinement, Amelia has a complicated dream about a compassionate "Ox of a Black Beauty." In her dream, the ox is more sensitive to a laboring woman's sufferings than she is to his improbable religious aspirations. The chapter occurs in a room furnished with history books, pictures, and tapestries that prescribe a female life of dreary rounds to nowhere. There are many religious icons, resonating with the initial "Jesus Mundane" chapter, and a late chapter in which two women are followed, one always going to and another always coming from church, a motif repeated in Robin's rounds of churches in *Nightwood*. The room holds a crucifix and depictions of Adam and Eve and friars, the latter doing rounds as endless of those of women. The dream woman's action is limited to the fitful lifting and replacing of trivial objects. The passage opens with a racially charged analysis of the source of the dream. The beautiful blackness of the ox may be an unconscious response to Wendell's paternal anxiety that a dark-complexioned child born to Amelia is not his.

Barnes's ox is humorous in the measured, repetitive cadences used to describe the movement of his "apexed quarters," his feet, and particularly his shadow. Barnes's ox aspires upward: "I am also" echoes the proclamation of the deity, and the egocentrism of Wendell. The "also," however, diverts the narcissistic human, undermines the word of God, and strikes a blow against speciesism as yet another form of hierarchical thinking. As a polite visitor to a bedroom, a speaker of English, and a detective of the emotions, the ox crosses the species barrier. It is well to remember that oxen are castrated bulls used as beasts of burden, now primarily in the third world. Barnes plays ironically upon a double meaning of "labour," as the dream woman in labor announces that labor, not thought, is the function of the beast. Yet she seems oblivious to the cultural assignment of women to the realms of the bestial and the natural. As the chapter concludes, the ox remembers and pities the laboring woman, regardless of how little heeded he has been by her or her god. This misfit male ox anticipates the role of the homosexual midwife/abortionist Dr. O'Connor in *Ryder*, and more so in *Nightwood*.[36]

The cycle of the book of *Ryder* ends with Wendell in his cornfield, regarded by a separate observer who asks, cynically, repeatedly, "Whom should he disappoint now?" as a succession of animals come to him. They look at him, are touched by him, breathe, and make sounds. They come close and go far, and assemble finally into a wave "closed over him, and he drowned, and arose while he yet might go." In T. S. Eliot's Prufrock, an overwhelmed "no-man" drowns in human voices.[37] He is denied the song of the beast/woman, the mermaid. In Lawrence's *The Rainbow*, Ursula nearly drowns among the surging horses, but finds her way out. In Barnes's version of near-death, a sexually proficient but unconventional male, Wendell, both drowns in bestial communion and resurfaces to provide endless cycles of disappointment. Sophia (who strongly resembles Barnes's grandmother Zadel) tells him that Julie, the child he has dismissed as "a hussy and a stubborn girl," "has always been you . . . you are exactly alike, except . . . that she is unhung, and you are slung like a man; it will make the difference." Wendell wants "to get back to me" in the conversation with his mother. But Sophia tries "to go beyond you" (222–23). The struggle to get beyond Wendell, the father who has partially disrupted patriarchy but kept himself at the center of creation—that is the knot of *Ryder*. Untangling and stitching over it is the future of the woman writer, and the feminist reader of Barnes's texts.

## Night Beasts

I see *Nightwood* as a book premised on constructions of the bestial. Jane Marcus has noted that there are more animals than humans in the work ("Laughing at Leviticus" 248). Being partially a novel of favored modernist cities (Paris, Vienna, Berlin, New York), it locates animals and marginal people at the circus. The circus also attracts many of the novel's major characters, including the Baron Felix (who finds other inauthentically titled people in the performers), Nora Flood (a professional journalist, like Barnes, who does advanced circus publicity), and Robin Vote (the mysterious central female of *Nightwood,* who meets Nora there). The circus allows the expression of marginality in social status, race, and sexual orientation. The presence of animals encourages an investigation of the boundaries between the bestial and the human. There is a new dynamic of power and understanding in the tamer's relationship to animals such as the lion. The exchange of animal and human gaze is as powerful as it was in *Ryder*. In the case of the big cats, there is the added dread of being eaten. Of course, vampirism and eating the beloved are regular tropes in Barnes's studies of intimacy.[38] *Nightwood* also employs frequent animal analogies, offered either by an anonymous narrator or by the talkative Dr. Matthew O'Connor. Ulrich Weisstein identifies "the reconciliation of man with God and nature" as O'Connor's primary goal (7).

In his famous introduction to *Nightwood*, T. S. Eliot finds that as a character, Robin is the "most puzzling of all, because we find her quite real without quite understanding the means by which the author has made her so" (xiv). At one time, he advised the omission of the final scene of the novel, in which Robin and Nora's dog engage in a strange ritual. Eliot admits to having been drawn at first to Dr. O'Connor, and praises him as a "disinterested" hero "squeezing himself dry for other people" (xiii). However admirable as a confidant, O'Connor is no more squeezed dry for others, and no less narcissistic, than Nora Flood. As noted in volume 1, a different aspect of the novel attracted Emily Holmes Coleman, who saw *Nightwood* as a study of love between women and encouraged Barnes to lay greater emphasis upon the relationship between Robin and Nora. The controversial cuts to *Nightwood,* in which Coleman, Eliot, Barnes, and Edwin Muir all took a hand, were made more to the stories told by O'Connor than to his philosophical statements or the parts of the text involving Robin. But Robin remains a problem in promoting the book. She is surely misunderstood in the jacket blurb on the 1961 New Directions paperback. This tells us that *Nightwood* "is the story of Robin Vote and those she destroys."[39] Robin's place in nature is probably the key to the understanding that Eliot sought.

The jungle in Robin's hotel room, noted earlier, is described as a "confusion of potted plants, exotic palms and cut flowers, faintly over-sung by the notes of unseen birds." While Robin remains silent about her sense of being among her plants, the narrator quickly starts interpreting the scene with powerful and poetic analogies that assign Robin to parasitic nature and sleep: "The perfume that her body exhaled was of the quality of that earth-flesh, fungi." "Her flesh was the texture of plant life, and beneath it one sensed a frame, broad, porous and sleep-worn, as if sleep were a decay fishing her beneath the visible surface" (34). She is called "the born somnambule, who lives in two worlds—meet of child and desperado" (35). At this stage, the description resembles the organic mystery of the feminine in Susan Griffin's ecofeminist *Woman and Nature: The Roaring inside Her:*

> What is she, in this night, becoming? And we are darkness. Like the carbon from the air which becomes the body of the plant and the body of the plant buried in the earth becoming coal or the body of the plant in her mouth becoming her own dark blood and her blood washing from her like tides. . . . Like a seed in the earth, in the soil which becomes rich with every death, animal bodies coming apart cell by cell, the plant body dispersing, element by element. . . . (167)

But Barnes does not rest with this; the description is embroidered further. Her scene becomes a "jungle trapped in a drawing room" like a Rousseau painting.[40] She is the "ration" for "carnivorous flowers." In terms of O'Connor's human hoax, "the set, the property of an unseen *dompteur,* half lord, half promoter, over which one expects to hear the strains of an orchestra of wood-winds render a serenade which will popularize the wilderness" (35). The machinations of the doctor, moving like a "dumbfounder" as he both revives Robin and steals her money, harmonizes with this cynical and artificial view. Barnes moves the narrative toward the perspective of Felix Volkbein, a successful banker, a worshipper of the past, and a frequenter of the circus, fated to marry Robin and become the father of a child she does not want. Felix takes in O'Connor's artful theft. He looks at Robin's eyes intently, during the brief interval when she opens them. In "their mysterious and shocking blue" he sees "the long unqualified range in the iris of wild beasts who have not tamed the focus down to meet the human eye" (37). What follows is an editorial on the fabrications of Felix, now identified with the "contemplative mind." Interestingly, Nora's faint now becomes a "pose" for a spectator. Robin's residence, the Hotel Récamier, makes the intertextual connection to Mme Récamier, the famous hostess of a Paris salon during the early nineteenth century, and herself the subject of Jacques Louis David's painting. We have already noted her humorous survival, in the form of a seal, in Barnes's late poetry. Mme Récamier's ability to attract male intellectuals and her eventual retirement to the Paris convent Abbaye-aux-Bois (which could be loosely translated as "chapel in the woods") are predictive of Robin's future.

> The woman who presents herself to the spectator as a "picture" forever arranged is, for the contemplative mind, the chiefest danger. Sometimes one meets a woman who is beast turning human. Such a person's every movement will reduce to an image of a forgotten experience; a mirage of an eternal wedding cast on the racial memory; as insupportable a joy as would be the vision of an eland coming down an aisle of trees, chapleted with orange blossoms and bridal veil, a hoof raised in the economy of fear, stepping in the trepidation of flesh that will become myth; as the unicorn is neither man nor beast deprived, but human hunger pressing its breast to its prey. (37)

Felix is making up both a myth and a mirage, incorporating imaginary beasts, and expressing his own hunger. This in turn makes him a predator, posed above a prospective mate like "Beast Thingumbob" of *Ryder*. The narrative grows increasingly savage as its predation is interpreted as the "hunger" for origins that obsesses Felix, as it had his father Guido: "We feel that we could eat her, she who is eaten death returning, for only then do we put our face close to the blood on the lips of our forefathers" (37). Felix is a highly cultured man, and an interesting juxtaposition is made when he stares at Robin, clad in an old brocade, over a piece of tapestry that he is pricing. Like the poor little rich girl of the opening quotation, Felix may be confusing tapestry with other things. Robin is described more as a "precipitation" (42) of destiny than a choice for Felix, and Robin has no "volition" to refuse (42). At the start of their marriage, Felix takes Robin to Vienna for the culture of museums. He lectures to her about great generals and statesmen, none of which makes much of an impression. All of this material of the past "dragged about her like a web" (119)—a figure of the web that is certainly not an enabling one. Only Robin's proclivity for the church gives Felix hope; she goes to the chapel to bring her mind to "this necessity," which I take to be the child Felix asks of her. This assignment is resonant with the "deed which must be committed," as Amelia Ryder apprehends the laws of nature. Like Gertrude Stein's Melanctha, Robin wanders the countryside "strangely aware of some lost land within herself" (45). When her time comes, Robin curses her labor pains and searches in her bloody childbed for something lost. Her only recorded act with her child is weird. As described by Felix, she was "standing in the centre of the floor holding the child high in her hand as if she were about to dash it down, but she brought it down gently." Can we trust Felix's "as if"? Is this perhaps better seen as a religious rite, the elevation of the host, the completion of the necessity she had pondered in the chapel? Unlike Amelia Ryder, Robin does not commit herself a second time to heterosexual procreation, and protests the first childbirth to Felix both physically and verbally. Robin does smash a doll/child she shares with Nora, perhaps never having involved this crafted product in a sacramental rite. The act seems a clear denigration of their lesbian alliance.

Robin's earlier flight to Nora and her salon in America is suggestive of a feminine culture and imaginary, and it makes an important connection of modernism back to an American position, where women work as agents. The house "was couched in the centre of a mass of tangled grass and weeds." The grain of Robin's face is described as "the tree coming forward in her" (50). Nora is set in the context of American women in the West: "With heavy hems the women becoming large, flattened the fields where they walked; God so ponderous in their minds that they could stamp out the world with him in seven days" (51). Nora and Robin had met at the Denckman Circus in New York. Robin comes to Nora's attention when the animals running around the ring turn the "orbit of the light" on Robin. In a profound but frightful gesture of interest in Robin, a "powerful lioness . . . turned her furious great head with its yellow eyes afire and went down, her paws thrust through the bars and, as she regarded the girl, as if a river were falling behind impassable heat, her eyes flowed in tears that never reached the surface. At that the girl rose straight up" (54). Nora sympathetically takes Robin's hand, and responds to her request to "get out of here" (54).

The home Nora makes for Robin in Paris becomes a "museum of their encounter," as had Guido Volkbein's for Hedwig a generation earlier. Notable among its furnishings are wooden horses from a merry-go-round— appropriate to Robin's childish love of toys and to the trope of crafted beasts. But, as she had with Felix, Robin leaves this second domestic situation. In her nocturnal wanderings to Paris cafés, Robin resembles a moth "who by his very entanglement with the heat that shall be his extinction is associated with flame as a component part of its function" (60). Pedestrians accordingly leave her alone. But Nora is tortured and confused, avoiding Robin even as she searches. As a nest builder and dweller, Nora perpetuates patriarchal female domesticity and is its victim.

Nora's dreams of her grandmother, on a night when Robin is wandering, suggest a doubled sense of loss. Her grandmother, like Robin, is in a continual process of leaving. In one remembered incident, she even departs from the secure sense of their relationship by appearing suddenly cross-dressed, and offering a "leer of love" (63). The same expression is used in Barnes's early lesbian verse "From Fifth Avenue Up," first published in *The Book of Repulsive Women* in 1915. There is a bird metaphor in the dream sequence. The bird has left the nest of the grandmother's room, though a plume and ink are left—perhaps for Nora to write with. The grandmother is dead, and in another dream Nora sees her "tangled in the grave grass, and flowers blowing about and between her; lying there in the grave, in the forest, in a coffin of glass, and flying low, my father who is still living; low going and into the grave beside her." While her father was "struggling with her death terribly," Nora "stepped about the edges, wailing soundlessly." She senses that even awake she is "burying them into the dark earth." Nora suggests that she also makes Robin die over and over within her (148–49), without knowing why. Nora's obsession with death and burials in the earth would seem to be an attempt to hold on to love. Dr. O'Connor suggests that Robin would feel safer if Nora were in a nunnery. As it is, Nora keeps " 'bringing her up' as cannons bring up the dead from deep water" (150).[41] It is significant that Barnes offers such pronounced difference in her two central female characters in this novel—particularly in their relation to nature.

The most controversial animal in *Nightwood* is clearly the dog, who engages in bizarre relational activity with Robin in the final chapter. Felix has complained that Robin is incapable of caring properly for her pets. It is another failure at (or rejection of) domesticity for Robin. What is going on here is clearly not a master/pet relationship—another combination alien to Robin. Nora's dog is better at tracking Robin than Nora had been at finding her in her drunken Paris wanderings. Rather typically, Robin is at her own form of worship in a chapel—this time a deserted one. In her long series of visiting church buildings, Robin has sought to define some necessity. Women are forever going to and coming from church in *Ryder*, where we have noted the conjunction of church trappings, the ox, and Amelia suffering childbed. The joining of church and animal is also present in the furnishings of the apartment shared by Robin and Nora, where merry-go-round horses and church embroideries serve as accents.[42]

Emily Holmes Coleman, like many later critics, saw the exchange of dog and woman in this final scene as sexual. Barnes insisted that the behavior was patterned on the antics of her friend Fitzi's dog. Without rejecting the physical suggestiveness of the scene, I wonder whether it might not also be appropriate to see it in terms of religious ritual. In *Epilegomena to the Study of Greek Religion* (1921), feminist anthropologist Jane Harrison discusses the totem animal as an important focus of primitive religion. We are all familiar with the animal/human combinations in Egyptian deities and Greco/Roman myths. Unable to bond to the organizing symbols of Felix Volkbein (whose name suggests the folk, the group), and unable to find the right sacred place by entering the churches of great cities, Robin comes to the derelict church associated with her former love Nora. Here perhaps the totemic animal finds her. The extended actions of dog and woman are suggestive of ritual healing. Both beast and human have a therapeutic run through the emotions, full of gesture, movement, and even pain. There is plenty of aural expression, but not through words—the preoccupation and limitation of Nora.[43]

The ritual begins as Robin goes into Nora's wild woodland country, circling as a bird or a tracking dog might, and quickly blending in: "The silence that she had caused by her coming was broken again by insect and bird flowing back over her intrusion which was forgotten in her fixed stillness, obliterating her as a drop of water is made anonymous by the pond into which it has fallen" (168). Robin's travel, her participation in ritual gestures, and the natural images setting the scene are all evocative of Rhoda's solitary scenes in *The Waves*. The distant barking of Nora's dog startles Robin into an upward position, as did the fiery look of the lioness in the circus. But with this beast, Robin can reverse the ritual, going down before the dog, as one might in honoring a god. Kristeva has drawn our attention to abjection to the mother figure in religion. This I think Robin has resisted in her own role with her child and in her avoidance of Nora's mothering. The dog has an anxious reaction to her bowing down, "rearing back . . . his paws trembling under the atrembling of his rump, his hackle standing . . . whining and waiting" (169). Robin comes on all fours, initiating a series of imitations. She whimpers, as he had. Advancing farther, "she struck against his side," eliciting "one howl of misery" and his attempt to bite her, barking and dashing about her. She too barks "in a fit of laughter, obscene and touching." Gradually they move more in parallel, both crying, "moving head to head" and then finally lying down together, "his head flat along her knees" (170). This repeats the gesture of the female gorilla in Barnes's journalistic piece "The Girl and the Gorilla." They go down to rest, woman and beast, together. Nora is a witness, already intimate with both the dog and the woman. Unlike Robin's male spectators in the Hotel Récamier, Nora leaves this text alone. Barnes refused to tell us more. Barnes wrote to Coleman:

> I do not go any further than this into the psychology of the "animal" in Robin because it seems to me that the very act with the dog is pointed enough, and anything more than that would spoil the scene anyway: as for what the end promises (?) let the reader make up his own mind, if he is not an idiot he'll know. (Barnes letter to Coleman, 2 July 1935, Delaware)

## The Beast Box of *The Antiphon*

In *The Antiphon*, we find a ruined ancestral house, "Hobb's [*sic*] ark," swarming with the family survivors of Titus Hobbs, a character comparable to both Wendell Ryder and Barnes's own father. Titus's wife,

Augusta, had pastoral origins like the maiden of "Rape and Repining." Miranda's story of her scythed innocence partakes of the fertile feminine field that we have noted in Barnes's earlier writing.

> Striking back at springtime, like a kid
> Hopping and skipping to the summer's day;
> Bawling and baaing out her natural glee ·
>
> . . . .
>
> Hopping and singing went she, when in one
> Scant scything instant was gaffed down (87)

Augusta has other mild animal incarnations. Her flank resembles a bird of paradise when she walks proudly. She recalls lost beauty like a dove "when I was thrown up for the gun," as doves typically were for target shooting.[44] This is Augusta's version of natural devastation with the advent of sexual experience. The mature Miranda is a more wily and dangerous animal, a "deadly beloved vixen" (99), or (in a vision rather like Yeats or Eliot) "a leopard in a land made desolate" (104) to her brother Jeremy. Her three brothers have uncharitable insect terms for their powerful grandmother, who aided and abetted their father. Like Sophia of *Ryder*, she is patterned on Zadel Barnes, briefly the hostess of a London salon. Victoria is a "skin-trussed boxer-hornet" living in London's Grosvenor Square, where she "hummed and shook beneath the midnight lamps" (153). Miranda, however, remembers her grandmother saving the ship for the family, and taking the children to the circus. The sons' resentment of Titus is expressed in epithets of virile farm animals and cruel sports with animals: he is an "old ram," a "cock-pit bully boy" (141), and a "stallion" (154). Instead of raising stock on his farm, Titus cultivated prostitutes, "his beasts, the girls" (128). The three brothers all play the cock whose crowing marked Christ's betrayal (173). Although they claim to be righting the wrongs of Titus for arranging the rape of Miranda, and of Augusta for letting it happen, they are abusive to both Miranda and Augusta. The women become scapegoats once Titus is inaccessible in death. Louise DeSalvo has sketched a broad pattern of family incest. She finds evidence that Augusta imposed sexual demands on Jeremy, who eventually fled. In the most abusive scene there are suggestions of sodomizing Miranda, as if she were a beast, when Dudley slaps Miranda's rump and comments on her best position (*Antiphon* 176; DeSalvo 307). For this scene, which Augusta tries to pass off as game play, the brothers Elisha and Dudley don masks of farmyard animals—a pig and an ass. The role of the big bad wolf is invoked as well, and appropriately, as they seek to blow the house down. The third brother, the lost Jeremy, is disguised as Jack the coachman, and equipped with whip and creel. He plays clown and sideshow barker as well, and has been Miranda's friend (and perhaps her lover) in Paris. "Jack" tells the dark family history of rape by presenting the dolls' house, "Hobb's ark." With this prop, he forces Augusta to replay the rape of Miranda. Miranda is remembered crying like the ewe "offering up her silly throat for slashing" (186). She is also seen "dragging her rape blood behind her, like the snail" (185).

Though she walks with difficulty, using a cane, Miranda has gained autonomy in middle age. She has seen the world and assumed an embroidered costume of the stage. In DeSalvo's parallel reading between the Mirandas of *The Antiphon* and *The Tempest,* paternal incest plagues both heroines. We have noted "tempest" used to describe the paternal rape in the field of "Run Girls Run." Miranda remarks calmly, "The wind that knocked our generation down was not a harvest" (212), words that pertain as well to World War II as to Titus. Barnes's Miranda has survived these tempests. She has no need to hunt the enemy or to seek revenge, as her brothers do in renewed cycles of abuse.[45] She thinks even of relieving her hateful brother when she tries to get Augusta to alleviate the "cramp in Dudley's hand," put there in the crib (181). Augusta, who has always favored her sons and sent Miranda "hunting for her crime" (164), now occasionally defends her. She declares her daughter "magnanimous" (168). She reassures Dudley, a stingy, successful watchmaker, that he won't have to support his sister: "Fie, fie! I've seen my daughter die before, and make it" (180).

*The Antiphon* has one more animal representation, a highly artificial and crafted one. The stage set calls for "a single settle facing front, at either end of which is set the half of a gryphon, once a car in a roundabout" (81). Barnes's inventory of merry-go-round figures collected for her Paris apartment included a gryphon, lending personal resonance to this prop. The gryphon is a creature of childhood amusement parks, fantasy, and terror. Part eagle, part lion, the gryphon stood guard over treasures. The eagle and the lion figure, respectively, on the national seal of the United States and in English heraldry. Barnes had combined them before for "Beast Thingumbob" in *Ryder.* Thingumbob contained eagle, ram, and lion in his even more polymorphous bestial form. The splitting of the gryphon, we learn, was the work of Titus. At the end of the second act, in order to make a bed for Augusta, Miranda asks her uncle to help her reconstruct the gryphon, to make "of this divided beast / An undivided bed" (189).[46] Miranda has slept on it at the start of the final act, and Augusta proclaims it "an excellent stage, fit for a play" (192). She wants to "play as girls" and recalls the donkeys, ducks, and drakes she had crafted for Miranda when she was a child. Miranda evokes a primordial maternal landscape dating from before her birth, and perhaps even before the ravaging of her mother, an event juxtaposed with her own rape:

> There was a time when we were not related.
> When I first loved thee—I say "thee" as if
> It were to use a lost endearment
> That in the loss has lost the losing world—
> When I first loved thee, thou were grazing:
> Carrion Eve, in the green stool, wading,
> In the coarse lilies and the sombre wood;
> Before the tree was in the cross, the cradle, and the coffin
> (193–94)

The gryphon accommodates Augusta like a magical carriage on a fantasy excursion to resorts, pleasure gardens, and imagined meetings with fashionable and famous women (an identity Miranda has rejected, to her regret).[47] These are no destinations for the "Trappist" Miranda. Mother and daughter are still struggling over the ways that they, like the gryphon, are split or united in one another. Their anxieties relate to the heart, and who is included in or cast out of it. The mother's heart seems interchangeable with the womb. Miranda is repeatedly sent birdlike from the portal, door, or gate. She has borne the guilt of mortals cast from the Biblical garden of Eden: "Scotched by the sword her people snatched / From the gate of Eden, for a whip / To beat her, reeling like an headless cock." She has just as grotesque an experience when, vixen-like, she is "bushelled in the mind's confessional, / Foxed down its gullet to the rump, / Quaking with unhouselled mouth agape, Lashing at the lattice with her paws" (215).[48]

Miranda offers several figures for the title-bearing metaphor, the "antiphon." The most obvious is the sympathetic vibration of strings of the viola. The first is a juxtaposition of animal and religious space: "Where the martyr'd wild fowl fly the portal / High in the honey of cathedral walls, / There is the purchase, governance and mercy." Another is a mutually consuming kiss when "loves so eat each other's mouth / Till that the common clamour, co-intwined, / Wrung out the hidden singing in the tongue." Such tonguing is reminiscent of the tongue as lesbian sexual instrument in Barnes's *Ladies Almanack*.[49] Love is eating the beloved—a suggestion with resonance in the fear of the lioness and the biting of the dog in *Nightwood*. But death itself, well timed, is also apt. "So the day, day fit for dying in / Is the plucked accord" (214). This proves to be Miranda's "day fit for dying in." Augusta and Miranda die together and "fall across the gryphon" (223). Augusta's ringing to summon back her sons brings down the bell that crushes them, and her last words to Miranda are ones of blame. But "being weary of the world," and having declared death "the hub that holds the staggered spindle" (218), Miranda cannot be seen as the loser.[50] Indeed, she seems to have plotted this resolution, which leaves her wicked brother at a loss.

It is Jeremy, still disguised as Jack, who begins to understand her drama, and to call himself fool, in his real name of Jeremy. In asking, "Could I know / Which would be brought to child-bed of the other," he begins to comprehend the feminine identification of mother and daughter, and to recognize the tormenting role of the daughter mothering her mother. He estimates "what price the token price / That cashing in the utmost treasure would exact"—a treasure I take to be Miranda, now guarded by the gryphon. He depicts himself as bestial: "The slayer snuffling 'round the kill / Breathing his contagion out before him / Draws up the victim with his steaming nose." He has "breathed up disaster and myself" and dug a home and "pushed my terror in" (224).

Just before she hears an ominous "stroke," Miranda has remarked to Augusta:

> It has been remarked from advent to the terror
> Woman is most beast familiar (205)

"Familiar": known, well-acquainted, of the family. Barnes takes on the patriarchal assignment of woman to nature. She survives those terms and finds in the beast both challenge and diversity. She lies as buried treasure in the earth, guarded by a gryphon, potential for our understanding.

# 3 West's Sense of Scaffolding

> Idiocy is the female defect: intent on their private lives, women follow their
> fate through a darkness deep as that cast by malformed cells in the brain.
> It is no worse than the male defect which is lunacy: they are so obsessed by
> public affairs that they see the world as by moonlight, which shows the out-
> lines of every object but not the details indicative of their nature.
>
> —*Black Lamb and Grey Falcon* 3

Writing in an experimental range and blend of genres, as did Woolf and
Barnes, Rebecca West addressed major cultural dilemmas of the twentieth century: women's political and economic rights, sexual freedom, so-
cialism, the conditions of labor, two world wars, religion, the arts, empire,
fascism, and Communism. She was able to study global problems on a
personal scale and to detect philosophical scaffoldings that often go unacknowledged or undetected—the most basic of these being the binary
thinking so fundamental to Western philosophy. West looked to art as a
symptom of health in a nation or an individual and as an antidote to
domination and corruption. She takes her place in this study as its most
deliberate political thinker and its most outspoken polemicist—qualities
that set her at odds with traditional, aesthetic definitions of modernism,
with the "charm" expected in an earlier generation of women (see volume 1), and with nonauthoritarian styles embraced by both feminism
and the postmodern practice of deconstruction.

The internal monologues of West's "The Strange Necessity" and *Harriet Hume* resemble contemporary work by Virginia Woolf; *The Judge* and
"The Strange Necessity" show a concern for vitalism and energetic forces
comparable to the thought of D. H. Lawrence and Wyndham Lewis. Yet
West is not contained by the combined modernisms of these figures. I
have noted her critiques of Lawrence and Lewis in volume 1. West missed
the treatment of "the long drive of the human will" in Woolf's *Jacob's
Room,* and we might infer that such monumental pursuits were important to her ("Notes on Novels" 142). West's concern with the intersection
of art and political praxis might be considered more postmodern than
modernist, or a continuation of the rhetorics of Fabian socialism, suf-

frage, Nietzsche, and individualism—all of them predecessors of high modernism. Her last works had a strong component of realism.

As an author who wrote in eight different decades, adapting to the changing political, economic, and artistic character of each of them, West is of strategic importance in these changing times, when we no longer wage a cold war against Communism but confront reasserted nationalism, neo-Nazis, and feminist backlash. We would do well to design as comprehensive a review of gender as she did over time. Critics of West have tended to divide her works into phases and genre types, missing a complex and integrated sense of her negotiations with culture. As early as the 1930s, West was aware of the problems her variety would pose for scholars. She warned a young woman writing her thesis that "the interstices [of her works] were too wide" for a good "picture of a writer." She was not eager to be pigeonholed into a "recognized school" (*BL&GF* 1084). The editors of her reissued works and the author of her obituary in the London *Times* are in agreement about the difficulties of her literary placement.[1] She expressed her own opinion of her fate to Doris Lessing: "In paranoid moods I may imagine some malicious deity who plans punishments to fit crimes, such as being beautiful, clever, strong, brave: 'We can't have that,' he mutters, directing downwards some bolt of retribution" (West letter to Lessing, 6 Feb. 1982, Tulsa). In better moods, she seems to have had a deep sense of having done what her inclinations and historical conditions permitted.

West was a lifelong advocate of feminism, and unlike Djuna Barnes, she was proud to be embraced by feminists. But even her feminism was questioned during the years from the late thirties through the mid-fifties, when she wrote relatively little fiction and a great deal of trial reportage, focusing upon problems of treason. West has appealed to women for different reasons over the years. The view of West as "upstanding and outspoken" goes back to Virginia Woolf (4 *L* 261), who respected her for taking a public, active role, speaking out in Parliament for married women's rights to earn. Her writing as a socialist feminist continues to hold its appeal, perhaps because it operates on clear historical ground, offering hope of problem solving based on political equality and life-giving virtues. This is the aspect of West made available by Jane Marcus when she edited *The Young Rebecca: Writings of Rebecca West 1911–1917*, collecting West's journalism from the *New Freewoman*, the *Clarion*, and the *Daily News*. Jill Craigie played an important role in encouraging West's interest in the project. West's 1914 short story "Indissoluble Matrimony" (also in the Marcus collection) was worthy of a place in *The Norton Anthology of Literature by Women* because its editors, Sandra Gilbert and Susan Gubar, admired its depiction of an activist woman winning at sex war.[2] However much Jane Marcus admires West's political journalism, she has less use for her fiction, which she considers too heavy-handed (see "Acting Out"). West is capable of psychodrama and melodrama in novels marked by traits of experimental modernism, such as *The Return of the Soldier, The Judge,* and *Sunflower.* She encouraged her publisher, Jonathan Cape, to market *The Strange Necessity* as a psychological study. *The Fountain Overflows,* which in 1956 ushered in West's late, largely realistic, autobiographical novels, may have appealed to a large female reading audience because of its emphasis on the experience of a talented family of women.[3] Together with *Family Memories,* this series probes the origins of the female self in several generations. The feminist Virago Press republished all of West's novels and several nonfiction works; after her death in 1983, it continued to issue previously unpublished novels and memoirs.

### The Binary Bind

The voicing of absolute, oppositional positions and the "scalping" of reputable writers won the youthful Rebecca West attention in the early decades of this century. Woolf's *A Room of One's Own* records the drawing-room explosion of Desmond MacCarthy, ignited by West's statement "All men are snobs." Despite her very different sensibility, style, and experience, Woolf's persona in *A Room* works around to substantial agreement with West. In the late twentieth century, after feminist and deconstructionist critiques of monological authority and binary division, Rebecca West's tone is alarming for different reasons.[4] West's case demonstrates the difficulty of rethinking and replacing basic patriarchal structures through the medium of literature. If West seems bound in the patterns she would escape, this is a problem of leverage that Myra Jehlen taught feminists to expect in her forward-looking article "Archimedes and the Paradox of Feminist Criticism."

West has been found unsatisfactory on a number of counts by recent feminists. Her consistent recourse to conflictual binaries, her focus upon heterosexual relations, accompanied by ambivalence regarding homosexuality, and the apparent repudiation of her early liberalism all strain against recent strands of feminism. In *Thinking about Women,* one of the founding literary critical works of the 1960s rebirth of feminism, Mary

Ellmann found a stereotyped polarizing of male and female qualities in West's work that she considered the very opposite of radical thinking. West joins Virginia Woolf as a practitioner of "the female aesthetic" in Elaine Showalter's *A Literature of Their Own*. To Showalter, she is no more successful than Woolf in offering models of female autonomy and success in the world. Showalter finds an overwhelming pattern of female punishment through self-betrayal and victimization by men in West's biography and in her novel *The Judge* (256–57). West's biographer, Victoria Glendinning, summarizes West's life as "a sadder story than I had expected," as West seemed to feel "like Job, persecuted by God (and by man, woman and child)" (*Rebecca West* 3). In a largely negative assessment, Moira Ferguson counters West's feminist reputation by emphasizing West's dark qualities—her inheritance of Calvinism from Scottish theology, and her interest in an interpretation of evil based on the Manichaean heresy. She also draws attention to West's anti-Communist writings and her most negative statements on homosexuality. West emerges as a "personal," psychologically oriented feminist, and not what would be more important to this critic—a "social feminist."[5]

West's judgmental, authoritative voice, used to typecast individuals and events, has struck many critics as masculine. It is certainly at odds with the anti-authoritarian, readerly voice experienced earlier in Woolf's essays. West's tone troubles Faith Evans, editor of the posthumously published *Family Memories:* "So overbearing is Rebecca West's . . . antagonism . . . that she risks failing to draw her readers into her condemnation. It is a typical weakness—or strength. Once Rebecca West has taken up a position, it is absolutely fixed: she will fight to the death, and the reader, unable to match her single-mindedness, is tempted to rebel, to consider the alternative view" (5). Evans makes these remarks in relation to West's portrayal of her mother's sister-in-law, who was credited with breaking up her grandmother's family. But the style is even more pronounced in West's antagonism for her elder sister Lettie, who is assaulted directly in *Family Memories,* and perhaps indirectly as Cordelia in the autobiographical novels begun with *The Fountain Overflows,* as noted in the family backgrounds presented in volume 1.

Jane Marcus locates West's "voice of authority" in a tradition shared by Mme de Staël, George Sand, George Eliot, Harriet Beecher Stowe, Mary Wollstonecraft, Olive Schreiner, and Woolf's *Three Guineas,* but acknowledges the problems this and other tendencies of West pose for "young American feminists." West's admiration of de Staël was expressed in a

1959 article that struck a very affirmative note with another long-lived and successful journalist and friend, Janet Flanner. Flanner wrote West to say that the essay, and more generally "pride in your writing, your mind, your scholarship," had lifted her out of a period of depression.[6] The voice of authority had its subscribers.

Some of the tendencies that have caused feminists concern have allowed others to deny West's feminist affiliations altogether. Skeptics of feminism typically gravitate to a different set of texts from those that attract feminist readers in order to make their point. *The Essential Rebecca West,* a collection of West's works selected primarily by her publishers at Macmillan in 1977, has little of the feminist and socialist West, and none of the experimental fiction from the twenties. It reprints nearly two hundred pages of *Black Lamb and Grey Falcon,* a work rarely cited in feminist analysis of West to date. In introducing *The Essential Rebecca West,* Samuel Hynes extricates West from associations with Virginia Woolf and "the woman novelist." He is relieved to find that in her 1928 essay "The Strange Necessity," West moves from an opening worthy of Woolf to a level of intellectual toughness and knowledge where Woolf could never have followed: "It is as if Dame Rebecca were acting out her liberation from the stereotypes of her sex, showing us how a free mind might play upon ideas" (ix, xii).[7] Hynes marks the start of her greatest creative period with *Black Lamb.* Peter Wolfe, who like Hynes prefers West's late nonfictional work, finds that *Black Lamb* "could do duty as a marriage manual," claiming that West credited "most of the book's best insights" to her husband (148). The husband-wife dialogues were satirized by Mary Ellmann as a play between feminine balloon and masculine ballast. Gordon Ray tried to suggest that West did not really mean what she said in the feminist *New Freewoman* (8–9).[8] Harold Orel points to a supposed paucity of writing by West on other women writers (32). Gloria Fromm has argued that West's best work is her essays, and that these are directed at men, the audience Fromm thinks that West favors. A clear exception to this is Doris Lessing, however. Lessing was drawn to *Black Lamb* in 1982, as support for her political activism. Lessing compared her state of mind to that of West at the start of World War II, and asked if she could cite West's work in alerting the public to the nuclear menace.[9]

The variety that critics find in West was determined to a large extent by historical and cultural forces, which include an ebb and flow in feminism, as characteristic of our day as hers. The basic themes that concern her are consistent. West found her place in the literary world by doing socially sensitive, independent-minded book reviews and essays, written in a voice notable for both amusing wit and scathing condemnation. As told in volume 1, Dora Marsden provided West's first significant literary home at the *New Freewoman* in 1911. The radical socialist editor Robert Blatchford liked her capacity to wield a "battle axe and scalping knife" (*YR* 89), and invited her to contribute to his paper, the *Clarion*. Ford Madox Ford and H. G. Wells sought her out in response to her book reviews. In 1914 Wyndham Lewis published "Indissoluble Matrimony" in his vorticist little magazine, *BLAST*. In the isolation of unwed motherhood, and supported for nearly a decade by Wells, West turned more to writing books. Her fiction and fictionalized essays of the teens and twenties—*The Return of the Soldier* (1918), *The Judge* (1922), "The Strange Necessity" (1928), and *Harriet Hume* (1929)—took on modernist forms and psychological interests, though always with undergirding social analysis and feminism. By the mid-twenties, when she needed independent financial support, she turned to writing regular columns for the London *Daily Telegraph* and an American paper owned by the Hearsts, the *New York American*. West always stated a preference for novel writing over journalism. As a novelist, she attracted Macmillan, Knopf, and Viking as publishers.

In the forties and early fifties, with World War II and its postwar trials, her political and court reportage found audiences on the conservative end of the political spectrum. Her American audience came largely through the *New Yorker*, where she had Janet Flanner and Emily Hahn as colleagues.[10] Her anti-Communist postwar position was expressed, among other places, in a set of articles for the *Sunday Times*. Some took these as a defense of the infamous Senator Joseph McCarthy. As West explained to J. B. Priestley, "I wrote those articles in the vain attempt to prevent the sabotaging of Anglo-American relations by the constant presentation of the United States as insane with anti-Communist hysteria," and feared she was "the last liberal left."[11] *The Meaning of Treason* includes reporting on Nazi and Communist trials. Though the theme of treason interested her, and could be applied to personal betrayals that she saw marking her own life, it was more or less an assigned topic.

By the thirties, West had done well enough financially to be able to indulge in some work that made no commercial sense, notably *Black Lamb and Grey Falcon* (1941). This work of multiple genre and tremendous length satisfied her unexpected passion for Yugoslavia, contracted while on a lecture tour for the British Council. In *Black Lamb*, she describes other of her works as attempts to find out what she knew about one thing or another—a love of London (*Harriet Hume*), the doom sounded in theology (*St. Augustine*), or the dangerous nature of rich people (*The Thinking Reed*) (BL&GF 1084). West's last project circled back to seeking an understanding of family, and was productive of a series of autobiographical novels (*The Fountain Overflows* [1956], *Cousin Rosamund* and *This Real Night* [posthumous]) and *Family Memories*—biography and autobiography assembled from drafts after her death in 1983.

In both her fiction and her prose works of social analysis, West seeks to detect and explore patterns of dominance and difference that shape human behavior, particularly in the mechanized, war-torn, patriarchal world of the early twentieth century. She repeatedly calls these patterns "myths," suggesting their wide influence, but also their constructedness and susceptibility to challenge and eventual change. West reads her myths in theology, history, literature, art, clothing, crafts, architecture, and personal dialogues. The Manichaean heresy is a favorite theological myth, offering a binary system where evil and death have pitted themselves against good and life, mixing with them in the original assault. People who follow this heresy extract positive elements from a chaotic world, rather than trusting in their eternal souls. Starting with the essay "Trees of Gold," West challenges the glorification of sacrifice in Christian theology. She finds it a life-denying paradigm, particularly costly to the young, and to women. Writing in 1917, West was encouraged by her experience of World War I to challenge "The New God" who sanctioned war, which is likened to a squandering of the harvest and an act of rape:

> Unmoved he looked upon the grey men who crept like rats through the yellow Belgian harvest that was never reaped. From his secure skies he looked down on the blue smoke curling from a Flemish farmstead and smiled in his beard, well content at the murder he knew would defile its hearth. He who on earth had nothing to say in praise of earthly love and permitted his servants to defame it did not move while men made from the sexual mystery a new torture and prelude to blood. ("The New God")

West uses this essay to blast the Christian God's aloofness to "earthy love," and in it she places value on "sexual mystery," as opposed to pious chastity. War is rape, and "one hates our fathers for having committed themselves to such a worship." As an alternative, West offers an appreciation of the human creativity brought to religion in architecture, song, and ritual. Speaking in her early journalistic tone, she hopes that through so-cialism, we may "see that life is ordered so that humanity may flower unstunted by poverty and unhappiness, so that there are the same oppor-tunities for courage and good deeds in peace and in war." Under these conditions, "a God will come to us born of the human will." In the po-litical sphere, West points to myths of superiority used to justify con-quest, empire, and the social and economic inequalities of race, class, and gender, under law and custom. West's myths are played out by recurrent types—the virile peasant, the regenerative mother, the rootless new urban class, and the destructive female parasite, a woman fed by class privilege and industrial production of nonessentials.

In this chapter, I will explore two sets of texts for their investigation of cultural myths of difference. I will look first at West's most recogniz-ably modernist and feminist phase, focused primarily in the novels *The Judge* and *Harriet Hume*. I will then turn to *St. Augustine* and *Black Lamb and Grey Falcon*—works of cultural analysis that occupied West in the 1930s, when many suggest that she had abandoned feminism. These enter the later phase of modernism also inhabited by Woolf's *Three Guineas* and Barnes's *Nightwood*. It is a phase which has been insufficiently un-derstood or integrated, particularly as feminism and modernism mesh with politics in social struggle.

## Maternal Politics in *The Judge*

Rebecca West opens *The Judge* with what seems a prophecy of doom: "Every mother is a judge who sentences her children for the sins of the father." It is an example of West's voice of authority, which dares to generalize about "every mother" and prejudges the father as a sinner. Patriarchal sins are as yet unspecified so that the father could be either an individual human or the uncaring God assaulted in her earlier war prose. The "sentence" is also undefined, inviting semantic or narrative, as well as legal, interpretation. Indeed, West's outrageous opening is best read as a challenge. The mother sentences the children "for the sins," not "to" them. The novel shows the efforts of several mothers to defeat a cycle of "sins of the father." West's redemptive mothers offer not a concept of in-born guilt or a retributive sentence but a fresh narrative.

H. G. Wells, very much involved with West and her work at the start of the 1920s, stated objections to *The Judge* that help identify how West was departing from her Edwardian male mentors. He had a hard time accepting the fact that the "judge" of the novel was not the man he expected him to be, but a mother. Wells expected West to stick with a simple, linear plot inspired by the life story of a real-life male judge they had met while on one of their vacations. He disliked the double plot of *The Judge*, which breaks in mid-novel from a young woman, Ellen Melville, in her Edinburgh setting, to relocate a generation earlier with Marion Yaverland during her youth in Essex. While Wells himself had offered naive, impressionable young women such as Ellen in his social romances, he was less apt to produce a Marion Yaverland.[12] Wells, the architect of *The Outline of History,* complained further that West "wanted history to be full of wonderlands" (Wells 100). It is interesting that, when West took up history in earnest with *Black Lamb and Grey Falcon* nearly twenty years later, she hit upon a mixture of genres that enabled "wonderlands" to coexist with history.[13]

Publication of *The Judge* in 1922 coincided with that of James Joyce's *Ulysses.* It may be better read in the company of Joyce's cyclical redoublings rather than Wells's factual analysis. As discussed in volume 1, West's reading of *Ulysses* in "The Strange Necessity" detected destructive cycles she associated with male violence, set against female generativity. This insistent, essentialist structure inhabits her own novel.[14] West's appreciation of Emily Brontë's *Wuthering Heights* is based partly on its presentation of gendered binary forces—a Byronic male vs. a redemptive, slain goddess (CC 109). She also appreciated Brontë's freedom with the prose genre. By doubling the women in *The Judge,* West articulates not just a heterosexual drama but also self-reviewing and renewing female agency within the human cycle, anticipating the work of Carol Gilligan. The self-reviewing process, which is worked largely through memory, also derives from another modern influence, Proust—one writer admired equally by West, Woolf, and Barnes.

West explained to S. K. Ratcliffe that her subject in *The Judge* was "the eternal swatting of that fly youth and beauty by the accumulations of evil done by careless handling of beautiful things" (West letter to Ratcliffe, n.d., Yale). This statement is milder than West's epigraph, but it does set up an implicit binary in which an evil of carelessness (whether individual or divine) attacks youth and beauty. West has a more cheerful side, in which she indulges in beauty, asserting the right of every youth to experience it. In her earliest journalism, she challenged puritanical denials of beauty and the class bias that denied equal access to it. She demanded healthful, appetizing food, attractive clothing, and the experience of music and art for working-class women in the essays "A New Woman's Movement: The Need for Riotous Living" and "The Sheltered Sex: 'Lotos Eating' on Seven-and-Six a Week" (YR 130–35, 184–88).[15]

The beauty under assault at the start of *The Judge* is Ellen Melville, an intelligent, progressive working girl of eighteen, already active in the suffrage movement. Each generation in the office where Ellen works, the boss seduces the working-class girl, but marries above her for economic and social class gain. Ellen is hired partly because she resembles a girl the boss had renounced as an unsuitable marriage partner forty-five years before. His son Philip repeats the act of seduction on Ellen. In his limited scheme of desire, she represents the "other" of class as well as sex: "Suddenly he wanted to enter into this world; not indeed with the intention of naturalizing himself as its inhabitant nor with the intention of staying there for ever, but as a navvy might stop on his way to work and refresh his horny sweating body by a swim in a sunny pool" (21). In this fantasy, Ellen is a passive, reviving solution for the self-pitying man to dip in at his pleasure. Philip fastens his male gaze and, nearly borrowing a phrase from T. S. Eliot's Prufrock, considers forcing the moment to its climax:

> The gas-jet was behind her, so to him there was a gold halo about
> her head and her face was a dusky oval in which her eyes and
> the three-cornered patch of her mouth were points of ardour. She
> had an animal's faculty for keeping quite still. He felt a pricking
> appetite to force the moment on to something he could not quite
> previsage, and found himself saying, "Will you have some Burgundy?" (25)

His voyeurism makes angel and animal of his object. The backlit female form is reminiscent of Gretta Conroy, shaped into a self-satisfying "symbol" by another man incapable of love, Gabriel Conroy in Joyce's "The Dead." Philip's "three-cornered . . . points of ardour" reduce female form to sexual geometry, the familiar triangle as woman.[16] For Philip, it is a target for practice; he is like one of the hunting males of Barnes's sexual scenarios. The "animal" metaphor permits Philip mastery over Ellen's one "faculty." He is attracted by stillness in a woman. In what is clearly a moment of passage into womanhood, Ellen experiences the proffered wine unpleasantly, like a "blow in the mouth" (26), but Philip seems to be enjoying the advantage experience (of wine, at least) gives him. Like Prufrock, however, Philip is denied his moment. Not content with what Gilbert and Gubar would term the "no-man" (*No Man's Land* 35–36, 108),

West provides Richard Yaverland, a larger, more exotic and virile male, who diverts Ellen's attention and neutralizes Philip's later attempts to assail her character.

As the novel doubles back in time, both Ellen's mother and her potential mother-in-law, Marion Yaverland, emerge as older custodians of beauty who have endured the assaults of evil. Mrs. Melville suffers from the loss of a treasured son, desertion by an unreliable Irish spouse, and subsequent economic and physical evils. Yet she and her daughter manage a degree of happiness as a couple, where Ellen fills in the masculine, supporting role. For her sources of this Scottish drama, West could go back to two generations of matriarchy in her own family: her grandmother Janet Campbell Mackenzie, widowed in her twenties, and her mother Isabella Mackenzie Fairfield, deserted by her husband when Rebecca was eight. The mother-daughter couple of *The Judge* seek out beautiful views within the compass of brief, economical outings. Mrs. Melville has remnants of former beauty—lovely arms and a fine dress she dons for the "beautiful party" she organizes for Ellen and herself (191–92). She has the sense to admit a young man to her daughter's life and the practical wisdom to revive roses he brings. In dying, Mrs. Melville reminds Ellen of the primal nourishment of the maternal body.

> In these moments the forgotten wisdom of the body, freed from
> the tyranny of the mind and its continual running hither and
> thither at the call of speculation, told them consoling things. The
> mother's flesh, touching the daughter's remembered a faint pulse
> felt long ago and marvelled at this splendid sequel, and lost fear. . . .
> The daughter's flesh, touching the mother's, remembered life in
> the womb, that loving organ that by night and day does not
> cease to embrace its beloved, and was the stronger for tasting
> again that first best draught of love that the spirit has not yet ex-
> celled. (185)

Though she is a rational, scientific, witty young woman, Ellen Melville communicates best in this scene through delicate and emotional hand pressure. In keeping with the theory of the semiotic chora advanced by Julia Kristeva, the figure of the mother becomes the basic signifying space for the regenerative cycle (93–98). Mrs. Melville's Dickensian death in a diphtheria hospital offers a critique of the recurrent social evil of poverty, but in Ellen's mind it asserts the inevitable assault of death upon life and beauty. The death of the mother—particularly in modernist texts such as

*Ulysses, To the Lighthouse,* and *The Judge*—may be death at its worst. It presents a loss of origin. Too often the mother must die in order that the unjust circumstances of her existence be seriously considered.[17]

Marion Yaverland becomes another model for female affiliation in the experience of Ellen Melville—a model so powerful that for many readers she dominates the novel, as it takes up her cycle in English coastal Essex.[18] The narrative shift is as remarkable as Joyce's beginning again, in the fourth episode of *Ulysses,* with the mature Leopold Bloom. West's narrative skip is regularly resisted by my students, who are at this point committed to Ellen Melville. The larger-than-life mythic and melodramatic mode of the latter part of the novel would seem equally uncongenial to materialist feminist readers. There is consistency, however, in West's Manichaean, binary theme of the assault on beauty by evil.

Marion Yaverland manifests and creates beauty throughout her life, despite adverse familial and social conditions. Early in her visit to Marion's home at "Yaverland's End," Ellen notes "windows of extravagant dimensions" that admit the "immensity" of the landscape (241). Marion considers her setting an oasis of beauty, pitying the "joyless lives" of commuting clerks "hurled physically" through "night and morning" (247). Marion has created a lavish interior in deliberate contrast to her stern ancestors; the ambiance also contrasts to the somber Scottish setting in which Ellen (and West herself when among her Edinburgh relatives) was raised. When she faces death, Marion finds this beautiful domestic creation difficult to leave.

Marion, when young like Ellen, was the target and victim of male desire and patriarchal judgment. Although he is the original love of Marion's life, the local Squire Harry is identified as the "evil" father in West's scheme of the novel.[19] Already married to a woman of the appropriate class, Harry woos Marion in the countryside. Their "natural" child, Richard, is the object of Marion's passion from the womb onwards. Before his birth, Marion endures desertion by her careless aristocratic lover, the scorn of her family, and even a stoning by village boys. Her recollection of nursing Richard at the breast is as stunning in its celebration of maternal passion as the much-discussed sexuality in the novels of Lawrence and Joyce. In name only, Marion enters a loveless marriage with Peacey, a man who shelters her from the stoning mob. But this only admits a new evil, marital rape. It takes a depraved system of aristocratic male privilege to give Peacey his opening with Marion. His violation is probably motivated as much by class and male rivalry as by sexual attraction; it seems partly the contest of a butler with his squire. West develops her own version of eugenics, which makes the mutual love of the parents the requisite for successful breeding. Roger, the product of a violent, loveless coupling, carries a seed of evil for the destructive work of the next generation.[20] West's description of a failure of mothering, from nurture in the womb to the meeting of the grown child's spiritual needs, is another significant investigation of maternal space on West's part. It relates directly to her epigraph on judgment and sentencing.

The final implied mother of *The Judge* is Ellen Melville, whose set of experiences prepare her to emerge from the maternal cycle with beauty more nearly intact.[21] Richard Yaverland is certainly a more attractive suitor than Philip James or either of the men who assault Marion Yaverland's beauty. He is aware of both Ellen's strength and her vulnerability, worrying about the tragic results which may come from the opposition of an active mind craving adventure and a feminine body. He is sympathetic to the aims of a suffrage meeting he attends at Ellen's suggestion, but in catching her eye across the assembly, he diverts her from this form of action (Peterson 193). When they visit one of Ellen's favorite landscapes in the Pentland hills, Richard thinks "pretty things" about Ellen that acknowledge an androgynous blend of beauty and utility in her nature. As noted in volume 1, his observations resonate with the central metaphors of web and scaffolding that recur throughout this study.

> It was so like her. It was beautiful and solitary even as she was. The loch that stretched north-east from the narrow neck of water under the bridge was fretted to a majesty of rage by the winds that blew from the black hills around it; but it ended in a dam that was pierced in the middle with some metallic spider's web of engineering; even so would romantic and utilitarian Ellen have designed a loch. (106)

Richard occasionally feels startling empathy over Ellen's passage into heterosexual love, censoring his impulse to infantilize her in diminutives, and placing a metaphor of maternal agency at the heart of her struggle:

> He had hardly believed in the positive reality of girlhood; it had seemed to him rather a negative thing, the state of not being a woman. But in the light of her gentle, palpitant distress, he saw that it was indeed so real a state that passing from it to the state of womanhood would be as terrible as if she had to give birth to her-

self. . . . It was such a helpless state too. She was, he said to himself again—for he knew she did not like him to say it!—such a little thing. (163–64)

Ellen is at first mildly repelled by the otherness of the male—"the faint bluish bloom" of his vigorous whiskers, forcing their way through soon after a shave. " 'There's something awful like an animal about a man' she thought, and shivered" (28). On their walk in the Pentlands (a landscape she was used to sharing with a close female friend), Ellen needs to free herself of Richard. She feels alien from someone who is "both a man and English," identifications which implicate Richard in cultural imperialism (109). Her mood is brightened when she spots a silver branch in the current of the stream where she has taken refuge. As she is drawn to Richard's first kiss, she is reluctant to relinquish the virginal textures and fantasies of girlhood: "the blue shadowed side of marble," gleaming ice, swift running, and romantic versions of love. The kiss is "hard, interminable, sucking pressure" that she experiences as "pain." But hearing his "deep sigh of delight," she has transformed. Ellen has already become maternal: "It was most foolish that she should feel about this great oak-strong man as if he were a little helpless thing that could lie in the crook of her arm, like an ailing puppy; or perhaps a baby" (156–57). Love for both of them involves the discovery of diversity in gender within each other, and careful handling of beauty.

While she resists identification with Marion Yaverland and her native Essex landscape, Ellen uncannily positions herself where Marion was as a young lover, recycling the past. In Marion's sight, she climbs to a spot by Roothing Castle where Marion first felt Richard move in her womb. With Richard, she visits a small marble temple where Squire Harry and Marion spent "night after night shut up with love . . . all the long time the moon required to rise from the open sea, fill all the creeks with silver, and drain them dry again as she sunk westwards" (266). The silver branch on the Pentland stream has been anticipated by Marion's silver creeks. Ellen wants Richard to lift her into an empty niche of the temple, and Richard senses that his father had placed Marion there and resists. But Ellen is capable of timeless wisdom when she re-reads a wider ritual significance to the monumental temple site: "She perceived that it was the silver circle of trees which was the real temple, and that the marble belvedere was but a human offering laid before the shrine" of a divinity that was to be found "along the ebony paths which ran among the glistening thickets" (410).

Ellen has refound the silver branch that vanished amid her fears of love by the Scottish stream. She may have rediscovered an ancient Druidic site. More important, she supplements architecture with nature, and denies the barriers and retentive economies of both worship and love. In contrast to the nonretentive silver temple of trees is the white marble memorial placed by Squire Harry's legitimate wife. Marion "knew that it had been erected not so much to commemorate the dead as to establish the wifehood of the widow who seized this opportunity to prison him in marble as she had never been able to prison him in her arms" (248).

This sense of love receives a fatal challenge, however, from the unloved brother, Roger, now a puritanical convert to evangelical religion who attacks Richard and Ellen (inaccurately) as free lovers. In Roger's conversion, West sustains her testing of religious scaffolding, questioning here its denial of passion and life. Marion, hoping to avert a violent struggle between the brothers, has majestically walked to her death in the sea. Richard has always had the seed of violence in his personality, however. It is most obvious in his wish to avenge his mother's desertion by his father—a wish frustrated by Squire Harry's death. But it takes on larger social resonance in his occupation. He is a manufacturer of explosives in the pre–World War I time frame of the novel. Thus the cultural scaffoldings of technology and religion emerge as evils in the crisis that occurs near the end of the novel. West also plays for the first time her scenario of sibling rivalry, as Richard responds to Roger's assaults upon his mother and lover by murdering him.

Richard and Ellen are united sexually, we are to infer, when all else in the plot has run to chaos. They walk into the marshes, Marion's landscape, which both of them had avoided previously. The marsh as regenerative site bears comparison to the pond, whose muddy depths generate the words for the future drama of Woolf's *Between the Acts*. Ellen first saw the marsh as a figure for Marion's "lethargy." She thought, "A plain of mud could not be beautiful. Yet the mind could dwell contentedly on this new and curious estate of nature, this substance that was neither earth nor water, this place that was neither land nor sea" (232). It is a place that avoids binary opposition in its very composition. It also comes to have potential for "grandeur" with her: "grand like the plain and yet composed of material that, as stuff for grandeur, was almost as uncompromising as mud" (233). It becomes a primal space for generating life: "It was as if this was the primeval ooze from which the first life stirred and crawled landwards to begin to make this memorable star" (232). In the swamps, Richard had previously sensed a feminine threat of the sort that Wyndham Lewis constantly denigrated as bad for the male artist (see *Tarr* 334):

> They stood at the edge of the primeval swamps and called the men down from the highlands of civilisation. . . . They served the seed of life, but to all the divine accretions that had gathered round it, the courage that adventures, the intellect that creates, the soul that questions how it came, they were hostile. . . . They hated the men who loved them passionately because such love was tainted with the romantic and imaginative quality that spurs them to the folly of science and art and exploration. (71)

But Ellen is born of highlands substance; partaking of this strength, Richard is prepared for his entry into paternity.

Richard makes a final "exorbitant" demand of Ellen "as if he had found a hidden staircase leading out of destiny." They go to the marshes, fulfilling a request she had made the day before: they will make love in a cattleman's hut. Marion had told Ellen that the hut was used by one of England's last magicians; it also re-creates a Christian manger scene. Life has transformed Ellen into a sibyl who takes her cues from the redshanks and the shadows that move over the primal landscape. Ellen at first feels complicit in an inescapable binary of gender: "the insane sexual caprice of men, the not less mad excessive steadfastness of women" (429). But hers is steadfastness with a difference; it is cautious, informed, and directed. She overcomes panic. Patiently she watches Richard in a final negotiation with fishermen, an exercise of charm and power that she knows gives him pleasure. She also waits for him to think about Marion, as he looks "to the open sea, over the country of the mud . . . the inexorable womb was continuing to claim its own." She avoids the mistake of alarming him—a mistake she blames for his violence to Roger. She knows that he, like Marion, is destined to be engulfed. But "in throwing her lot with them and with the human race which is perpetually defeated, she was nevertheless choosing the side of victory" (430).

Why victory? And who is the other side? Marion, Richard, and Ellen all manage social victories—over prudish relatives and employers who deny a life/love/beauty principle, and religious and class-based institutions such as Roger's Hallelujah Army that perpetuate such denials. They also seek victory over death through Ellen's and Richard's child. Will

Ellen's single motherhood be a mere repetition? Hopeful readers will recall that Ellen brings to this experience the caution learned from her foremothers' mistakes, which include an overinvestment in sons. Ellen welcomes a child of either sex. She retains the tools of social analysis learned from suffragettes, the womb-knowledge of her mother, and the celebration of beauty by Marion. She has situated herself in both the stern Pentland landscape and the primal mud of Kerith Island. Grown wily about ways of destruction, Ellen now times her moves to avert catastrophe. If she can summon all of these resources, built up over generations, she will conceive and conserve beauty, not just in her child but in her ongoing self.

## The Magical Feminine of *Harriet Hume*

*Harriet Hume* is a very different book from *The Judge*. Textual play qualifies it as traditionally modernist in form, and its minimal cast of a single couple satisfies the pared-down version of modernism approved by Pound and achieved in Joyce's *A Portrait of the Artist as a Young Man* and West's own first novel, *The Return of the Soldier*. West deliberately played with gender, creating a character of what Glendinning describes as "undiluted femininity" (*Rebecca West* 126).[22] Jane Marcus has written of its fantasy component (signaled in the subtitle, *A London Fantasy*) as a significant subgenre of female modernism, where it joins works such as Woolf's *Orlando* and Sylvia Townsend Warner's *Lolly Willowes*.[23] Its fantasy and play may have discouraged West herself from taking the work nearly so seriously as she had *The Judge*. West wrote to Sylvia Lynd, "I hope you will like it in its unpretentious way—it's only an hour's crazy entertainment" (West letter to Lynd; quoted in Glendinning, *Rebecca West* 126). We leap through time, and from one character's thoughts to the next; trees are transformed to maidens, and (as in Joyce's *Finnegans Wake*) we wonder whether it is an account of death or life.

*Harriet Hume* was published in 1929, after West had freed herself from Wells and his scorn of "wonderlands." She had become a frequent traveler to the United States and, like Harriet, a confident woman about London. As her disclosure to Sylvia Lynd suggests, this novel is more the product of female associations than was *The Judge*. West's admiration for Woolf's *Orlando*, expressed in her 1928 review "High Fountain of Genius," helped establish the importance of 1928 as a banner year for feminist modernism in volume 1. In a letter reacting to West's review, Woolf suggested that West was the ideal reader of her fantasy, her mind "working along where mine tried to go (what a lot more of my meaning you have guessed than anybody else) & expanding and understanding, making Everything ten times more important than it seemed before" (Woolf letter to West, Tulsa). In somewhat mixed terms, Woolf defended *Harriet Hume* against Vita Sackville-West's charge that the work was "a brew of Meredith, *Orlando* and Amanda Ross." Woolf notes that West's play on style "helps her to manufacture some pretty little China ornaments for the mantelpiece" (4 *L* 88). The metaphor is appropriate to Harriet, who enjoys beauty on a smaller scale than Marion of *The Judge*. Harriet is a collector of fine little artifacts.[24]

*Harriet Hume* works even more insistently than *The Judge* with binaries of gender. It follows its central couple, Arnold Condorex and Harriet Hume, from youth to death in six encounters and near-encounters, in all seasons. A less sympathetic male than Richard, Arnold has a traditional set of masculine expectations for a career in public life. He begins as a poor lawyer without family connections or class stature, and rises as a politician through a series of playoffs and betrayals that he represents as triumphs of negotiation. Aspects of his rise derive from H. G. Wells, while his political dealings suggest West's brief but distressing affair with Lord Beaverbrook.[25] West's cultural critique is more subtle here than in her early socialist articles, but it persists. Condorex's ugly surname suggests the trade names of modern products (Playtex, or the condom Durex) and a carrion-eating bird. He is further identifiable with materialism in his amassing of great debts to support the lifestyle expected by the politically well-connected, parasitic wife he acquires, quite peripherally to the novel.[26] There is a dimension of empire in Condorex's career. As a young man, he moves on from lovemaking with Harriet to experiencing "a spasm of desire" over the prospect of commanding a dispatch box in the foreign service (62). He becomes Lord Mondh (lord of *le monde,* the world, perhaps) by fraud. Condorex covered the ignorance of the British Raj by pretending to discover the location of Mondh. West's narrator makes the cynical aside "No white man must ever admit to a Mango that he does not know everything" (69).

Harriet begins her novel as a far more established young woman than Ellen Melville of *The Judge*. She lives on her own, enjoys sexual freedom, and pursues a career as a pianist, all attributes of the new woman. In ad-

dition, she has mystical qualities and narrative skills that escape a historical category.[27] Musical accomplishment and self-expression could be considered another tradition in female modernism. Margaret Stetz has argued that it provides women writers with an alternative to affiliation with
male writers.[28] Within West's works there are numerous female musicians
modeled on her mother, whose talent as a pianist is well described in *Family Memories*. Most notable are Mrs. Melville of *The Judge* and Mrs.
Aubrey and two of her daughters in *The Fountain Overflows*. Among
other female modernists, Dorothy Richardson found piano playing a useful extension of Miriam Henderson's language and psyche in *Pilgrimage*.
Music functions similarly for Rachel Vinrace in Woolf's *The Voyage Out*
and for Lucy Honeychurch in E. M. Forster's *A Room with a View*. Jane
Campion's film *The Piano* picks up on the same expression of sexual force
in women.

Harriet's cultural command is developed further by her choice of
rooms in fine old Blennerhassett House, her informed appreciation of
eighteenth-century architecture and Adam brothers' stucco work, and her
collection of exquisite little art objects, as permitted by her limited funds.
West's diaries betray a similar passion for buying small, affordable art objects; the taste for the work of the Adam brothers goes back to her family
in Edinburgh (*FM* 84). Harriet's possession of a portion of former privilege—the apartment carved from the house and garden of an aristocrat—
suggests a redistribution of beauty as well as wealth. It was a scheme of
urban reform that West would continue to advocate for cities—Vienna,
for instance, as she discusses its architectural errors in *Black Lamb and
Grey Falcon*. Though she knows and appreciates artists such as the Adam
brothers and Sir Joshua Reynolds, West engages in play with their famous
works. Headless sheep haunt the Adam brothers, as the throwaway parts
of artwork that featured only the ram's head. Unlike the puritanical scaffolding rejected in *The Judge*, the eighteenth century offers a matrix for
art and exuberance, transformed to Harriet's purposes.

Victoria Glendinning has detected the underlying binary division in
Harriet's art vs. the politics of Arnold Condorex ("Introduction"). Seen
another way, Harriet positions herself in the stereotypically masculine
domain of culture, as performer, critic, and owner. She does this, however,
without relinquishing what is usually placed in opposition to masculine/
culture. She in no way gives up woman's traditional association with nature. But hers is a creative and active relation. Harriet situates herself in

gardens, both the parks of London where she strolls with Condorex and her own piece of an old Kensington garden. She grows flowers. She remakes male accounts of nature.

Harriet recasts Joshua Reynolds's painting of the three graces to explain the presence of three extraordinary trees in her garden, in the process recycling with a difference the myths of Daphne and Persephone. As babies, three sisters were stolen away from their parents. It is likely that they were taken into nature, since when they were restored, they were bound together by floral garlands. The garlands are reminiscent of girls' school pageants, and were a notable motif in Sylvia Pankhurst's murals for the WSPU exhibition in 1909. Their collective absence in nature is an inversion of the Persephone/Hades myth. Deprived of the connective garlands when married, girls were never so beautiful or spirited again. They assumed their final form as trees when, Daphne-like, they fled potential rapists. Harriet's culminating achievement with nature comes at the close of the novel, when she brings on preternatural spring.

*Harriet Hume* is organized around Harriet's personal role as wise woman, attempting repeatedly to intervene spiritually in the destructive cycles of Condorex's political life. Her capacity at mind reading discomfits him from the start, as he refers to her with annoyance as "witch" and "this Cassandra," disliking her appearance as "sibylline" (193). On the other hand, as a performer of the feminine, Harriet gives Condorex some encouragement to think of her as delicate and yielding. He can take satisfaction from "how kindly she had bent herself to his will" (21). She lets him think that he has fashioned her like Pygmalion. Harriet is presented as a bestower of gifts, dependent upon the attitude of the receiver. If the gift is not appreciated, the woman may just seem "easy" (55–56). Harriet shows symptoms of tremendous physical and emotional drain when she has epiphanies about his political intentions. On the first of these occasions, Condorex must catch her in his arms; in a late meeting she must recline on a couch.

The most violent potentials of dualism are realized in late scenes of the novel. The couple meet on the night of his political ruin, when apparently Condorex already plans murder/suicide. In reviewing their past relations, she reminds him, "You yourself once explained that there was a mystical confusion of substance in us" (203). But he is more interested in seeing them as opposites, a structure which means destruction. "There is no room in the world of spirits for opposites. . . . To concede to one's opposite, in the most infinitesimal degree, is to die" (204–205). Harriet does not see harm in opposites: "There is the North and there is the South, and there is no war between them" (203). Condorex nourishes two traditional male visions of gender differences, and would control Harriet by them. In one, he plays the role of Orpheus, as an artist depicts him in one of Condorex's wall decorations: "a young man lion-ruddy with the hues of health, stretching out his arms in eternal desire towards a young woman that stands in the recesses of a cave, all black and white, and bloodless and perfect, like yourself" (208). He also longs to transport her "to a purer world where things sit more stably in their categories. I would clang an iron gate on you, and shut you in a garden, where there are no coloured flowers, but only tall lilies standing in wet black earth, and no trees save the decent cypress" (209). It is Hades, the land of deadly entrapment, the idea of which makes Harriet wrench herself from his bear-like hug.

Condorex's lust for orderly categories, secure economies, and the survival of his own oppositional being gets uglier when he is left on his own, talking to a mirror. He suggests that in the physical world, opposites such as lion and lamb can live safely apart "until the mawkish smell of her herbivorousness seeks him down the wind and draws him to her by its insult to his difference; and her terrible meek breath on his fierce muzzle posits a relationship and makes him her murderer" (229). Sounding like a character out of Wyndham Lewis, Condorex expresses fears of disorder and contamination, expressed in the metaphor of a stain spreading relentlessly from a single drop: "Why, its headstrong alchemies, the confusion of substances it not only permits but procures with delight, are most dangerous. They prevent a man from standing upright, they cut out his most vital parts, they yield him utterly to his opposite, who by necessity must wish his death" (230). So, apparently killing himself with a revolver, Condorex becomes a lost spirit, blundering through tangled streets and a natural landscape deprived of season, intending to murder Harriet.

The spirit he encounters admits her own limitations, extracts good from his difference, and suggests complementarity rather than conflict:

> "What was the use of me being so innocent in this g-g-garden,"
> she bleated into her handkerchief, "when I had no power to impose
> my state on the rest of society? I may have been innocent, but I was
> also impotent. . . . Humanity would be unbearably lackadaisical if
> there were none but my kind alive. . . . When you were not pursu-
> ing the chimera of greatness, you performed many very worthy
> achievements that enabled our species to establish itself on this

globe more firmly. Did you not see to the building of bridges, the teaching of children, the suppression of riot and bloodshed?" (266–67)

Harriet's vision includes some acceptance of the British imperial enterprise which has employed Condorex. On his side, Condorex appreciates the integrity of Harriet's timeless aesthetic contemplations, contrasting the destructive effects of political negotiation:

> For that principle forbids one ever to let the simple essences of things react on each other and so produce a real and inevitable event; it prefers that one should perpetually tamper with the materials of life, picking this way with the finger-nail, flattening that with the thumb, and scraping that off with one's knife and stamping it on the ground at one's feet; and the most ambitious performance in that line, ay and the most effective . . . was murder. (267–68)

The mind that betrays truth or commits murder would continue to fascinate West, carrying into her reporting on both criminal and treason trials in the 1950s.

*Harriet Hume* is in some ways a more mature version of West's 1914 story "Indissoluble Matrimony," which Gilbert and Gubar have read as all-out sex war, based on "the dis-ease of no-manhood" exhibited by its male protagonist, George.[29] Arnold Condorex is a more intelligent and successful man than George, a dull clerk condemned to live out a routine existence, returning nightly to a shoddy development house. Harriet takes more pains to know Arnold than the story's heroine, Evadne, does with her husband, George. Harriet does not believe in a God of war; both Evadne and George do, at least momentarily, just before they grapple in a deadly vortex of water. Indeed, Evadne is a more combative female than Harriet. She is fighting partially for her own identity as a spokeswoman for socialism; Harriet's more aesthetic occupation is never challenged. Like *Harriet Hume,* the story has a surprising ending. Contrary to George's assumptions, Evadne has not been drowned. Death is beyond George's capacity, even for himself. As executioner of the supposed evils of Evadne, he had planned a martyr's suicide via the gas main. But Evadne has routinely shut it off for the night, and George falls asleep, frustrated. Gilbert and Gubar suggest, finally, that he was not worth killing. I suspect that West wants to realize a primal, maternal feminine in

Evadne. Not a disciple of a war ethic, she becomes the "child's god" that George had thought of as he struggled in the water. Evadne's slumbering embrace of George resembles the final meeting of Harriet and Condorex at the end of *Harriet Hume*. Published in BLAST, "Indissoluble Matrimony" had a feminine vision that went beyond the violent surface articulations of BLAST editor Wyndham Lewis and the aestheticized violence of vorticism.

The final magic of Harriet Hume includes her ability to transcend the barriers between minds and between species (she is lamb-like, cat-like, and capable of speaking to a dog in his own language). In this she is resonant with Djuna Barnes's Robin Vote of *Nightwood*. Despite her nonviolent nature, Harriet will not yield her own life. She is renovating without being masterful, and sets a tone which is less discomfiting to readers than West's other sibylline women, including Marion of *The Judge*, Rose Aubrey of *The Fountain Overflows*, and West's persona in *Black Lamb*. Harriet restores the natural cycle by bringing the missing season of spring into the garden. She hands out refreshments to Condorex and the two deceased police officers who have protected her. Harriet overcomes her own sloppiness by putting her house in order before taking Condorex in for the night. Yet, never an agent of total control, she cannot tell what the next day will bring.

The meeting of redemptive female with self-destructive establishment male is revisited by West in *The Thinking Reed*, "The Abiding Vision" (one of the novellas included in *The Harsh Voice*), and even the crime story "Mr Setty and Mr Hume." None of these heroines is as active or imaginative as Harriet, however. Mrs. Hume is merely oblivious. Into a story that seems to focus upon murder, detective work, and courtroom drama, West inserts this new mother, remarking, "Women of her type resemble artists in their failure to feel surprise at the exceptional event." While West's work will exist "only on the printed page," Mrs. Hume may untangle "the snarl in [her murderer husband's] genetic line" (318–19). Less optimistically, the wife and mistress of Sam Hartley support his career as an American businessman in turn, sacrificing themselves to exhaustion—the condition that Harriet was sometimes left in by Condorex. The female hero of *The Thinking Reed*, Isabelle, carries the name of West's own redemptive mother into a novel concerned with wealth and the destructive lifestyle of a male industrialist, her husband, Marc. Isabelle understands the ministering type of woman represented in another female character in the novel, Luba, whom she befriends. Isabelle speaks in West's authoritative voice. She offers an understanding of Luba's needs that applies to all humans, and crosses gender: "Surely in each human being there is both a hungry, naked outcast and a Sister of Charity, desolate without those she can feed and clothe and shelter; and these cannot minister to each other. That is the rule which has been put in to make it more difficult. They must find a stranger outside the skin to whose Sister of Charity the outcast can offer his sores, to whose outcast their Sister of Charity can offer her pity" (165–66). Isabelle saves Marc from corruption, but in doing so suffers a miscarriage—yet another sacrifice of youth and beauty to cultural evils.

## The Sexual Politics of *St. Augustine*

Rebecca West's exploration of dualistic binaries and the social scaffolding of imperial cultures reached back to the struggles over sexual and material guilt experienced in the days of early Christianity by St. Augustine. She made him the subject of a monograph in 1933. Augustine appealed to West for a number of reasons. She was impressed by the "modern" method of his *Confessions:* "He works in the same introspective field as the moderns. In his short violent sentences, which constantly break out in the rudest tricks of the rhetoricians, rhymes, puns, and assonances, he tries to do exactly what Proust tries to do in his long reflective sentences, which are so unconditioned by their words, which are so entirely determined by their meaning. He tries to take a cast of his mental state at a given moment" (165). This suggests that West's definition of modernism favors subjective truths and ideas, acknowledging the limitations of words, as did Woolf.

West also shows interest in Augustine's marginal socioeconomic and political position in fourth-century Africa, then part of a fading Roman Empire: "that stony yet not infertile land, which engendered tremendous crops, tremendous men, violent events" (168). As a Numidian, Augustine was of a conquered race, and thus motivated to prove himself. On the verge of its fall to the vandals, the urban population of Rome had been "castrated" of their "will" by a routine of providing civil amenities, and by the censorship of negative information. In this era of "spiritual mischance," Christian individualism and intellectualism gained in appeal with certain people, according to West. These included individuals temperamentally attracted to movements, and "people whose ethical fastidiousness led them to desire some of that peculiar and delicate wisdom which is only learned in defeat" (161–62). Numidian conditions of marginality and difference might be compared to the situation of another former Roman conquest, Yugoslavia, which West would explore a few years later in *Black Lamb and Grey Falcon*.

West's work on Augustine allows her to explore the heresy he held, Manichaeanism. West presents her summary of Manichaeanism not as a law or fact but as "a beautiful myth": "How nearly it corresponds to a basic fantasy of the human mind is shown by its tendency to reappear spontaneously in age after age" (SA 180). The myth is figured metaphorically: "Light and darkness, good and evil are the same pair under different names," as are spirit and matter. West's retelling of the myth adds a second metaphor of seeding, where soil and seed are perversely antithetical. Satan, ruler of the kingdom of darkness, made war on God's kingdom of light; God begat Primal Man as a defender. Man was captured, and though he was released after God's victory over Satan, the two kingdoms had become confused in the course of battle. "Seeds of darkness had been scattered widely in the soil of light, innumerable seeds of light found themselves sown deeply in the darkness. . . ." The mixture persists in earthly humans. "Demons seek his darkness; prophets enfranchise light" (ibid.). This blend provides the makings of complex psychological characterization, in which binary oppositions play within and between individuals, as we have seen them do in Richard of *The Judge*, in the exchanges of Harriet and Condorex in *Harriet Hume*, and in *The Thinking Reed*. Extracting the good requires spiritual wisdom, and very often West's maternal figures possess this wisdom. It was a drama that West never tired of, sustaining it through the final series of novels that began with *The Fountain Overflows*.[30]

The story of St. Augustine's passionate relationship to God is explained by West as an alternation between gender-marked, parental poles of influence. This personal story resonates with the historical challenge Christianity posed to Rome. The particular force that brought Augustine to the Church, by her account and most others, was his mother, Monnica. Jane Marcus suggests that in this "psycho-biography," West "studies Augustine entirely in terms of his relationship with his mother" ("A Speaking Sphinx" 153). Monnica offered the prophetic vision that the Christian standard "would rise him at one step above the greatest man in Rome, would utterly condemn the accomplishments of civilization, and indeed reward him for lacking them, and what was more, would ensure him pre-eminence in the future life as well as in this" (SA 171). In effect, it would lift him out of destructive patriarchal cycles. Monnica is notable for her "steady self-control" which gives her patience through Augustine's period of sexual experience and is rewarded with their "climax," a supreme ecstasy which finds the two of them talking "of the purity of life with God, unstained by sensuous experience, and they were lifted up towards it" (198). West sees Augustine's search for the invisible universe as a search for his mother, after her death (203). West would return to the problematics of renouncing life for immortality in *Black Lamb and Grey Falcon*. She poses some difficulties with Monnica's agency, finding it "unforgivable" that Augustine separated his son from his mistress at his own mother's instigation. Monnica's encouragement of her son to renounce heterosexual love has its self-serving aspect, according to West: "It was fortunate that in her religion she had a perfect and, indeed, noble instrument for obtaining her desire that her son should not become a man" (171). West finds that Augustine exaggerated the importance of sex, yet had "an unreasoning horror of it." She is interested in his complaints about the undignified anatomy of men. But her own speculation on the subject compares the powers of the sexes in the reproductive act, finding the advantage with women, predictably on account of maternity. She points to the "disadvantageous situation of man in the sexual act, who finds that for him it ends with physical collapse and surrender of power, whereas for his partner it ends with motherhood and an increase of power" (170).

West follows Augustine beyond his period of spiritual identification with his mother into a late masculine phase when he was an administrator of the convent at Hippo. She suggests that from early childhood the political and social dimensions of life were "all associated with his father, or at least the male side of life" (170). Augustine's masculine aspirations would have been to rise out of his provincial African contexts. Indeed, a similar rise out of obscurity and social disadvantage had been achieved by H. G. Wells. West's own path out of Edinburgh and her attraction to political subjects can be taken as an index of her own diversity in gender orientation.

A maternal principle, operating in cyclical time, is the final theory offered in West's essay on St. Augustine. Setting her story into the monumental cycles of history, West remarks that Augustine and Roman civilization were gone. "Nothing remained except the Church to which his mother had given him, the Mother Church, where as much of the human tradition was stored as would permit man to repeat in another place the cycle of building up and tearing down to which, as yet, he has been limited" (236).[31] The mother is the source of rebuilding, but regrettably lacks the capacity to break the cycle of recurrent destruction.

Apart from the parental binaries that contribute to the character of St. Augustine, West discusses another implied binary in Augustine's philosophy of sexual and material guilt. Augustine briefly practiced homosexuality. West endorses Augustine's analysis of what she terms, in her authoritative voice, the "real offence of homosexuality." It is that "it brings the confusion of passion into the domain where one ought to be able to practice calmly the art of friendship" (174). Augustine's denigration of sexuality and of material possessions, done in order to placate God, has roots in all religions. It even has restrictive effects upon Shakespeare and a set of male modernists, according to West. Where modernists examine these Augustinian tensions, they contribute to West's refiguring process and resultant new strategies.

> Lawrence tried to investigate the complex of ideas and test its validity by exposing himself to its emotional effects, which have long been disregarded in the one-sided discussion of its intellectual bases. Proust made a colossal effort to justify his sense of dualism by marshalling all the evidence for the horrid oddity of matter collected by his senses, and to soothe the sting by propounding that experience could be converted into beauty by being removed into the immaterial and therefore clean world of memory. James Joyce in *Ulysses,* representing the spirit by the unstained boy Stephen Dedalus and matter by the squatting buffoon Leopold Bloom finds a myth that perfectly expresses the totality of facts and emotional effects of the Augustinian complex. It is the ring-fence in which the modern mind is prisoner. (SA 233–34)

By calling the modern mind a prisoner, she clearly sets the goal of release.

## Ideas of Empire in *Black Lamb and Grey Falcon*

In West's 1913 essay "Trees of Gold," travel through rural Spain had served as an antidote to her young female rage about the political situation back home in London. *Black Lamb and Grey Falcon* offers more complex therapy. It is still based on cultural contrasts—a formula also observed in the Edinburgh-Essex contrasts of *The Judge,* and more so in the Russian-English parentage of the female hero of *The Birds Fall Down.* *Black Lamb* is a book of compound genre—scholarly history, art appreciation, travel guide, anti-imperial tract, mystical meditation, and auto-biography. It probes the processes and assumptions of Western culture by looking off-center at its Slavic margin. For West, Yugoslavia is the colonial "other" of numerous invading cultures, and a resource for seeing the psychological "primitive" which West sees as the basis of the modern Western mind. John Gunther, an intimate friend of West and himself a commentator on Western culture, found *Black Lamb* "not so much a book about Yugoslavia as a book about Rebecca West" (Gunther letter to West, quoted in Glendinning, *Rebecca West* 155). As with all writing on a culture not one's own, we must be wary of the writer's finding what she wanted, to confirm familiar paradigms. Larry Wolff credits West with breaking away from the self-serving idea of Eastern Europe: "The idea of Eastern Europe as the continent's backward half was invented in Western Europe, to illuminate by contrast the greater glory of 'Western' civilization. Rebecca West was a journalist on the trail of that dishonest, self-serving appropriation of Eastern Europe, seeking to invert a tradition of condescension and to redefine the mapping of civilization in Europe" (28). In doing so she abandoned "the figure of the cultivated traveler to the dark lands of Eastern Europe," which "was as old as the idea of Eastern Europe itself" (29). Writing in April 1941 to Alexander Woollcott, the American drama critic and playwright whom she considered a "twin-soul," West explained herself:

> The Yugoslavian book now seems to me a preternatural event in my life. Why should I be moved in 1936 to devote the following 5 years of my life, at great financial sacrifice and to the utter exhaustion of my mind and body to take an inventory of a country down to its last vest-button in a form insane from any ordinary artistic or commercial point of view—a country which ceases to exist? I find the hair raising on my scalp at the extraordinary usefulness of this apparently utterly futile act. (West letter to Woollcott, Harvard)

Her British and American publishers, Macmillan and Viking, gave her minimal contracts.[32] That done, they did not balk at the 1,187 pages of a book even she described as an "acute case of literary elephantiasis" (West letter to Roughead, Texas). This liberty with form and length was a very different state of affairs from what Djuna Barnes met with Eliot at Faber, where she was forced to cut both *Nightwood* and *The Antiphon* drastically, as noted in the previous chapter.

The Manichaean myth, which West explored extensively in *St. Augus-*

*tine*," recurs in this text. West informs us that the heresy visited Yugoslavia in Catharism, which flourished in the Dalmatian walled city of Trogir as well as in Bosnia. West studies the Manichaean disposition in a sculpture by Radovan on the portal of a thirteenth-century church of Trogir. She suggests that this work "instantly recalls the novels of Dostoievsky," and she uses the qualities of this art to generalize about the temperament of Slavs. In her final memoirs, West even traced a Slavic ancestor on her father's side, thus claiming a Slavic disposition in herself (*Family Memories* 204–205). Her remarks bear comparison to Woolf's sense of the "Russian influence" on modern fiction, her interest in Dostoyevsky's powers with the creation of character, and particularly her description of the "utmost sadness" and inconclusiveness of Russian mind: "It is the sense that there is no answer, that if honestly examined life presents question after question which must be left to sound on and on after the story is over in hopeless interrogation that fills us with a deep, and finally it may be with a resentful, despair" ("Modern Fiction," CR 158). At Trogir, West finds scenes of Christ that "are depicted with a primitive curiosity, but also make a highly cultured admission that curiosity cannot be wholly gratified. It is as if the child in the artist asked, 'What are those funny men doing?' and the subtle man in him answered, 'I do not know, but I think . . . ' " More earthly scenes are of Adam and Eve, animals, and a common working man, about which the same questioning of child to man within are posed. Since in the Manichaean belief there may be particles of light even in the common man, "each individual and his calling had to be subjected to the severest analysis possible"—a different state of affairs from the orthodox practice to be followed with beings possessed of souls (BL&GF 174). She traces this into a difference in discourse, where Slavs "will try out all kinds of conduct simply to see whether they are of the darkness or of the light," leading to "debate and experiment which to the West seem unnecessary, and therefore, since they must involve much that is painful, morbid" (175). Such discussions are recorded with delight in *Black Lamb*. West considers the Manichaean a "useful conception of life," but is critical of its excesses, including the literal rather than allegorical interpretation of the process for recovering light, nastiness about sex, and practices that verged on necrophilia and suicide (172–73).[33]

Introducing Woollcott to *Black Lamb,* West directs his attention to the St. George's Eve section. She also sends him the typescript of an article on St. George, who "had an extraordinary adventure with a wild beast amounting to a powerful intervention on the side of life against death,"[34] words echoed in *Black Lamb* (811). The rituals of St. George's Eve in heavily Muslim Macedonia all encourage fertility—one of the attributes of St. George. In one place, women lay in a ritual trance around a cross. In another, veiled women embraced a rock. Despite the sameness of this ritual and the patriarchal rule that they be "undifferentiated female stuff, mere specimens of mother ooze," West finds their gestures highly individual, and of value (*BL&GF* 803). These rituals have some resemblance to the trancelike state entered by Robin Vote in Djuna Barnes's novel *Nightwood.* The culminating ritual of St. George's Eve provides the black lamb of West's title, and a deep faulting of religion. In a place called The Sheep's Field there stood a flat, irregular rock, about six feet high and "red-brown and gleaming, for it was entirely covered with the blood of the beasts that had been sacrificed on it during the night." It is not new to West, "for we are all brought up among disguised presentations of it" (823). She watches as two lambs in succession are sacrificed atop the rock, by having a knife drawn across their throats. Many pages later she recollects the victim in greater detail: "the lamb forcing out the forceless little black hammer of its muzzle from the flimsy haven of the old man's wasted arms" (914). West makes an equation to Christianity: "All our Western thought is founded on this repulsive pretence that pain is the proper price of any good thing. Here it could be seen how the meaning of the Crucifixion had been hidden from us, though it was written clear" (827). She consistently challenged the scaffolding of sacrifice.

The second symbol of her title, the falcon, is introduced in a poem well known in Yugoslavia. The bird (really St. Elijah) comes from Jerusalem to the Tsar Lazar, leader of the Serbs. On the eve of their battle with the Turks at Kossovo, the falcon gives Lazar his choice between an earthly kingdom and victory, or a heavenly kingdom in defeat. He chooses the latter, and hence, the falcon also suggests that "sacrifice is a valid symbol" (914). West views this defeat as comparable to that of Western liberals, who "never speak as if power would be theirs tomorrow," who "want to be right not to do right" and feel "no obligation to be part of the main tide of life" (914). Hers seems a postmodern challenge to the old left, a call to political praxis. While W. B. Yeats's well-known falcon of "The Second Coming" can no longer hear the falconer, West's gets new orders. For West, Yugoslavia "writes obscure things plain, which furnishes symbols for what the intellect has not yet formulated" (914). By being "dear to the primitive mind," it is vital also to her, since the primitive mind is the foundation of the modern mind (914). West looks to art to "understand the whole of life" and ultimately "destroy the myth of the rock," though she does not expect this for a thousand years. "No wonder we reach out to lay hold on such a force when we are beset with disgusting dangers" (1127).

While West was writing *Black Lamb and Grey Falcon,* Yugoslavia went through a coup in an attempt to mount resistance to the Nazis, and was rapidly defeated by them. The poem of the grey falcon was revived, somewhat inappropriately, as West admits, to describe the flight of the young Serbian king Peter from Yugoslavia through Jerusalem to London, even as his country fell to the Nazis. This poetic appropriation forces her to recognize poems as "palimpsests," and to sense the throb of the death wish in life.

Although West's affection for Serbs is undeniable, she does resist the Serb-Croat-Muslim division that afflicts the former Yugoslavia as I write this. She has admiration for many Yugoslavians: the Bosnian heretics of Sarajevo, the embroiderers of Macedonia, and a solitary woman on the road at Montenegro, who sought to understand the process of her destiny (1012). What seems, to an unappreciative companion, a "mish-mash" of "primitive" people offers to West a fascinating problem: "It is precisely because there are so many different peoples that Yugoslavia is so interesting. So many of these peoples have remarkable qualities, and it is fascinating to see whether they can be organized into an orderly state" (662). The latter was of great value to West, explaining much of her later conservative writing.

Yugoslavia offers an ideal setting for the study of empires, from the Greeks through the Nazis, and including Roman, Ottoman, Byzantine, Turkish, Venetian, and Austro-Hungarian remnants in history, architecture, painting, dress, and embroidery. Early in the work she notes the basic religious difference between the Croats, who typically follow Roman Catholicism, and the Serbs, who are Orthodox Christians. As far as imperial influence goes, West suggests that, largely because of their northern situation, the Croats took on values of their Germanic, Austro-Hungarian dominators, the Habsburgs.[35] West reviews the history of imperial intrigues, murders, and insults to the Slavs and their colonial administrators resulting from this connection. She shows how her understanding grows, from distant memory of the news that reached Britain in her childhood, through visits to numerous sites that played into history, and further from conversations with Yugoslavs who have their own interpretations of events. The Serbs have a more independent history in regard to imperialism, in West's interpretation. She credits them with valor in warding off the Turks from much of Europe, and admires their institutions, which include the code of law and foreign policy established by King Michael (533–35). But she does not oppose Serb and Croat; like her principal host, in reality the scholar and writer Stanislav Vinaver, she puts her hope in a united Yugoslavia, able to withstand the next superpower.[36] West's skepticism about empires extends to Britain: "her bustling polychrome Victorian self..that would assume, at a moment's notice and without the slightest reflection the responsibility of determining the destiny of the most remote and alien people" (1115).

West heaps scorn on all evidence of German domination and incipient fascism in Yugoslavia. She occasionally explains that she does not dislike all Germans. Her mother had been well treated when serving as a musical governess for a German family living in London. Her husband, Henry Andrews, had numerous German contacts. He had spent part of his childhood in Hamburg, and until the rise of fascism did business for German banks (see *FM* 105ff., 223ff.). But she is displeased to find Germanic hearts and flowers invading the embroideries of Zagreb. West begins her German analysis with domestic contact, as she and her husband share their train travel into Yugoslavia with vacationing Germans. The men of the group are professionals who talk guardedly about the impact of the Nazi regime on their business lives. They care much more for the seaside than they do for Yugoslav nationals or their culture. West constructs a rather loaded incident in which they eject a Latin-looking, epicene young man from the train compartment because he has only a second-class ticket, when it turns out that they too have second-class stubs. She also provides a compulsive eater. German tourists are typically portly and rude when they reappear on her route.

West's treatment of German tourists is mild compared to her portrayal of Gerda, a German expatriate living in Yugoslavia. She is the wife of Constantine, the government official who plays host to West's traveling persona. Constantine is a temperamental poet, a Serb, and a Jew—the last category adding complexity to the German question. West tries to understand Constantine's repeated defenses and placations of Gerda, sharing the project with her own husband, who finds Constantine "preposterously good" to Gerda. The Jewish and Slav respect for Germany and Austria is explained by West as the effect of Western culture coming to Eastern Europeans through Germany. She also suggests a self-hatred, induced by the process: "an uneasy suspicion that if Germans and Austrians despise the Slavs and the Jews there must be something in it" (666). As their travels progress, Gerda plays the role of connoisseur, which fits her into West's most scorned category of women—the cultural parasites of the privileged classes. Gerda deadens the enthusiasm of the traveling couple, whom she expects to hold Eurocentric values. To an extent that strains the imagination and spoils her characterization, Gerda disparages things Yugoslavian and glorifies things German, even down to the war monuments.

Virginia Woolf thought of going to see Rebecca West "about fascism" in 1935 (4 D 321). An explanation is provided, with Yugoslavian focus, in *Black Lamb and Grey Falcon*. West looks to a new, deprived urban order as the basis for catastrophic events occurring on the periphery of Yugoslavia. West dates her interest in Yugoslavia to the day when she heard of the assassination of its king, Alexander, in 1934. This brings a flashback to the 1898 assassination of Queen Elizabeth of Austria, announced to West as a child by her mother. Switching between the political and the domestic, West suggests that Elizabeth might have "medicined the sores of empire, if only the medium for this work—her marriage—had been bearable." The queen's murderer, Luccheni, is West's first fascist—the product of the "new towns which the industrial and financial developments of the nineteenth century had raised all over Europe," towns planned in the interest of the rich, and "careless of the souls and bodies of the poor." Hitler and Mussolini came of the same economics of deprivation. West puts on here the battling voice of the *Clarion*. As in *The Judge*, she is finding evil in the careless waste of human resources.

> The new sort of people have been defrauded of their racial tradition, they enjoyed no inheritance of wisdom; brought up without gardens, to work on machines, all but a few lacked the education which is given by craftsmanship; and they needed this wisdom and this education as never before, because they were living in conditions of unprecedented frustration and insecurity. (612)

Already in Zagreb, West saw pasty-faced children, denied the peasant right to fresh air in winter. But craftsmanship and sense of tradition survive among even the poorest of inhabitants of the older cities and countryside of Yugoslavia.

The politics of Yugoslavia, as analyzed by West, implicate gender difference, in both sex roles and analogies. West uses feminine strategy as a basic metaphor for Yugoslavian survival under its various invaders. She suggests that Slavs have twice "played the part of . . . woman in the history of Europe. The woman she has in mind is one who resists by yield-ing." Though he "takes possession of her and perhaps despises her for it . . . suddenly he finds that his whole life has been conditioned to her." He "has not conquered her mind, and . . . he is not sure if she loves him, or even likes him, or even considers him of great moment." She may even have let him into her life because "she hated him and wanted him to ex-pose himself" for her own despising (302). Napoleon, allowed entry into the snowy core of Russia, was one victim. The Bosnians who submitted to the Turks were able to live in high style and to practice their own re-ligious heresies in the Free City of Sarajevo. Sadly, we now know of an-other turn of fate.

West finds masculinity she can appreciate in Yugoslavia. Neither in-ability to produce crafts nor uncertainty about sexuality afflicts the boat-makers of Korchula: "These were men, they could beget children on women, they could shape certain kinds of materials for purposes that made them masters of their worlds" (BL&GF 208). West contrasts them to the bespectacled, delicate, and effete male types of Western cities. At sev-eral junctures, West hints that homosexuality is rare in Yugoslavia, imply-ing that this is a relief from the sexuality she is experiencing in her own country.

Through the 1950s, in novels and letters, West uses denigrating terms of her era such as "pansy" in referring to gay males.[37] Still, figuring out her attitude toward homosexuality seems to have been a long-term pro-ject for West. In *Family Memories* she recalls that, as ladies, her grand-mother and mother were expected to be ignorant of homosexuality, even when her uncle got into trouble for being at a gay brothel when a murder occurred. West ponders the love arrangements of Proust, one of her fa-vorite authors. She sets up different categories of gays. She rehearses the arguments for and against toleration of homosexuality, worrying finally about men's danger to one another: "It has been impossible, because of the masculine tenderness for their painful and unreasonable situation, to debate this matter coolly; and therefore, as I write, homosexuals have been put into a position of peril. Homosexual practices have been made legal; but a very large part of the population still abhors them and will turn on any homosexual who avails himself of the legal rights accorded his kind, should his activities become public, and will rend him to pieces without mercy" (FM 90).

West is drawn to a number of women in the course of her travels. Her diary of 1975 suggests that life might have been happier if she had been lesbian in orientation (Glendinning 125). The exotic dancer is a recurrent attraction, present in her writing since 1913, when she wrote her first travel essays for the *New Freewoman* on a visit to Spain. In one of these, "Nana," a flamenco dancer, served the maternal, regenerative role West would develop further in *The Judge:*

> In all directions she presented smooth white surfaces and pleasant bulges; her hair rose from bright low forehead like a solid and newly-blackleaded iron fender; her shoulder beamed like a newly-enamelled bath. And this amazing incandescence was only the glittering facade of an attractiveness whose rich texture pleased the eye as the pile of a Benares carpet pleases the finger. . . . A sudden generous smile of the big brilliant mouth showed it to be something of the very dearest charm. For about her glowed the rarest warmth in the world, the comfortable warmth of hot bread-and-milk consumed beside the nursery fire: and in the bosom which should have been sheathed in starched linen one would certainly find the sympathy that gives its kisses freely and barges no price of repentance. (26–27)

In *Black Lamb and Grey Falcon,* West's persona renews her acquaintance with a belly dancer called Astra, whom she had met on the previous year's visit. West offers a technical description of Astra's breasts, revolving in opposite directions: "This gave the effect of hard, mechanical magic; it was as if two cannon-balls were rolling away from each other but were for ever kept contingent by some invisible power of attraction" (308). On the previous visit, Astra had given West dancing instructions. They had shared information about their lives, reaching a level of physical and personal familiarity that the British traveler's current chauffeur finds intolerable.

West frequently singles out women embroiderers for appreciation, considering them producers of "uncorrupted merchandise." In one outstanding example "there was an effect of darkness stirring with the colours of creation. But the little suns and trees and stars would not take creation too seriously, it was as if fun was being poked at it" (*BL&GF* 783). This embroiderer is thus respected for achieving an independent world view. West finds some women who find a place in the tradition and politics available. In one region, women dance with a heaviness comparable to the Orthodox Christians' religious icons (93). An old Macedonian woman was deprived by Turkish misrule of supposed Western advantages, but she fed on "the sweetness spilled from the overturned cup of Constantinople. Therefore she was Byzantine in all her ways, and in her substance. When she took up her needle it instinctively pricked the linen in Byzantine designs," and when she sat, it was with a stiffness that "was a symbol of her beliefs about society," and the posture taken by people who were to be respected (638–39).

Yugoslavia is not a utopia for women. There are places where customs suggest oppressive views of women. One such place is Skopska Tserna Gora, where women dance "the kolo" dressed in "shapeless piles of assorted haberdashery, mixed up with coins and cords and false hair and flowers" (673). Here again, West sees a more general principle. Such garments do not happen by chance. "They are usually imposed by a society that has formed neurotic ideas about women's bodies and wants to insult them and drive them into hiding, and it is impossible for women to be happy in such a society" (673).

In discussing the configuration of gender in Yugoslavia, West continues to make authoritative statements about the needs and beliefs of "all men" and "all women." The outcome of these dispositions by gender can differ in Yugoslavia, however. Take, for example, her discussion of the rationale behind women's self-abasement, as it occurs in "picturesque symbolic rites, such as giving men their food first and waiting on them while they eat." West suspects that "women such as these are not truly slaves, but have found a fraudulent method of persuading men to give them support and leave them their spiritual freedom." She offers an absolute of male disposition: "It is certain that men suffer from a certain timidity, a liability to discouragement which makes them reluctant to go on doing anything once it has been proved that women can do it as well." But with the fraudulent abasement of their women, "men will go on working and developing their powers to the utmost" (330).

West suggests that in contemporary Western culture, women lose both ways. During the Depression, when women supported the family, "their husbands became either their frenzied enemies or relapsed into an infantile state of dependence." But abasement is also risky since it abnegates economic and civil rights. In the West, employment is so insecure that women's "sacrifice" alone cannot hope to restore men's "primitive power" of productivity. Women also risk abandonment by a man no longer tied to one village, and able to take the next train to a new job (330). Ultimately, West would do away with fraud between the sexes. This is part of the fantasy of Harriet Hume, who is both restorative and clairvoyant.

West finds the Yugoslav arrangement a compromise with the merit of giving women some "freedom from male prescription."

Gerda represents not just German opinions but a type of a modern Western woman detested by West because of a nonproductive relationship to art and the economy. In 1913, West wrote disparagingly about parasitic women in a set of essays for the *Clarion*. One factor in the ruin of Arnold Condorex in *Harriet Hume* is the economic demands of a parasitic wife. In her 1918 World War I novel, *The Return of the Soldier*, West condemns the home-front economy presided over by Kitty, the spoiled, upper-class wife of the soldier. Kitty consumes the unnecessary products of the empire and British industry, remaking her husband's home into a place worthy of display in the "illustrated papers," thus entering a media cycle of self-perpetuating desire. Kitty's hatred of the novel's representative of primitive life force, Margaret, is comparable to Gerda's response to Yugoslavia.

West uses the Yugoslavian context to make contrasting statements about masculine and feminine spirituality. She suggests that men "find it difficult to live without the help of philosophical systems which far outrun ascertained facts, but are wholly unsuitable to women, who are born with a faith in the unrevealed mystery of life and can therefore afford to be skeptics" (167). Equally unsuitable to women is a Mithraic hieroglyph of a god, a bull with exaggerated sexual organs, and a gargantuan scorpion in deadly struggle:

> Grossness was being grossly murdered, with gross incidentals. No wonder women were not admitted to this worship, for it was distinctively masculine. All women believe that some day something supremely agreeable will happen, and that afterwards the whole of life will be agreeable. All men believe that some day something supremely disagreeable will happen, and that afterwards the whole of life will move on so exalted a plane that all considerations of the agreeable and disagreeable will prove petty and superfluous. (430)

Despite its passivity, West prefers the female creed as more logical and enhancing to life. The "supremely disagreeable event" will only "strain and exhaust those who take part in it. It is not true that the vine and the wheat spring from the blood and marrow of a dying bull, the beasts from its sperm. The blood and marrow and sperm of the dead clot and corrupt, and are a stench" (431).

The most disagreeable human event is surely war. West was not a pacifist along the lines of Virginia Woolf. Once a state was at war against an enemy such as the Germans or the Turks, West appreciated bravery and support from the home front. During World War I she wrote an appreciative article on women munitions workers, and repeated May Sinclair's account of nurses beneath the bombs in Belgium (*YR* 305). Her opposition to war was more fundamental. War was a denial of life. *The Return of the Soldier* is a complex and ironic study of life denials in both war and the marital arrangements of the privileged classes. Amnesia, occasioned by shell shock, takes the World War I soldier back to his vital first love, Margaret, a woman he could not marry because of rules of class. But Margaret is so tempered to sacrifice that she cures him of amnesia by nurturing him like a mother. She realizes she can return him to the present with a toy that reminds him of his child. Yet the rehabilitated soldier, unlike the lover, has a "dreadful decent smile" and "a hard tread upon the heel," having nothing to look forward to. Another soldier departs in West's *This Real Night*. Richard Quinn, the idealized and carefully nurtured little brother of the narrator, dies as suddenly in war as does Andrew Ramsay of Woolf's *To the Lighthouse* or Jacob of *Jacob's Room*. In *Black Lamb and Grey Falcon*, West is "filled with feminist rage" by a model for a war monument that uses peasant women in endorsement of war:

> Since men are liberated from the toil of childbirth and child-rearing, they might reasonably be expected to provide an environment which would give children the possibility to survive and test the potentialities of humanity. The degree of failure to realize that expectation revealed in this disgusting little room could not be matched by women unless ninety per cent of all births were miscarriages. (488)

This is West at her most authoritative and dramatic. She essentializes, dividing the functions of humanity into feminine nurture and masculine culture. Whereas their part of the labor should be to provide a potentializing, truly "cultural" environment, men inflict the institution of war instead.

I want to conclude my study of the political and polemical West with a consideration of her aesthetics. It is a mistake to focus only upon the evils West finds in Western society, in warring men, and in parasitic women. In the course of her work she shares many delights with us—environments of productive intellectual discussion, beauty, and art. Whether

Rebecca West takes us through Paris with the young female persona of "The Strange Necessity," through London with Harriet Hume, or through Yugoslavia in a fictionalized palimpsest of her own visits of the late 1930s, she tested a culture or an individual in two areas: the care for life and human potential, and the production and comprehension of art. In her early essay "The New God," West preferred the workers on the Gothic cathedral to any God of war or sacrifice who might have motivated the work.

We may have some reservations about West's own art. Virginia Woolf, whose chapter has wrestled more with artistic form, abandoned her reading of *The Judge* because of aesthetics. Stuffed sausage was Woolf's metaphor for West's packed and explosive style. I often long to cut out two or three phrases from her sentences, which become particularly labored when she analyzes underlying causes of traits of character. Indeed, I think her influence has contorted my own syntax. A labored effect is often true of her frequently used dialogues as well, though these have the merit of dispersing authority. While awkwardness may be believable for Yugoslavs not speaking their native tongue, there is little excuse for the elaborateness with which ideas are expressed between husband and wife in this work.[38] Victoria Glendinning finds a host of other faults, including imbalance and the familiar charge of excesses of authority:

> She was in *Black Lamb* uninhibitedly judgemental, sweepingly certain about things about which no one on earth can be certain; and she spun vague, mystifying, lovely webs of words around ideas that could have been expressed simply. Some passages sound like self-parody. Her sense of scale was distorted, perhaps deliberately. Significant people or events were deflated by images drawn from kitchen or nursery, to comic effect, while the gesture of a stranger glimpsed for a second might be drenched in an intense, apocalyptic significance not always accessible to the reader. (*Rebecca West* 167)

West's style is hardly compatible with Glendinning's own even, practical, straightforward manner. But some of West's strategies can be defended, and we may learn to live with others. It is probably necessary to live with her absolute statements, taking them less absolutely as her personal understanding—the product of her attempts to see what she knows from experience. Her boldness of expression is compatible with her desire to expose basic cultural assumptions—the scaffoldings of belief. If her tone shocks us, it also forces us to re-examine the sources of our resistance.

In the course of her works, West qualifies some of her earlier attitudes, and she finds new categories of difference that challenge binary division. West's deflating images from kitchen and nursery bring these feminine realms of responsibility and experience to bear on art; they give implied endorsement to common women's wisdom. More often than not, the stranger elevated to apocalyptic importance is poor or female; in these selections, West shifts the accent of history. West has a mystic aspect, as is appropriate to the various religious rituals and sites examined in *Black Lamb and Grey Falcon*. In complicating the original conception of the work in a diary, West investigated memory and examined the process by which early impressions are confirmed or qualified, with increased experience. West's violation of simple genre definitions is her most important contribution to the much-vaunted modernist quality of experimentation.

West's definition of art, written in response to Dalmatian churches and Macedonian embroideries, helps to explain her own literary form, and her sense of the necessity of art to life and to the viability of a culture.

> For of course art gives us hope that history may change its spots and man become honourable. What is art? It is not decoration. It is the re-living of experience. The artist says, "I will make that event happen again, altering its shape, which is disfigured by its contacts with other events, so that its true significance is revealed"; and his audience says, "We will let that event happen again by looking at this man's picture or house, listening to his music or reading his book." It must not be copied, it must be remembered, it must be lived again, passed through those parts of the mind which are actively engaged in life, which bleed when they are wounded and give forth the bland emulsions of joy, while at the same time it is being examined by those parts of the mind which stand apart from life. At the end of this process the roots of experience are traced; the alchemy by which they make a flower of joy or pain is, so far as is possible to our brutishness, detected. What is understood is mastered. (*BL&GF* 1127–28)

West offers a vast collection of art in her works. She is sensitive to traditions of many art forms—ritual, visual, textile, musical, literary. She ranges and rearranges these by nation, philosophy, era, or gender, and mixes them with discoveries in science and industry. In defining her experience, West declared an early relation to culture through a female tradition of music, a male tradition of journalism, and an urban experience of fine architecture. West associated art with pleasure and vitality, and proclaimed it the right of all classes, not just the privileged (which she clearly was not). West thought little of people who consumed decorative objects for prestige, instead of actively learning from art. Thus art was not a thing apart, but the substance and test of the life of an individual, or a culture. Her movement across cultures became a project of salvaging the material and the will for revitalization, all the while reassessing the scaffoldings of philosophy, state, and religion that had failed in the past.

# 4  1939 and the Ends of Modernism

Let us try to drag up into consciousness the subconscious Hitlerism that holds us down. It is the desire for aggression; the desire to dominate and enslave. . . . Hitlers are bred by slaves.

— Woolf, "Thoughts of Peace in an Air Raid" 245

So many of these peoples have remarkable qualities, and it is fascinating to see whether they can be organized into an orderly state.

— West on the people of Yugoslavia, *Black Lamb and Grey Falcon* 662

I expect to see myopic conquerors
With pebbled monocles and rowel'd heels,
In a damned and horrid clutch of gluttony
Dredging the Seine of our inheritance.

— Barnes, *The Antiphon* 91

By 1928—the focal date of volume 1—Virginia Woolf, Rebecca West, and Djuna Barnes achieved the conditions necessary to launch out into work that made modernism, with a difference. Each developed distinct arrangements for her life, coping with obstacles and sources of enervation. They also found appreciative audiences, and were at least temporarily well paid by journals that reached beyond the *avant-garde*. They tackled substantive feminist issues, including lesbian identification and women's access to new professional and technical fields. Woolf valorized the rapture of human relations in her ever-varying experimental process with words and form, setting a different spin on a privileged modernist focus. Barnes unstitched woman's representation in nature, springing the family trap, and attending to the views of lesbians and homosexuals. West scrutinized new books and old cultures, extracting the embedded systems of belief and loosening the bonds of binary thinking.

In the following decade, markets—including literary markets—changed, as did the world political scene. Life was attached at all four corners to grim and threatening circumstances. This drove some of their male colleagues—Yeats, and Eliot mildly, Pound overtly—toward fascism. All three women looked on as writers a half-generation younger than themselves began a long flirtation with Communism. Barnes and West were firsthand observers of the Depression as it took its toll of lives in New York City.

Barnes suspected a shift in the American market in the mid-thirties, when she had trouble placing *Nightwood* with a publisher. At the same time, Woolf got rejection slips from *Harper's*. Noting recent competition from Erskine Caldwell and William Faulkner, Barnes described what she thought was salable to Natalie Barney: "bloody crimes, rape (casual and not passionate), murder by the carload, in a rapid staccato style and so easy to read that an idiot could finish the book in the course of his daily insanity" (Barnes letter to Barney, 9 Apr. 1934, Jacques Doucet).

Nineteen thirty-nine—the year focused upon in this chapter—saw the publication in English of Hitler's *Mein Kampf,* though his intentions for Europe were already clear. Hitler's voice boomed over the radio, now a part of the collective consciousness of Europeans and Americans alike. Woolf's family had experienced recent losses of war with the death of her nephew Julian Bell, who was serving in the ambulance corps in the Spanish Civil War—another manifestation of a changing order. On September 1, 1939, Woolf gave what was to become her routine political report to her diary:

> War is on us this morning. Hitler has taken Dantzig: has attacked—
> or is attacking—Poland. Our P[arliamen]t meets at 6 tonight. . . .
> Now at 1 I go in to listen I suppose to the declaration of war.
> (5 D 233)[1]

Woolf helped stock a cottage for mothers and children evacuated from South London, and found it more pleasant and possible to sew blackout curtains than to read. But she was not prevented from writing for long. A walk cleared her head for her next project, suited to her changed times:

> This book will serve to accumulate notes, the fruit of such quickenings. And for the 100th time I repeat—any idea is more real than any amount of war misery. And what one's made for. And the only contribution one can make—This little pitter patter of idea is my whiff of shot in the cause of freedom. . . . (5 D 235)

When the war began in earnest, she wrote at Monk's House under the air raids. Leonard made a suicide plan in the event of German invasion; we have since learned that they were on the Nazi hit list. The Woolfs' London home in Tavistock Square was bombed to ruins.

Barnes had to be extricated from Paris as the Germans approached.

Dispatched by boat to America, she lost the European territory that had given spiritual sustenance to her work since 1920.[2] A journalistic piece she wrote in 1941 is titled, tellingly, "Lament for the Left Bank." Settling alone into Patchin Place in Greenwich Village, Barnes published little until *The Antiphon* appeared in 1958.

West took up the safer country life at Ibstone House, where she prospered financially by producing dairy products and shared her skills in canning fruits and vegetables with the community. She and her husband provided housing and organizational expertise to refugees, particularly ones from their beloved Yugoslavia. Using the examples of past history to urge liberals to fight, West contributed letters on "Italy in Albania,"[3] "War Aims," and "A Challenge to the Left" to *Time and Tide*. In their continuing journalism, Woolf and West expressed, with deep concern, differing positions in regard to war. Both were alert to the state of the profession they had transformed by entering it, and eager to make the most of it in 1939.

Important figures and forces of modernism were disappearing or diminishing in influence. As Virginia Woolf was "bubbling along" with the writing of *Between the Acts* in 1939, she recorded T. S. Eliot's difficulties with dialogue in his new play, *Family Reunion*. His resignation from the *Criterion* marked the end of an era to her. There was a gulf between Woolf and Bloomsbury men over her 1938 pacifist work, *Three Guineas*. When they met, Maynard Keynes could offer only silence on the subject. Her ongoing biography of Roger Fry, who had died in 1934, brought reconsideration of the heyday of the Omega Workshops and Fry's critique of her modernist prose lyricism. Leonard showed an unusual lack of enthusiasm for the biography. William Butler Yeats and Sigmund Freud both died in 1939, but not before Woolf had a poignant meeting with Freud that year. *Finnegans Wake,* a work with affinities to *Between the Acts* and *The Antiphon,* was published in 1939, as Joyce's last work. With his death in January 1941, Woolf recalled predictions of his prominence in literary history by T. S. Eliot and Katherine Mansfield. She noted cynically, "Now all the gents are furbishing up opinions, & the books, I suppose, take their place in the long procession" (5 *D* 353). We know now that she was close to her own death.

This chapter reviews for the sake of comparison the issues, attitudes, and forms of what are arguably the last modernist works of Woolf, West, and Barnes. Woolf was writing *Between the Acts* in 1939, while West worked on *Black Lamb and Grey Falcon*. The action of Barnes's *The An-*

*tiphon* is set at Dover in 1939, amid a mass migration from the German takeover. Though not published until 1958, this poetic drama belongs in spirit and form to modernism.[4] John Graham has identified "antiphonal exchanges" in the first reunion scene of *The Waves* (w:H 217). One definition of "antiphon" is the sympathetic vibration of strings on musical instruments. This differs physically from attachment—a process we have attended to throughout this study—but still suggests empathy in shared vibration. Toni McNaron has suggested, based on diary entries from 1940, that one reason Woolf took her life was that she no longer felt an echo, meaning a "repercussion," or relationship to an audience for her work (502). This chapter allows us to sense resonances, as all three made the dangers of fascism obvious to their compatriots, finding its presence even in British and American domestic settings. They planned a survival strategy through a new relation to language.

Though 1940–41 provides the traditional endpoint for modernism and a time of retreat for Barnes, I should like to step beyond it. Barnes was one of a number of women through whom modernist writing extends into the 1950s and beyond. Jean Rhys and H. D. are also of this group. Decades later, they resumed work begun in the 1920s, producing new versions of suppressed subjects, acting as postmodern pioneers. Though she died in 1941, there was more of Woolf to come—rejected early versions of published texts and newly published autobiography, including another text of 1939, "A Sketch of the Past" (published 1976), which has been eagerly received by a new feminist generation. Political and legal reportage became West's privileged genres of the 1940s and early 1950s, as she admitted, saying that in that era history required that she write on politics (Bookshelf interview). Realism predominates in her fiction, resumed in the mid-1950s, including *The Birds Fall Down* and the autobiographical trilogy begun with *The Fountain Overflows*. Still, West's abiding modernist interest in psychology, seen particularly in her representation of women's minds and visions, erupts in essays and fiction that otherwise follow more realistic conventions.

Woolf's *Three Guineas* appeared in 1938, framed as a woman's response to a prosperous, educated man—a middle-aged lawyer who had written asking for her opinion of how war can be prevented. By turning the question to an inquiry into men's psychological motivations for going to war, Woolf offered her most forceful and probing feminist polemic, very late in her career. As a collector of cultural evidence, she clipped newspapers, culling photographs, quotations, and economic statistics, documenting "facts" as never before.[5] This method was as close to the cultural journalism of Rebecca West as she was ever to come, though at cross purposes—West feeling, more like Leonard Woolf, that war must be waged against Germany. Refusing to participate in institutions that foster war, instead of entering them to perform an ongoing critique, Woolf's political method remained that of the deliberate outsider. West enjoyed becoming the insider, as noted in volume 1, where we considered her long relationship with Lord Beaverbrook. Among his varied credentials, Beaverbrook was a war minister with several portfolios. Not only did West work for legal change within state systems. She upheld a morality of mutual loyalty which, while it fostered the individual's rights to spiritual freedom and bodily health, also rooted out and severely condemned treason to the state, and even to family members.

Woolf's *Between the Acts* and Barnes's *The Antiphon* were both set in 1939 in English country houses already sustaining the reverberations of war. As shown in chapters 1 and 2, violence extends into the Oliver and Hobbs families of these respective works, taking such forms as incest, rape, homophobic violence, bestiality, suicide, and even murder. West's *Black Lamb and Grey Falcon* offers a long historical view of the horrors of imperial incursions into Yugoslavian territory. She treats male impositions upon women, whether in the arrangements of one couple or in the enactment of cultural rituals, as symptoms of political dysfunction. On the other hand, she nostalgically celebrates Slavic men employed in productive crafts and prepared to beget children as a virile emblem of cultural health.

The destructive force of fascist authority threatens to smash and silence culture, whether found in high art or in local crafts, in all of these works. Rather than defeat the writing process for Woolf, West, and Barnes, war and fascism give it new material and purpose. All three authors were moved to collect scraps from older traditions, wherever they lay among the people, working them into new productions of mixed genre. As writers, they also seem to have learned a new meditative attitude, placing their writerly selves into readerly reserve as they waited for words, ideas, and human relations to emerge. In Yugoslavia, West recorded native dress and gesture, architectural fragments, embroidered motifs, and ancient rites, many of them organizing concepts of gender and ethnicity. The scraps of poetry that became the basis of Woolf's *Between the Acts* are matched by Barnes's struggles from the 1950s onward with fragments of her own verses.[6] In their respective verse/drama/fictions, Woolf and Barnes have characters perform cultural scraps, in genres ranging from Elizabethan and Jacobean theater to music hall and gramophone songs—performances that capture the subversiveness of M. M. Bakhtin's carnivalesque. It is in some places an art of reversal, in which evidence of the bestial or the "primitive" puts into question the supposed upward direction of human evolution, as recorded in a cataclysmic period of history.

Rebecca West undertook *Black Lamb and Grey Falcon* partly as a means to counter fascism. From the first, *Black Lamb* was a political project, conceived during West's British Council lecture tour through Yugoslavia in 1936. In this capacity, West represented Britain in postimperial outreach. She filed reports on political and cultural leaders she met in her travels, registering uncertainty that she had been worth their expense, suggesting what sort of speaker would have been more suitable to given audiences, and quite aware that "propaganda" was the goal of the Council (Letter to Col. Bridge, British Council Archive). Before the Nazi invasion in 1940, the British Council urged the BBC to accept a series of broadcasts based on West's work in progress, stating that "conditions make it important to do everything possible to increase British influence" (Charles Bridge letter to Cecil Graves, 27 May 1936, BBC Written Archive). West's enormous volume attempts to record what was about to be lost by taking an "inventory of a country down to its last vest-button."[7] As noted in the previous chapter, she considers it a "preternatural event in my life," and not the stuff of a sound professional decision. It is "useful," but in a new sense of that word, bordering on the visionary, and realized only over time (West letter to Woollcott, Harvard).

As I write this concluding chapter, Sarajevo, where West looked down upon "the minarets of a hundred mosques" (298), is being blown to pieces. Daily we learn more of civilian deaths—the latest outrage the bombing of the marketplace; earlier there were reports of secret concentration camps and programmatic rapes, all of this affecting the Muslim population most severely. These deeds, supported by Serbian leader Slobodan Milosevic, "the Butcher of the Balkans,"[8] resonate with the Nazi menace West hoped to confront. In December 1992, Lawrence Eagleburger, then U.S. Secretary of State, condemned Milosevic and others as war criminals, calling for a new version of the Nuremberg trials—an event West recorded in 1946 as a journalist. There are abundant ironies to this tragic repetition. In her epilogue of *Black Lamb,* West applauds the Serbs for their futile resistance to the Nazis and credits them with resisting the imperial expansion of the Turks. She reminds us of Croat complicity with the Nazis. In telling her tale, West settles on powerful symbols—such as the legendary falcon that served as a messenger from Jerusalem to Tsar Lazar, fourteenth-century leader of the Serbs. Kossovo, where Lazar's army was martyred, has became one of Milosevic's own symbols in rallying the Serbs for his projects of ethnic cleansing and domination.[9] I suspect that were she here to advise the British foreign minister today, West would propose as a healing agent the grandson of King Peter, the 1930s Grey Falcon, Crown Prince Alexander Karageorgevitch.[10] Throughout World War II, West provided a home in exile for Yugoslavians, saving them for the day when their nation could be reconstituted—a project suspended by Communism after the war. The epigraph records her appreciation for the variety of people in Yugoslavia: "So many of these peoples have remarkable qualities, and it is fascinating to see whether they can be organized into an orderly state" (662). The latest indicators are pessimistic indeed, though they are largely the product of those who stayed behind with the Nazis and then Tito, to be armed with Communist weapons and methods. West denounced in no uncertain terms the British switch to supporting Tito's legitimacy as the ruler of postwar Yugoslavia.

As noted in the previous chapter, *Black Lamb and Grey Falcon* offers a theory of fascism, linked to a long sequence of murdered royalty. Elizabeth of Austria's murderer, Luccheni, is West's first fascist, a product of "new towns which the industrial and financial developments of the nineteenth century had raised all over Europe." Such towns were cut off from the countryside and designed "in the interest of only the rich, and careless of the souls and bodies of the poor. The new sort of people [had] been defrauded of their racial tradition,[11] they enjoyed no inheritance of wisdom" (612). West's sense of "tradition" here is vastly different from that of Eliot, criticized by West (see volume 1). Her sense of tradition is an experiential base, facilitating wise decisions regarding spirit and body. I have no doubt that West would place the Communist-trained Milosevic in this fascist category today, as Anthony Lewis did convincingly in a series of articles for the *New York Times*.

Woolf and Barnes were also keenly aware of the advance of fascism, with some of their important insights coming from female colleagues. Barnes reports having met Janet Flanner (also a colleague of West) in April 1936, "riding high" after the appearance of her series of articles on Hitler in the *New Yorker* (Barnes letter to Coleman, 1–3 Apr. 1936, Delaware). Woolf considered consulting Rebecca West about fascism in 1935, and she joined Leonard Woolf at antifascist gatherings. Quentin Bell set the pattern of dismissing Woolf as a political activist, suggesting that she was unable to fit with the "machinery" of politics. He pointed to her pacifism and her association of war with masculinity as obstacles to political involvement (2 Bell 186–90). Yet we have noted her sense of involvement on the plane of ideas.

I do not wish to locate Woolf and Barnes in the midst of political machinery, or on a political side of what Andreas Huyssen has called the "great divide." Woolf, West, and Barnes convince me of the need to question the mapping of such a divide. Read by postmoderns, Woolf's feminist pacifism and outsider position are political tools operating on the conceptual level. In both "Thoughts on Peace in an Air Raid" and *Three Guineas* she brings into consciousness a new pressure group who must teach themselves the power that thought has to bring about change. West has been conceded a place in politics, winning a misleading "masculine" label for being there. Yet no one tracked a more complex path across the supposed political divide than West, who constantly uses domestic metaphors to illuminate and deflate men's political postures, and finds a species of madness in the extreme limitations of both sexes. She values supremely life-giving activities. Woolf, West, and Barnes cope with a treacherous era by questioning power structures and hierarchies, traversing outsides, differences, and "betweens," offering antiphons, "primitive" reversions, sexual inversions, and heuristic visions.

*The Antiphon* is set in the bombed-out family home of Augusta Burley Hobbs—its damage resonant with the fate of Woolf's London home. Barnes's set displays a gap in one wall, a paneless Gothic window, and a main hall cumbered with "a dressmaker's dummy, in regimentals, surrounded by music stands, horns, fiddles, guncases, bandboxes, masks, toys and broken statues, man and beast" (81). Miranda, the daughter of the family, is followed onto the set by the mysterious Jack, who has served as a coachman, carries "a whip and creel," and is clearly performing an "act," such as Barnes might have experienced in Berlin cabarets. Reporting on the condition of Europe, he greets Miranda:

> Mischief Madame! I expect to be,
> In this knock-about of general war,
> Up to my neck in steeples; starting stoats,
> Hens in hats, and sailing ships in lanes.
> And by the edging off of custom, get me bit
> By grounded gargoyles that once staled the sky
> With rash Orion's water. Mischief lady?

> I expect to see myopic conquerors
> With pebbled monocles and rowel'd heels,
> In a damned and horrid clutch of gluttony
> Dredging the Seine of our inheritance. (91)

Jack is Miranda's brother in disguise and may have been her lover. It is a resonant constellation that brings fascism home, extending Barnes's apparent experience of incest from father to son. Though dead, Titus, the patriarch, haunts a revenge tragedy scripted by his sons. The actions of the mother, Augusta, make clear her abiding preference for her sons. This sets the stage for Miranda's death, as well as her own.

*Between the Acts* seems tame by comparison. Pointz Hall is intact, though airplanes in wild duck formation menace the skies (we see from Barnes's doll house and Woolf's wild duck that both are post-Ibsen productions). We are constantly reminded that language falls in "scraps, orts, and fragments" (BA 192). Rape is openly reported in a newspaper read by Isa, which she superimposes on her own family's history, as studied in chapter 1. In this family, incest games (if not the acts themselves) are implied for Isa's father-in-law, Bart, with his sister Lucy. Like it or not, Isa has continued Bart by bearing his grandchildren, who can be expected to be stockbrokers, or—in the economy of war—fodder for the guns. "The father of my children," his breeding role, is the first identification for Isa's husband. Giles, like Jack in Barnes's more bizarre work, is costumed down to the boots for various acts—stockbroker, sportsman, gentleman, and, we might add, fascist, as he smashes the "monstrous inversion" of snake eating frog. Giles aims at homosexuality, but the act serves to suggest a multitude of exterminations. His boots connect him to the rugged defenses of Mr. Ramsay, who almost demands that his boots be admired, and the dead Jacob Flanders, whose legacy is a pair of useless shoes. One of the scraps of *Between the Acts* is an allusion to the poetry of the fallen World War I soldier Edward Thomas.

All of these late modernist works cast humans, and particularly women, in complex relation to nature. Isa is likened to a peacock; Miranda, to a ewe "offering up her silly throat for slashing" in her rape (186). Comparable sacrifice of the black lamb is the ritual that celebrates the birth of a child in Muslim Macedonia, as described by West. The patriarch has his dog, or horse, or falcon in the respective works. Various forms of sexual inversion are suggested by the most complex natural images of these works. A snake, choking as it tries to swallow a large toad, is the inversion of birth, the suggestion of homosexuality Giles strikes at in *Between the Acts*. The officers' story of a horse with a green tail leads a girl into gang rape in Woolf's novel. In another animal metaphor for rape, Miranda of *The Antiphon* is compared to a vixen

> bushelled in the mind's confessional,
> foxed down its gullet to the rump,
> quaking with unhouselled mouth agape,
> Lashing at the lattice with her paws. (215)

The lesbian kiss, likened to eating and the ringing of the bell, is one of Miranda's definitions of the "antiphon":

> Loves so eat each other's mouth
> Till that the common clamour, cointwined
> Wrung out the hidden singing in the tongue.

Mother-daughter sexuality is accommodated by the most extraordinary artifact of *The Antiphon*, the gryphon. Reassembled by Miranda to make a bed for her mother and herself, it becomes a bed of memories. Augusta recalls the animal crafts she had made for Miranda when she was a child. Miranda envisions a primordial maternal landscape predating even the ravaging of her mother, as noted in chapter 2. Mother and daughter are still struggling over the ways that they, like the gryphon, are split or united, and borne by one another.

The female authority figures of these two works, Woolf's Miss La Trobe and Barnes's Miranda, have mysterious pasts of rape or illegitimate offspring, of wandering outside England, or former occupations that can only be guessed and gossiped at. West was herself the traveler who became the subject of gossip. She does not place comparable emphasis on a female wandering type, but she encounters a number of women wanderers. Her persona in *Black Lamb and Grey Falcon* renews her acquaintance with a belly dancer, Astra, and expresses concern about her fortunes, which vary depending upon location. There are less desirable cafés where Astra is subject to masculine abuse. Amiable, fleshy, and maternal, yet skilled in something West's persona cannot do, she receives a brief, admiring portrait.[12]

The itinerant activities of Miss La Trobe, Miranda Hobbs, Astra, and West's own persona suggest that they are independent and survivors. Miss La Trobe's loss of her actress lover and her dread of living alone echo Nora's loss of her partner Robin in Barnes's *Nightwood*. Miranda and La

Trobe have moments of threatening command. Miss La Trobe makes use of a mechanical device, the gramophone, to play patriotic songs that elicit the desired emotional responses from her audience. Her device compares to BBC broadcasts of Hitler's booming rhetoric, or of parliamentary speeches declaring war, recalled in Woolf's diary. La Trobe is not content when two of her audience, Giles and Cobbet, fail to see her point. La Trobe has one image of capturing and cooking undirected beings that is a horrific anticipation of Nazi body-works: "She was one who seethes wandering bodies and floating voices in a cauldron, and makes rise up from its amorphous mass a re-created world. Her moment was on her— her glory" (153).

Miranda of *The Antiphon* is tall and elegantly clad, as if for her ulti-mate performance. Her use of a cane suggests experience as much as in-jury. Her calm remark "The wind that knocked our generation down was not a harvest" (212) applies as well to the waste of the present war. Miranda seems to have organized her fatal visit home. She tells her mother's story, and mothers her mother. By providing the gryphon as psy-chological transportation, she facilitates her mother's childish delight in the past, also unburdening it. In choosing this hour for her death, Miranda leaves her brother feeling the fool. He has misgauged his own losses in his elaborate scenario for evoking maternal guilt. While seeming both victim and martyr, Miranda ultimately turns the terror of lost mas-tery upon itself.

As the world boomed and brandished threats of annihilation, Woolf, West, and Barnes collected themselves to patiently attend to the re-emer-gence of mental and cultural resources. West's designation of *Black Lamb and Grey Falcon* as "a preternatural event in my life" suggests that it was an act of faith, outside her normal course of operation. The ending of both *The Antiphon* and *Between the Acts* suggest potent burials, from which new words and ideas would emerge. Jack, the self-proclaimed predator "snuffling 'round the kill," had dug a hole and "pushed my terror in" (224). Barnes exposed this double-edged terror in a text that admits only gradual comprehension. Jack had cashed in his mother, in a desper-ate seeking after home. This system of fear and predation represented fas-cism, both in Europe and in the dysfunctional family. Miss La Trobe gives up much of her authority as her part of *Between the Acts* concludes. She allows increasingly for gaps and pauses that make independent demands on her audience. She finally plays the patient attendant, waiting for new words to emerge from the mud, where old efforts have sunk. La Trobe may be summoning forth a new scenario for Giles and Isa. When the novel switches to them, the coming hours are cast like a nightmare of primordial beasts as the "dog fox fights with the vixen, in the heart of darkness, in the fields of night" (219). But this ending also calls for digging back into caves before houses were built. Referring back to one of her most pervasive creative models, perhaps only by digging or illuminating the tunnel or the cave differently, the heterosexual couple, Giles and Isa, as reconceived by the lesbian Miss La Trobe, will bring forth a new life for culture.

The late modernism of Woolf, West, and Barnes is as resourceful and challenging as anything they wrote. They did not attempt to shore themselves up against their ruin, nor do they regret the loss of "master narratives."[13] They compounded anew, from scraps and orts, styles and genres of the past, disappearing within them. They treated the end of a literary era as a space between, hoping, I think, that the gains they had made in opening the writing profession for women, and exploring questions of sexuality, politics, and experimental form, would be summonable again, given a new feminist era and dedicated, deciphering readers. When we bring back both the venturesome writing and the complex cultural contexts of modernist women such as Woolf, West, and Barnes, we prepare for our own intellectual work. We learn to gauge support systems, whether institutional or conceptual, privileged or neglected. We decide when we must leap beyond them. We learn to salvage and meditate. Patiently, potently, we take up the strand.

# Notes

1.     Useful direction away from traditional patriarchal forms has been provided by an array of postmodern theory, including that of Jacques Derrida, Jacques Lacan, Michel Foucault, Jean-François Lyotard, Andreas Huyssen, and Gilles Deleuze. Volume 1 begins with an extended discussion of available theory.

## 1. WOOLF'S RAPTURE WITH LANGUAGE

1.     Norman Friedman uses "double vision" to mean a state of balanced subjective and objective perceptions in *To the Lighthouse,* a more passive, stable paradigm than I am suggesting. His discussion of the feminine aspects of water imagery is relevant to my treatment of this metaphor, however. For a more deconstructive model of "conditions of seeing" in Woolf, see Matro, who provides a list of earlier Woolf criticism that, like Friedman's, offers paradigms of aesthetic order and androgynous balance (212–13).

2.     For "Phases of Fiction" Woolf settles on five "phases" that partake of different categorical systems, cutting across history and genre, and including formal and attitudinal aspects: "Truth-Tellers," "Romantics," "Character-Mongers and Comedians," "Psychologists," and "Poets." The essay frequently presents an ideal of wholeness, only to suggest the disadvantages of its achievement. Woolf notes that the reader may "think himself . . . in possession of a whole world as inhabitable as the real world. Such a world, it may be urged against it, is always in process of creation. Such a world, it may be added, likewise against it, is a personal world, a world limited and unhabitable perhaps by other people" (93). In her "Letter to a Young Poet" of 1932, Woolf advised resistance to the period designations erected by reviewers, lecturers, and broadcasters: "A pistol shot rings out. The age of romance was over. The age of realism had begun" (*The Death of the Moth* 211).

3.     Sandra Gilbert and Susan Gubar also resist the "foreign land" positioning of Woolf in relation to language, and offer their own set of productive Woolfian fantasy types. In one, a "voyeuristic" role is directed toward interpreting her "affiliation" with earlier women writers. A second fantasy relates more closely to language and male modernists such as Joyce—a "fantasy about a utopian linguistic structure—a 'woman's sentence' " used to

overthrow "the sentence-as-definitive-judgment, the sentence-as-decree-or-interdiction" (*No Man's Land* 196–205, 228–31). I find more variety in Joycean sentencing than they do and more use for French feminist paradigms of writing the female body, though both of these may reflect the greater emphasis upon metaphors (as opposed to characters and plots) in my analysis.

4.   In her "Revolution in Poetic Language," Kristeva defines the "genotext" as "not linguistic (in the sense understood by structural or generative linguistics). It is rather, a *process*, which tends to articulate structures that are ephemeral . . . and non-signifying" (121). Pamela Caughie sustains this concept of literature as process when she suggests that one should see Woolf's writings as "a dynamic model for narrative rather than a dualistic one, that is in terms of possibilities, not fixed positions, in terms of functions, not appropriate forms" (8). On reading Woolf through Kristeva, see Nikolchina. Bette London offers a critique of the fantasy constructions noted above.

5.   Joyce's exposition of epiphanies occurs in *Stephen Hero* (210–11), which was written 1904–1906 and published in 1944. It is the concept of a young Stephen Dedalus, and is part and parcel of a deliberate aesthetic theory. Stephen's epiphanies are voyeuristic and retentive. They credit the artist with the capacities of keen focus and achievement of wholeness. In his 1971 comparison of "moments of being" to Joycean epiphany, Morris Beja initiates a new attitude toward Woolf-Joyce comparative study, with the caution that "the immensity of [Joyce's] influence on her has been more often assumed than demonstrated" (116). He finds more concern in process than final discovery in Woolf, likening her more to Pater than to Joyce in this aspect (114–16). Beja compares the revelatory element in the two concepts, their "irrational and intuitive" nature, and their unifying role. Yet he hints at a failure to define the revealed "it," or the "reality" of moments of being, with the mildly patronizing "one can hardly blame her" (115). Indeed, we have come to see that one can appreciate this as a revolutionary move on Woolf's part.

6.   The same applies to Woolf's character Rachel Vinrace, who has a similar thought of amazement at her existence: "She was next overcome by the unspeakable queerness of the fact that she should be sitting in an armchair, in the morning, in the middle of the world" (*vo* 125).

7.   This is also a central tenet of *Three Guineas*.

8.   Rebecca West would recall the same gender distinctions in her own final work, *Family Memories*. All three authors engage in auto-analysis, centering on their childhoods—West beginning with *The Fountain Overflows*, Barnes with *Ryder*, and Woolf with *To the Lighthouse*. See also chapter 1 of volume 1, "(Dys)functional Families."

9.   *Epilogomena to the Study of Greek Religion* (1921; New York: University Books 1966), 475. The quoted summary comes from Andrée Collard, who

uses the Harrison sense of holophrase as a basic concept in her eco-feminist work *Rape of the Wild* (Bloomington: Indiana University Press, 1989). A more standard definition of holophrase describes a single-word utterance that functions as a phrase or sentence. Psycholinguists situate this early (before eighteen months) in their longitudinal study of the acquisition of syntax.

10.  Djuna Barnes was not a student of foreign and classical languages and, despite her extended residence in Paris, was not fluent in French. West studied Latin, but not Greek. She told an interviewer that Greek was not on the curriculum of her Edinburgh school because its founder feared that the young women might be infected by the Greek Orthodox religion. She seems not to have minded this lack as Woolf did. West did pride herself on the ability to pick up languages, including a bit of Serbo-Croatian, while she was writing *Black Lamb and Grey Falcon*.

11.  Woolf's notebooks give evidence that she continued doing Greek translations long after the lessons ended, though analysis of their grammar must await another scholar.

12.  As a formative example, Wyndham Lewis said of *Mrs. Dalloway*, "Often the incidents in the local 'masterpieces' are exact and puerile copies of the scenes in his Dublin drama (cf. the Viceroy's progress through Dublin in *Ulysses* with the Queen's progress through London in *Mrs Dalloway*—the latter is a sort of undergraduate imitation of the former, winding up with a smoke-writing in the sky, a pathetic 'crib' of the fireworks display and the rocket that is the culmination of Mr. Bloom's beach-ecstasy)" (*Men without Art* 168).

13.  Schlack places Peter in the tradition of eighteenth-century critics of female foibles (55–56).

14.  Richard Pearce suggests that Peter gets the "culminating vision, the last word" (153), fulfilling the romance plot.

15.  Abel has sought out a "clandestine" pre-Oedipal plot of "female development," which can be found for Clarissa Dalloway, Rezia Smith, and even Elizabeth Dalloway. Her original matrix is "the early symbiotic female bond that both predates and coexists with the heterosexual orientation toward the father and his substitutes" (173). Bourton emerges as "a pastoral female world spatially and temporally disjunct from marriage and the sociopolitical world of (Richard's) London" (176). She finds Clarissa's attachment to this world unresolved by the marriage plot. Abel usefully draws attention to the gap in the narrative of Clarissa's early childhood, focusing upon the loss of the maternal bond and the creation of her sister Sylvia, only to have her obliterated by male carelessness (171). The loss of her childhood consciousness also prevents us from making comparisons to Woolf's early discovery of a scaffolding of words in moments of being. Pursuing repressed materials from another angle, Suzette Henke presents evidence that, in moving from her notebook, "The Prime Minister," to the

final version of *Mrs. Dalloway,* Woolf muted connections that she had made between marriage and war as patriarchal institutions.

16.   He offers almost no discussion of her great moment with Sally, and is far more concerned with Peter's reports of access between his mind and Clarissa's, and her moment of understanding Septimus (see 190–92, 195–96).

17.   Woolf said at one point that she had "no scaffolding" for *Mrs. Dalloway* (2 *D* 13–14). I am using the sense of scaffolding she developed in "A Sketch," rather than the more readily identified mythical parallel of a work such as *Ulysses,* the sense of scaffolding she is probably using in the diary entry.

18.   See, for example, DiBattista, "Joyce, Woolf and the Modern Mind" (107–109).

19.   The opening of *The Voyage Out* offers a comparable scene, in which Helen Ambrose, while walking through a commercial district of London, contends internally with her grief over leaving her children (12).

20.   Jane Marcus discusses the importance of Woolf's revision of Lewis's "taking the cow by the horns" to "taking the bull by the udders," and her coy attribution of the phrase to Vanessa Bell, in *Virginia Woolf and the Languages of Patriarchy* (136–39).

21.   Joyce's use of iron railings in evoking the limits of women's lives in the *Dubliners* stories "Araby" and "Eveline" is worthy of comparison here.

22.   J. Hillis Miller identifies her song of vanished love as "Allerseelen," by Richard Strauss (190). The lyrics feature flowers, heather, and "last red asters." Miller's interpretation emphasizes a return from the dead, a regaining of lost loved ones. While it offers a cyclical paradigm, this takes a more retentive form than the one which is offered in my analysis.

23.   That the urban underclass finds only a semimythical embodiment here is a useful point of discussion. Susan Squier makes a positive argument for Woolf's "street haunting" in "The City as Landscape."

24.   See Showalter, "On Hysterical Narrative," for a useful summary, and Patricia Laurence's *The Reading of Silence* for the best application to Woolf to date.

25.   Morrison's M.A. thesis on Woolf and Faulkner offers complex preparation for her art, and was itself a connective strategy in the American academy of her day. The richest exploration of Woolf in the African American context occurred at the 3rd Annual Virginia Woolf Conference at Lincoln University, a historically African American institution, in June 1993. See the collected papers, ed. Vara Neverow-Turk and Mark Hussey.

26.   Elizabeth Abel and Louise DeSalvo are notable exceptions to this pattern. See Abel's "Cam the Wicked" and DeSalvo (175–79).

27.   Louise DeSalvo gives a startlingly negative reading of Mrs. Ramsay's intervention. See her *Virginia Woolf* (177–79). Helen also fails to address the wa-

tery depths of her niece Rachel, even though she suspects Rachel's father, Willoughby, of something—perhaps abuse of both wife and daughter.

28. In her "Foreword" to *Pilgrimage*, Richardson notes that two figures stood out among the writers who joined her in fiction of the early century, hinting at Woolf and Joyce. Her own caricature of Woolf is represented as "a woman mounted upon a magnificently caparisoned charger," suggestive of privilege as well as skill (Scott, ed. 430).

29. "The Narrow Bridge of Art" is frequently invoked in discussions of the form of *The Waves*. See Rosenbaum and Minow-Pinkney.

30. To clarify their differences, I attempted to assign them to types by using the Myers-Briggs Type Indicator—a model based on Carl Jung's personality types. Myers-Briggs measures preferences on four scales. These relate to focus (extroversion/introversion), acquisition of information (sensing/intuition), decision making (thinking/feeling), and orientation to the outer world (judgment/perception). In my Myers-Briggs approximations, I did not find any type repeated.

|         | Focus | Information Acquisition | Decision Making | World Orientation |
|---------|-------|-------------------------|-----------------|-------------------|
| Louis   | I     | N?                      | T               | J                 |
| Bernard | E     | S                       | F               | P                 |
| Neville | E?    | S                       | T               | J                 |
| Susan   | I?    | N                       | F               | P                 |
| Jinny   | E     | N                       | F               | P                 |
| Rhoda   | I     | S                       | T               | J                 |

To be adequate to Woolf's approach to personality, Myers-Briggs would need another category—relation to language, where pairings of poetic/narrative or, in our poststructuralist age, semiotic/symbolic would help to elucidate differences.

31. James Haule has pointed out that Woolf filled the early drafts of Part II of *To the Lighthouse* with extensive references to World War I. In its final form, the war still advances on metaphorical "stray airs, advanced guards of great armies" (*TTL* 128–29), gets lettered in "cool cathedral caves" (127), and breaks out in the horrific parenthetical report of Andrew's death (133).

32. As noted in volume 1, Beerbohm created a highly unflattering imaginary sketch of Rebecca West, cross-dressed and swelling in a three-piece suit, her hair pulled back into a tight bun, for a letter to George Bernard Shaw. It is further evidence of his sense that the woman writer is a monstrosity.

33. *The Waves* became a book of the day cycle—no time for moths. Its reigning deity is a solar woman who is relentless in carrying out her cycle, and heedless of humans. She is partly obscured by her fan, just as in an intermediate stage Woolf's "she" had become hooded. This ominous, unap-

proachable, and indifferent deity is comparable to Woolf's earlier mythic women—the "nocturnal women beating great carpets" who suggest the rumblings of war in *Jacob's Room* (175), or the giant figure that looms at the end of the fantasy ride of the self-styled lonely traveler Peter Walsh, affecting his treatment of mortal women (*MD* 57).

34. Only slightly less relevant is one of Woolf's "Lives of the Obscure" published in the first *Common Reader,* which treated the entomologist Eleanor Omerod. Her accurate observations of more ruthless insect life began as a child in a high chair, watching grubs cannibalize a dead member of their group.

35. Of eleven references to keywords involving "moth" listed in the *Concordance to the Waves,* four are attributed to Susan. Neville and Bernard have two references, and Jinny and Louis one each. Only one moth survives in the intervals. Its effect is in harmony with Rhoda's imagination: "All for a moment wavered and bent in uncertainty and ambiguity, as if a great moth sailing through the room had shadowed the immense solidity of chairs and tables with floating wings" (*W* 183).

36. Laurence writes in reaction to Lee Edwards, whose concept of "schizophrenia as narrative" serves as a literary symptom of Woolf's manic-depressive states (Edwards 28–29), neglecting Woolf's "broader explorations of the mind" (Laurence 146).

37. Beverly Ann Schlack attributes Rhoda's question and her "breathless diction" to her reading of Shelley (105).

38. Rhoda's question is elaborated in the first holograph draft, where it is used to strike a contrast with Bernard (then called John). John makes up a nosegay to present to Miss Davies, and thinks of it loosely as a symbol, a means of fertilizing barren ideas (*W:H* 39–40).

39. He has one remarkable predecessor in Woolf's gallery of characters—Terence Hewet, another androgynous male; his project in *To the Lighthouse* was a novel on "silence." Rachel, often compared to Rhoda of *The Waves,* evades Hewet as Rhoda does Bernard.

40. Woolf had tried another form of consolation in her first draft. Bernard (then called Archie) had followed Susan into another retreat—a cellar where green bottles were stored, rather than the beechwood. She admires his clear, active attitude toward problems: "All this is clearer much (*sic*) than what went on within her heart; what he said, was so sensible: so kind: & also, so matter of fact. He said that one could take a bottle & shy stones at it. . . . And what perhaps happened then was that while Archie knocked the bottles over, & she felt, well if he is so active & has no sort of fear, & if he makes a mess down here, & we shall certainly get into trouble for it (*W:H* 8). In quoting from the holograph drafts, I do not include crossed-out words.

41. This has irresistible similarity to the "cracked looking-glass of a servant," Stephen Dedalus's clever phrase in *A Portrait of the Artist as a Young Man.*

42. Compare to this Stephen Dedalus's recourse to "the spiritual-heroic refrigerating apparatus, invented and patented in all countries by Dante Alighieri" (*A Portrait of the Artist as a Young Man* 252).

43. Joyce's characters Stephen Dedalus and Leopold Bloom both go through Byronic phases, in resonance with Bernard.

44. This is taken from his postscript to Remy de Gourmont's *The Natural Philosophy of Love*, considered at greater length in volume 1.

45. Patricia Maika identifies Lucy as Themis, a unifying spirit that "ranges all over earth sea and sky." Woolf would have known of her in Jane Harrison's 1912 volume *Themis: A Study of the Social Origins of Greek Religion* (30–32).

46. In an early draft, William takes notes on Bart and Lucy as an example of how brothers and sisters were different in the nineteenth century (*PH* 547). Their bond is founded in part on a sexually charged childhood fishing incident, when Bart insisted that Lucy do the bloody business of taking the fish off the hook.

47. To me this seems related to the point made in *Three Guineas* that in 1938 women still could not be members of the London Stock Exchange.

48. There is resonance here with Rhoda's dissatisfaction with her mirror image, noted above.

49. Marilyn Brownstein pointed out to me that the Latinate word "copulation" is used for the fertilizing process in the early typescript (*PH* 177).

50. Trees figure in the reassuring cycle of immortality imagined by Mrs. Dalloway: "Somehow in the streets of London, on the ebb and flow of things, here, there, she survived, Peter survived, lived in each other, she being part, she was positive, of the trees at home . . . being laid out like a mist between the people she knew best, who lifted her on their branches as she had seen the trees lift the mist, but it spread ever so far, her life, herself" (12).

51. Maria DiBattista sees this final creative act as an act without an audience (*Virginia Woolf's Novels* 234). I feel that it demands a reader's collaborative turning inward. On words in *Between the Acts*, see also Nora Eisenberg and Sallie Sears.

52. Although Rebecca West strongly endorsed many of Woolf's works, she did not feel that Jacob, as a young man about to lose his life in World War I, was a success: "She is at such a distance from it that she makes no discoveries" (*CC* 220). It should be remembered that West took on a comparable problem with *The Return of the Soldier*, and may have prided herself on the creation of male characters.

53. The boot has become a favored object in Fredric Jameson's *Postmodernism, or the Cultural Logic of Late Capitalism*, which features Andy Warhol's "Diamond dust Shoes" on the cover and additional footwear by Vincent Van Gogh, René Magritte, and Walker Evans within (10–11). Magritte's shoes becoming human feet make the best postmodern sea change, according to Jameson.

54. Woolf dropped a cynical remark, "Another stock broker has been born!" from an earlier version in which Isa had just spotted Haines and was fantasizing about bearing his different breed of children.

55. "Old man's beard" was a useful plant to H. D. as well. In *Bid Me to Live*, her persona writes a letter to explain her aesthetic to Rico, a character closely resembling D. H. Lawrence, whose pronouncements on gender once influenced her strongly. He mixed in her imagination with Merlin and supplied names of plants: "But when I think of Merlin, he is not an old man. Old man's beard? No it was ladies' bedstraw and then you stopped writing me their names" (176).

56. In the later typescript, the author was to tell the reason for "suffering"—an insertion later replaced with "our behavior"—in this appearance outside the bushes (*PH* 435).

## 2. Barnes's Beasts Turning Human

1. The perplexities of the unhappy children in Barnes's stories carry over into her most celebrated works, as Carolyn Allen has suggested in her study of little girls' seduction stories ("Writing toward *Nightwood*").

2. I agree with Alan Singer's suggestion that Barnes has her own way of working metaphors, liberating them from Aristotelian theories of transference and the referential troping commonly practiced in linear, representational narratives, and leaving them "contingent and mutable" (67, 81). See also Messerli, who cites the "radical" metaphors of the early stories such as the one cited above. Susan Lanser discusses the "dense and highly allusive prose" of *Ladies Almanack*, noting that "metaphors often make one strain desperately and still end up not quite making sense" (in Broe, ed. 157–58). Elizabeth Pochodo examines ways that "excessiveness of style" goes beyond metaphor in *Nightwood*.

3. I tend to view Barnes in the class of "constructionists," as opposed to "essentialists," as defined by Diana Fuss in *Essentially Speaking*. She delays rather than denies essentialism through her discursive practices. See Fuss (1–6).

4. Barnes described her family (a source for both *Ryder* and *The Antiphon*) as a tapestry in which "threads intermingle" (Barnes letter to Emily Holmes Coleman, Delaware). Djuna may have been doing some sort of needlecraft when she reported to her grandmother, "I have got a foot & a half of the chain done already" (Barnes letter to Zadel Barnes Gustafson, 26 Feb. 1909, Maryland). Critics have favored metaphors of needlework to describe Barnes's style. Louis F. Kannenstine compares "the descriptive field" of her early poetry to "a Gothic tapestry" (30). See also Field (21) and Herzig

(266). Cheryl Plumb's symbolist interpretation of her works through *Ryder* and *Ladies' Almanack* is titled *Fancy's Craft*.

5. Nancy Fraser and Linda Nicholson resist the totalizing tendency of early feminist theories, starting with the biologism of Shulamith Firestone, but including also social-role differentiation that assigns woman to a domestic sphere, or to the activity of mothering, and the acquisition of gender identity, as in the work of Nancy Chodorow (26–30). In "A Manifesto for Cyborgs," Donna Haraway discusses Susan Griffin, Audre Lorde, and Adrienne Rich as theorists who "insist on the organic, opposing it to the technological." Haraway prefers to explore "the breakdown of clear distinctions between organism and machine" (216). Griffin's readings of lions, cows, and other animals are resonant with the bestiary of *Nightwood*. Diana Fuss gets around the deterministic aspects of essentialism by studying its strategic deployment, as noted above in n. 3.

6. Kannenstine finds that Barnes's art evokes a tormented middle state for those who would be whole in one direction or another. While Eden is an important unified state of innocence for Kannenstine, Alan Williamson suggests a hermetic rather than an orthodox Christian state of innocence. The bisexual Adam of the hermetic scheme offers a sexual middle ground, escaping binary extremes of gender.

    Cheryl Plumb discusses social/natural images in Barnes's story "A Night among the Horses," finding both sets destructive (57). She considers the early Barnes a social satirist of middle-class values, and works with a binary of art/physical world, in the symbolist tradition of Baudelaire and Gourmont. This was the tradition also valued by Pound.

7. Karen Kaivola's *All Contraries Confounded* also proceeds on nonbinary assumptions.

8. In *Beasts of the Modern Imagination*, Norris studies "a tradition in modern thought and art" that offers "a critique of anthropocentrism at the hands of beasts." Norris considers this tradition, as exemplified by Max Ernst, Nietzsche, Darwin, Kafka, Hemingway, and Lawrence, a "*cul-de-sac*" for which she finds little evidence after 1930 (1). She suggests that its alternative of "biocentrism" offers a new way of formulating the distinction between culture and nature. Animals live for themselves, not the other. They proceed on instinct, express desire directly, and submit to biological fate. Desire in the cultural human is felt in terms of a "lack" which gives birth to language—a concept familiar to readers of Lacan. Thus human desire is mediated. "The salient difference between Nature and culture in this new way of formulating their distinction is the 'political' function of mediation and, by extension, mimesis" (5). Nietzsche condemns the mimetic cultural human as a panderer.

    The aggressive, vital predator hero of Nietzsche and Lawrence is one trope of the biocentric tradition that seems applicable to Barnes's depiction of Ryder. She is also wary of the panderer in her verse fragments: "There is no gender in a fossil's eye, Pander, pass by" (ms., 21 May 1970, Maryland).

Also useful is Norris's sense that this tradition is at war with itself, and the "beasts serve as masks of human animals who create them" (1).

9.    I thank Phil Herring for first suggesting this to me.

10.   When I reproduced this drawing for a paper presented at the Djuna Barnes Centennial Conference (October 1992), Annette Leavitt noted their phallic quality. At that same conference, Jane Marcus later cited a long list of phallic limbs advancing ahead of Barnes's characters.

11.   As described at greater length in volume 1, the baroness brought the art of Dada to Greenwich Village, and was cared for in many ways by Barnes, who became her executor after her suicide.

12.   I derive my description from Doughty (143), who notes that Barnes had mounted a set of such illustrations on cardboard.

13.   The same illustrations strike Jane Marcus as "Pennsylvania Dutch surrealism" ("Laughing at Leviticus" 226).

14.   In an early draft, Augusta suggested that Titus "pulled his house apart while weaving—a Penelope," but she is left wondering what he (as a Penelope) waited for (quoted in Curry 294). Though Augusta seems to blame Miranda for pulling down her web, her sons are the most obvious agents of destruction in the drama.

15.   This craft calls to mind Sylvia Plath's *The Bell Jar*, in which Esther is appalled by the fate of Mrs. Willard's painstakingly braided rag rug, which ends up sodden and muddy before the kitchen sink.

16.   Hagar is a good choice for a novel in which bigamy is practiced. The advancement of male children by ambitious mothers is implied in both subjects. This is a regular practice of mother figures in *Ryder, Nightwood,* and *The Antiphon.* All parenthetical page citations to *Ryder* use the St. Martin's Press edition.

17.   I am grateful to Patience Phillips for pointing out the lesbian content of this scene in graduate work done at the University of Delaware.

18.   For more thorough discussion, see Benstock (260).

19.   "Run Girls Run" is among the drafts rejected for *Nightwood.* It is an extension of the "Rape and Repining" chapter of *Ryder.* Barnes published a piece called "Run Girls Run" in *Caravel* in 1936. At about this time Djuna Barnes received secondhand underwear from Peggy Guggenheim. Though she was indignant to find that the garments had been darned, she enjoyed writing in them, as Peggy discovered on an unexpected visit.

20.   In her social critique, Marcus goes over the ornaments in considerable detail. She suggests that the caravel may be a slave ship. She draws attention to the racist, anti-Semitic overlay, which of course is invited in the allusion to *Othello.*

21.   "Rape and Repining" was published in *transition* at the same time that *Finnegans Wake,* then called "Work in Progress," was being serialized. For an extensive comparison of Barnes and Joyce, see my " 'The Look in the

Throat of a Stricken Animal': Joyce as Met by Djuna Barnes." This essay reuses some portions of that work.

22. James Scott interprets them as fallen, sleeping maidens (66), which suits the chapter but not the actual postures, or the single victim. I am grateful to my son Ethan for observing that the women in the picture look like they are listening for something. The original drawing has the erased caption "ears to the ground."

23. Andrew Field connects to *Nightwood* the "bloody wood" of Eliot's "Sweeney among the Nightingales," a poem in which Agamemnon's murder is combined with the setting of Philomela's rape.

24. I find it interesting that in 1911, Virginia Woolf attended a ball dressed as a Gauguin savage. Thus Barnes's character is not exceptional in her role play.

25. The Hippodrome circus is mentioned in a 1909 letter in which Zadel Barnes uses the institution as a favorable comparison to family-imposed suitor Percy Faulkner. It seems likely from the description of the grandmother taking the children to the circus in *The Antiphon* that Barnes may have first attended with Zadel.

26. Both Rebecca West and Virginia Woolf also took on assignments at the zoo. Woolf was fascinated by the new aquarium at the London Zoo, and wrote on it for *Time and Tide*. West took on a BBC assignment on the 100th anniversary of the London Zoo.

27. "The female of the species is more deadly than the male." From "The Female of The Species," Stanza l. The Kipling of *Just So Stories* and *The Jungle Book* presents obvious material for reworking and parody in the Barnes bestiary. There are other possibilities, particularly in *Nightwood*. Compare, for example, the title of Kipling's poem "Watches of the Night," and the chapter title for *Nightwood*, "Watchman, What of the Night?" Dr. O'Connor's statement that "though those two are buried at opposite ends of the earth, one dog will find them both" (NW 106) echoes the line from Kipling's "Ballad of East and West Is West": "When two strong men stand face to face / though they come from the ends of the earth." Gender, pose, and number have all been altered, however. See Plate 15 for the original layout.

28. Barnes mentions Mme Récamier repeatedly, and usually in a negative manner, as if to reject the form of salon in which the hostess becomes an admired object. Mme Récamier attracted both literary and political figures, including Murat and Chateaubriand. But she was also a friend of Mme de Staël.

29. The second line of course parodies the final line of Yeats's poem "Under Ben Bulben," and more specifically the verses he had inscribed on his gravestone, made of "limestone quarried near the spot": "Horseman, pass by." Barnes refers to Dante in her marginal notes on the sheets.

30. Kannenstine remarks on Barnes's apparent unawareness of the dictates of imagism in her poetry (31).

31.  Ulrich Weisstein invokes the great chain in his discussion of Robin Vote in *Nightwood*, identifying as its lowest rung "the beast, whose three principal accessories are 'excrement, blood and flowers' " (8). This subordination is, I think, inappropriate to Barnes's organization of values and avoidance of categories.

32.  Modernist women writers regularly present music as female expression and/or vocation. Further examples are found in Dorothy Richardson's *Pilgrimage*, Rebecca West's *Harriet Hume* and *The Fountain Overflows*, and Virginia Woolf's *The Voyage Out*.

33.  Wendell's ox and beast stories resonate with Joyce's version of Ovid's *Fasti*, shared with Barnes in one of their Paris dialogues. In this story the farmer Hyrieus brings forth his son Orion from the side of a bullock first feasted on and then urinated upon by the gods ("Vagaries Malicieux"). As storytellers, Wendell and Dr. O'Connor take up a discourse of talk that Joyce recommended to Barnes. Barnes was working on a new version of this story of birth from a dead beast in the rejected "Bow Down" manuscript for *Nightwood*.

34.  The father as failed schemer is also a theme in Rebecca West's last series of novels, starting with *The Fountain Overflows*.

35.  In his attempt to move among women for the maximal breeding opportunity, and his confusion of them with cows, Wendell is fulfilling the masculine text of Susan Griffin's "Cows" chapter (67–68).

36.  For a comparison of this chapter to Joyce's childbirth chapter in *Ulysses*, "Oxen of the Sun," see my " 'The Look in the Throat of a Stricken Animal': Joyce as Met by Djuna Barnes."

37.  I use no-man here as it is in Gilbert and Gubar's *No Man's Land*. They provide the following examples: "From the betrayed and passive narrator of Ford's *Good Soldier* to cuckolded Leopold Bloom in Joyce's *Ulysses* and the wounded Fisher King in Eliot's *The Waste Land* to the eunuch Jake Barnes in Hemingway's *The Sun Also Rises*, the paralyzed Clifford Chatterley in Lawrence's *Lady Chatterley's Lover*, and the gelded Benjy in Faulkner's *The Sound and the Fury* as well as the castrated Joe Christmas in *Light in August*, maimed, unmanned, victimized characters are obsessively created by early twentieth-century literary men" (35–36).

38.  In Barnes's early play "The Dove," the demurely named title character, who has "the expectant and waiting air of a deer" (148), bares the shoulder and breast of one of two sisters she has been living with and "sets her teeth in" (163). The sisters keep an unexplained assortment of guns and knives. Reference is made to numerous animals, including a seamstress's monkey, and a bat, who may have entered the apartment. The *Creatures in an Alphabet* also engage in self-consumption.

39.  This is a narrative line favored by Joseph Frank, but challenged ably by Gerstenberger.

40. "The Dreamer" by Rousseau is an ideal candidate. A female nude half reclined on a chesterfield sofa occupies the foreground, left. There are numerous jungle birds, an elephant, and two lionesses, one at the center, staring at the viewer through prominent irises. A black native becomes visible because he holds a yellow pipe. He may be the conjurer of the Rousseau work.

41. Barnes's admiration for Mark Twain is worth mentioning in conjunction with this observation. Cannon were used in the search for Huck's supposedly drowned body in *The Adventures of Huckleberry Finn.* Huck had of course staged his own death. He was in a position for a return of the self; this is not the way that Nora's lesbian relation to Robin had defined itself. Twain also inspired Rebecca West. See volume 1, figure 2.

42. These items were on Barnes's own inventories of her Paris possessions (ms., Maryland).

43. Donna Gerstenberger remarks that the "novel ends in a tableau—a wordless scene of Nora and Robin, the latter seemingly bereft of human consciousness." Robin and the dog make "sounds that exist outside of (and perhaps beyond) language" (137). The dog is another consciousness to Robin, whereas it is a pet to Nora.

44. Barnes used this same metaphor of the beautiful game bird as victim in recalling the tragic Marilyn Monroe.

45. On this point I disagree with Benstock, who reads a scenario of mother-daughter hate in *The Antiphon* (236).

46. Earlier Augusta requested that, when she died, Miranda should lay her in a tree (147).

47. As revealed in the next chapter, this desire is fulfilled in part with the travel writing of Rebecca West.

48. In this role, the bird is comparable to the moth, as ghost of Rachel Vinrace, at the end of Woolf's *The Voyage Out.*

49. See Lanser.

50. Helen Westley, in her memorable interview with Barnes (see "The Confessions of Helen Westley"), declares the central importance of "ennui," and claims mature vision.


3. WEST'S SENSE OF SCAFFOLDING

1. See Hynes (xviii), Marcus ("A Speaking Sphinx"), Hutchinson, and the London *Times,* 16 March 1983. Identifying West as "author, journalist and critic," the *Times* obituary notes that "into no one of these departments of literary activity did Rebecca West fit with entire ease."

2. For the analysis summarized here, see 1 *No Man's Land* 96–101. Gilbert and Gubar reassign dominance from male to female, but retain an oppositional

binary system, and thus do not refigure the binary. The militancy of the model does correspond well to the historical period of the outbreak of World War I, and to West's early involvement with the militant arm of the suffrage movement. I will argue greater subtlety to "Indissoluble Matrimony" later in this chapter.

3. For statistics on its success, see Glendinning, *Rebecca West* (209–10).

4. For a summary of binaries as problematized in feminist theory, see Jardine (71–73). Victoria Glendinning notes the "early origins" of West's concepts of "opposing dualities," relating this to the "dialectics of gender" (*Rebecca West* 127). Evelyn Hutchinson, who gave West needed attention and support at Yale University in the 1950s, was able to view her binarism as a dialectic of antinomies in the best tradition of British empiricism, "whose tools . . . are continually modified . . . to handle new situations" (250).

5. Late in life, West still identified herself as a socialist. Sue Thomas offers another set of categories for West when she describes her feminism as "romantic vitalist feminism." She charts a move during the 1920s from materialist to more essentialist work, characterized by innovative work with psychoanalytic theory.

6. Letter from Janet Flanner, 6 July 1959, University of Tulsa. Flanner's summary of de Staël suits West: "Yes, she knew who and what could cause tyranny, could muffle the liberal spirit and the word and fought frantically, alternating with dignity and creation of defined ideas, against the oppression of such a personality."

7. Quite the opposite, in "The Strange Necessity of Rebecca West," I tell of my first attraction to West via this initial personality—"a dynamic, outspoken female intellectual, serving as critic of literature and life" (266). While the "stereotype" of the feminine is restricting, it is now very difficult to see Woolf in "stereotype." Woolf's interest in sharing process with readers, as discussed in chapter 1, permeates "The Strange Necessity," and makes its voice of authority less daunting than in some of West's other texts.

8. Ray remarks: "If she . . . expounded feminist doctrine with an assurance amounting to fanaticism, this was after all what subscribers to the *Freewoman* expected for their three pennies; no doubt she had her private reservations" (8–9). Ray has West working for the earlier version of Dora Marsden's journal, when she in fact wrote for the *New Freewoman*. His claim that West "lost her faith in the suffrage cause" is also inaccurate.

9. Lessing was planning an article for the *Guardian*, which was to point out the government's "grey and negative defeatist attitudes, amounting to a death wish"—a position bound to appeal to West's interest in a life principle. Lessing wanted to quote some of the most famous lines from *Black Lamb*—ones that John Gunther had emphasized in a letter to West:

> Only part of us is sane: only part of us loves pleasure and the longer day of happiness, wants to live to our nineties and die in peace, in a house

that we built, that shall shelter those who come after us. The other half of us is nearly mad. It prefers the disagreeable to the agreeable, loves pain and its darker night despair, and wants to die in a catastrophe that will set back life to its beginnings and leave nothing of our house save its blackened foundations. (*BL&GF* 1102)

10.  Barnes was also a contributor (though a rare one) to the *New Yorker*. Several prose sketches appeared there in the late twenties: "Reproving Africa" and "The Woman Who Goes Abroad to Forget" (both in 1928), and "Lady of Fourteenth Street" (1929). It also received two late poems by Barnes.

11.  Letter to J. B. Priestley, 22 June 1955, Texas. In this long letter West takes pains to set the articles in context. They were written, she suggests, when the Senate committee had met only a few times, and before his attack on MIT. She suggests that, as a result of her journalism and *The Meaning of Treason,* the Communist party would have reason to spread lies about her, including the notion that she would "suddenly fall for a half-baked gorilla from the Middle West."

12.  For a revisionary survey of these, see my article "Uncle Wells on Women." One novel with an older woman who achieves some degree of personal growth, though not much mental life, is *The Wife of Sir Isaac Harman* (1930).

13.  Among West's works on history is *1900,* a lavishly illustrated coffee-table book with generous cultural analysis, published in 1982, the year before she died. West was predictably interested in politics, technology, literature, the arts, and empire, as found in the U.S. and France as well as Britain.

14.  I have discussed this pattern and its contortions in *Joyce and Feminism* (120). To fulfill her paradigm, Leopold Bloom must play a destructive, materialist role and be implicated in the death of Rudy Bloom. Molly Bloom is an ideal generative figure; Stephen Dedalus, an ideal son.

15.  These essays were written for the *Clarion* in 1913. Correlatively, West condemns the home-front economy of the spoiled upper-class woman Kitty in her 1918 World War I novel, *The Return of the Soldier.* Kitty remakes the home that her soldier husband returns to worthy of display in the "illustrated papers" (12).

16.  This triangle is used by Djuna Barnes in the opening chapter of *Ladies Almanack* (published 1928), and by James Joyce in representations of ALP for *Finnegans Wake.* The abstraction of sexuality to geometry pervades cubism. Wyndham Lewis was among the geometricians known to West, and he has his own chapter in volume 1.

17.  For another very powerful death scene of a mother, see the final pages of West's *This Real Night.*

18.  There are others, most notably a suffragist leader, Mrs. Ormiston, and Mary Queen of Scots, who still walks the streets of Edinburgh in Ellen's fantasy (*The Judge* 16).

19. Letter to S. K. Ratcliffe, n.d., Yale.

20. Though illegitimate, Richard is a vigorous, virile child; Roger, his legitimate brother by a violent, unloved father, is not. Neither is the ill-conceived Philip, Ellen's seducer in Edinburgh. In *The Return of the Soldier*, the children of Chris and Margaret by unloved partners both perish, presumably deprived of essential vigor. Passion grounded in love, not reliable support, is requisite of the father; hence the viability of the autobiographical heroine of *The Fountain Overflows*.

21. This assessment is due largely to numerous discussions of the ending of *The Judge* with my graduate students, and particularly Shirley Peterson, who treats *The Judge* in her dissertation.

22. Glendinning also provides a summary of critical reactions, including Wells's positive one, which somehow derives from the book a notion of the "secondariness" of women.

23. *Harriet Hume* comes out second best in Jane Marcus's comparison of it to *Lolly Willowes*. She feels greater liberation in the rustic, independent spinsterhood achieved by Lolly in Warner's work than she does in Harriet's death and reconciliation with a male in *Harriet Hume* ("A Wilderness" 148–49, 157). Both works offer a valuable questioning and subversion of patriarchy by spritely female heroes, but Marcus charges Hume with a retreat from politics into art that handicaps her power to act. I think that part of the appeal of Warner's novel is that it offers a practical, happy ending to the solitary woman—too frequently a victim in patriarchy. West's more abstract fantasy has greater scale; it extends beyond death, relentlessly pursuing the deadly cycle of dualistic destruction. Marcus's article provides an excellent overview of *Harriet Hume* and a model of the sort of comparative, resisting reading that is useful for female as well as male modernists.

24. The remark also recalls Woolf's mild satire of collectors in *A Room of One's Own*—the students at her lecture who hope for "a nugget of pure truth to wrap up between the pages of your notebooks and keep on the mantelpiece for ever" (3–4).

25. *Harriet Hume* can be seen as a comeback from West's unsuccessful effort to fictionalize the end of her liaison with Wells and her frustrations and loss of self-esteem over Beaverbrook in *Sunflower*. She never completed this novel, though it was published posthumously in 1986. In her afterword to *Sunflower*, Victoria Glendinning cites an important binary from West's notes. This lies between women who remain close to the primitive because they continue its work and great men demanded by civilization, but overly strained by it (276).

26. West's attacks on the parasitic woman began in essays such as "The Future of the Middle Classes: Women Who Are Parasites," published in the *Clarion* in 1912, reprinted in *The Young Rebecca*. I am grateful to Jane Voss for the "Durex" connection and to Barbara Gates for the condor.

27. Glendinning traces her origin to "a visual memory of her friend Harriet Cohen waving from the balcony of a house in Regent's Park," and considers Harriet, more narrowly than I care to, "her creator's idea of undiluted femininity" (*Rebecca West* 126).

28. Stetz suggests that West developed an acceptable sense of "affiliation" (in the sense of that word, derived from Harold Bloom's usage, by Gilbert and Gubar in vol. 1 of *No Man's Land*) with "literary mothers." For the father role, however, she chose male composers and painters instead of "interfering" male writers. Wells could not follow her into these areas of expertise (49).

29. This story has been republished in *The Young Rebecca* as well as the Gilbert and Gubar anthology *The Norton Anthology of Literature by Women*. "Sex war" was a familiar term in West's day, particularly in journalism. She used it in the title of an article, "The Sex War: Disjointed Thoughts on Men," which appeared in the *Clarion* in 1913.

30. Evil forces have taken over a home in *The Fountain Overflows*. It is never determined whether they are poltergeists (pre-Christian explanations of evil as restive spirits of the dead) or ruses fabricated by a gifted but disruptive father figure. In either case, a "good" mother can work them out, not violently but with firm spirituality and compassion for restive humanity. A recent novel with considerable resonance to this is Toni Morrison's *Beloved*.

31. In developing her concept of monumental time, Kristeva remarks on the Virgin as a perpetuation in Christianity of anterior maternal cults ("Women's Time" 191).

32. Glendinning summarizes her agreements as follows: £200 on publication from Macmillan in advance of royalties. No royalties from Viking for the first 4,000 copies, then 15 percent to 6,000 copies, and 25 percent above that (*Rebecca West* 154). Viking plans a new edition, capitalizing, it seems, on the current Bosnian tragedy.

33. I find too little acknowledgment of these critiques of Manichaeanism in Moira Ferguson's article "Feminist Manichaeanism: Rebecca West's Unique Fusion."

34. "If Worst Comes to Worst," carbon typescript, West Collection, HRHRC, University of Texas at Austin.

35. The alliance was renewed in late 1991, when Germany led the way to recognition of a separate Croatia. Ironically, this seems to have precipitated ethnic cleansing, by Serbs as well as Croats.

36. Victoria Glendinning and numerous reviewers of *Black Lamb* detect West's preference for Serbs. Glendinning says rather too simply, and without a reference, "Rebecca was not keen on the Croats, because they reminded her of the Catholic Irish" (*Rebecca West* 155). I do not find West simply anti-Catholic. Her tolerance was displayed in an era when Anthony considered

conversion, and she sent him to consult with her sister, Lettie, who did become a Catholic.

37. She reports of attending a hairdressing show run by "voluptuous pansies" in 1950 (West letter to G. B. Stern, 6 March 1950, Tulsa). In 1971 West wrote to Emanie Arling about Beverly Nichols's party, where "there were 4 women to 11 queers and one heterosexual (the Judas, obviously)" (West letter to Arling, 24 February 1971, Tulsa).

38. Mary Ellmann objected to the gender stereotyping of the arrangement. She summarized their discourses as masculine ballast vs. feminine balloon, though as Victoria Glendinning notes, the West character supplies both factual ballast and imaginative flight in the text (*Rebecca West* 167–68).

## 4. 1939 AND THE ENDS OF MODERNISM

1. It came two days later, on September 3. She and Leonard fought over whether the prime minister should have been urged toward the declaration of war (Leonard finding it justified; Virginia, unable to take up the militant position, feeling always the outsider, in the mode of *Three Guineas*).

2. Barnes had an alcoholic breakdown while staying in Paris. Emily Coleman extracted her from a nursing home as the German occupation impended. Her fare was paid by Peggy Guggenheim (Field 216).

3. This was actually a plea to England to help arm Yugoslavia against the advance of Italy in April 1939. West had been aware of an Italianized Albania since 1936, and complained about the failure of the British government to pass on this information to the press.

4. It also belongs to 1950s experiments with verse drama, and to Barnes's continuing interest in the work of T. S. Eliot, who was writing in the same form.

5. For an excellent discussion of the evolving formal use of "fact" in Woolf's *Three Guineas* and *Between the Acts*, see Patricia Laurence's "The Facts and Fugue of War."

6. Only two fragments appeared in her lifetime, both published in the *New Yorker*: "Quarry" (27 Dec. 1969) and "The Walking-mort" (15 May 1971).

7. It is 1,179 pages long. *Black Lamb*'s encyclopedic, salvaging tendency is shared by Joyce, from *Ulysses* onward.

8. Milosevic is given this title in the leading entry of James Walsh's summary of Europe in 1992 for *Time* magazine. See *Time* 141.1 (4 Jan. 1993): 44–46.

9. Milosevic traces his rise to power to a successful nationalist speech in Kossovo (National Public Radio, 21 Dec. 1992). Like Hitler, he accused a politically weak ethnic group, the Albanians, of endangering a strong one, the

Serbs, and used this as an excuse to strip ethnic Albanians of political power, and even access to education in their own language.

10. Karageorgevitch welcomed this role in an article on the Op-ed page of the *New York Times* (11 Aug. 1992).

11. We would probably substitute "ethnic" for "racial" in West's phrase today. Stephen Dedalus uses "race" in the same way when he takes on his missionary impulse at the end of Joyce's *A Portrait of the Artist as a Young Man.*

12. "Nana," title character of one of her articles in the *New Freewoman,* and Luba of *The Thinking Reed* are others, both discussed in chapter 3.

13. The term is from Lyotard. For an analysis of comparable reactions by H. D., Anais Nin, Barnes, and Barnes's acquaintance from Morocco Jane Bowles, see Ellen G. Friedman, "Where Are the Missing Contents?" As Friedman points out, Bowles has her own reaction to the Nazis, deliberately naming a character in *Two Serious Ladies* "Miss Goering," for the Nazi murderer.

# Bibliography

Abel, Elizabeth. "Cam the Wicked: Woolf's Portrait of the Artist as Her Father's Daughter." In Marcus, ed., *Virginia Woolf and Bloomsbury*, 170–94.

Allen, Carolyn. " 'Dressing the Unknowable in the Garments of the Known': The Style of Djuna Barnes' *Nightwood*." In *Women and Language*, ed. Sally McConnell, Ruth Baker, and Nelly Furman, 106–18. New York: Praeger, 1980.

———. "Writing toward *Nightwood*: Djuna Barnes' Seduction Stories." In Broe, ed., *Silence and Power*, 54–66.

Barnes, Djuna. "Against Nature: In Which Everything That Is Young, Inadequate and Tiresome Is Included in the Term Natural." *Vanity Fair* 18 (August 1922): 60, 88.

———. *The Antiphon*. In Barnes, *Selected Works of Djuna Barnes*, 77–224.

———. *A Book*. New York: Boni and Liveright, 1923. Reprinted as *A Night among the Horses*. New York: Boni and Liveright, 1929.

———. *The Book of Repulsive Women: Eight Rhythms and Five Drawings*. New York: Bruno Chap Books, 1915.

———. "The Confessions of Helen Westley." In Scott, ed., *The Gender of Modernism*, 40–45.

———. *Creatures in an Alphabet*. New York: Dial Press, 1982.

———. "The Diary of a Dangerous Child." *Vanity Fair* 18 (July 1922): 56–58.

———. "Djuna Barnes Probes the Souls of Jungle Folk at the Hippodrome Circus." In Barnes, *New York*, 190–97.

———. "The Dove." In Barnes, *A Book*, 147–64.

———. "The Girl and the Gorilla." *New York World Magazine* (18 October 1914): 9; rpt. in Barnes, *New York*. 180–84.

———. *I Could Never Be Lonely without a Husband: Interviews by Djuna Barnes*. Ed. Alyce Barry. London: Virago, 1987.

———. "James Joyce: A Portrait of the Man Who Is, at Present, One of the More Significant Figures in Literature." *Vanity Fair* 18 (April 1922): 65, 104; rpt. in Barnes, *I Could Never Be Lonely without a Husband*, 288–96.

———. *Ladies Almanack*. 1928. Elmwood Park, Ill.: Dalkey Archive Press, 1992.

———. "Lament for the Left Bank." *Town and Country* 96 (December 1941): 92, 136–38, 148.

——. Letters to Zadel Barnes Gustafson, Barnes Collection, McKeldin Library, University of Maryland.

——. Letters to Natalie Barney, Natalie Barney Collection, Bibliothèque Jacques Doucet, Paris.

——. Letters to Emily Holmes Coleman, Coleman Collection, Morris Library, University of Delaware.

——. "Love and the Beast." Unpublished ms., Barney Collection, Bibliothèque Littéraire Jacques Doucet, Paris.

——. *New York.* Ed. Alyce Barry. Los Angeles: Sun and Moon, 1989.

——. "A Night among the Horses." In Barnes, *Selected Works of Djuna Barnes,* 29–35.

——. *Nightwood.* 1936. New York: New Directions, 1961.

——. Poetry fragments. Barnes Collection, McKeldin Library, University of Maryland.

——. "Run Girls Run." Unpublished ms., Barnes Collection, McKeldin Library, University of Maryland.

——. *Ryder.* New York: St. Martin's Press, 1979.

——. *Ryder.* Elmwood Park, Ill.: The Dalkey Archive Press, 1990.

——. *Selected Works of Djuna Barnes.* New York: Farrar, Straus and Cudahy, 1962.

——. *Smoke and Other Early Stories.* London: Virago, 1983.

——. "There Is No Gender in the Fossil's Eye." Unpublished ms., Barnes Collection, McKeldin Library, University of Maryland.

——. "Vagaries Malicieux." *The Double Dealer* 3 (May 1922): 249–60.

Barnes, Zadel. See Gustafson, Zadel Barnes (Buddington).

Beja, Morris. *Epiphany in the Modern Novel.* Seattle: University of Washington Press, 1971.

Bell, Quentin. *Virginia Woolf: A Biography.* 1972. 2 vols. London: Granada, 1976.

Bell, Vanessa. *Notes on Virginia's Childhood: A Memoir by Vanessa Bell.* Ed. Richard J. Schaubeck. New York: Frank Hallman, 1974.

Benjamin, Walter. "The Work of Art in the Age of Mechanical Reproduction." In *Reflections: Essays, Aphorisms, Autobiographical Writings,* ed. Peter Demetz. New York: Harcourt, Brace Jovanovich, 1978.

Benstock, Shari. *Women of the Left Bank: Paris, 1900–1940.* Austin: University of Texas Press, 1986.

*BLAST: Review of the Great English Vortex.* Nos. 1–2 (1914–1915). Ed. Wyndham Lewis. New York: Kraus Reprint Corporation, 1967.

Bridge, Colonel Charles. Letter to Cecil Graves. BBC Written Archive, University of Reading.

Broe, Mary Lynn, ed. *Silence and Power: A Reevaluation of Djuna Barnes.* Carbondale: Southern Illinois University Press, 1991.

Burke, Carolyn. "Accidental Aloofness": Barnes, Loy, and Modernism." In Broe, ed., *Silence and Power,* 67–79.

Caughie, Pamela. *Virginia Woolf and Postmodernism: Literature in Quest and Question of Itself.* Urbana: University of Illinois Press, 1991.

Conrad, Joseph. *Heart of Darkness: Norton Critical Edition.* Ed. Robert Kimbrough. New York: Norton, 1972.

Curry, Linda. "Tom, Take Mercy: Djuna Barnes' Drafts of *The Antiphon.*" In Broe, ed., *Silence and Power,* 268–86.

"Dame Rebecca West: Author, Journalist, Critic." *The Times* (London), 16 March 1983.

DeSalvo, Louise. *Virginia Woolf: The Impact of Childhood Sexual Abuse on Her Life and Work.* Boston: Beacon, 1989.

DiBattista, Maria. "Joyce, Woolf and the Modern Mind." In *Virginia Woolf: New Critical Essays,* ed. Patricia Clements and Isobel Grundy. 77–95. London: Vision, 1983.

———. *Virginia Woolf's Novels: The Fables of Anon.* New Haven: Yale University Press, 1980.

Doughty, Frances M. "Gilt on Cardboard: Djuna Barnes as Illustrator of Her Life and Work." In Broe, ed., *Silence and Power,* 137–54.

Eder, Doris. "Louis Unmasked: T. S. Eliot in *The Waves.*" *Virginia Woolf Quarterly* 2.1–2 (1975–76): 3–27.

Edwards, Lee. "Schizophrenic Nature." *The Journal of Narrative Technique* 19.1 (1989): 25–30.

Eisenberg, Nora. "Virginia Woolf's Last Words on Words: *Between the Acts* and 'Anon.' " In Marcus, ed., *New Feminist Essays on Virginia Woolf,* 253–66.

Eliot, T. S. *The Letters of T. S. Eliot.* Volume I: *1898–1922.* Ed. Valerie Eliot. San Diego: Harcourt Brace Jovanovich, 1988.

———. *The Waste Land.* In *The Complete Poems and Plays, 1909–1950,* 37–55. New York: Harcourt Brace and World, 1952.

Ellmann, Mary. *Thinking about Women.* New York: Harcourt Brace Jovanovich, 1968.

Evans, Faith. "Introduction." In West, *Family Memories,* 1–12.

Ferguson, Moira. "Feminist Manicheanism: Rebecca West's Unique Fusion." *Minnesota Review* 15 (Fall 1980): 53–60.

Field, Andrew. *Djuna: The Formidable Miss Barnes.* Austin: University of Texas Press, 1983.

Forster, E. M. *A Room with a View.* 1908. London: E. Arnold, 1977.

Frank, Joseph. *The Widening Gyre: Crisis and Mastery in Modern Literature.* New Brunswick, N.J.: Rutgers University Press, 1963.

Fraser, Nancy, and Linda J. Nicholson. "Social Criticism without Philosophy: An Encounter between Feminism and Postmodernism." In Nicholson, ed., *Feminism/Postmodernism,* 19–38.

Friedman, Ellen G. "Where Are the Missing Contents? (Post)Modernism, Gender, and the Canon." *PMLA* 108.2 (1993): 240–52.

Friedman, Norman. "The Waters of Annihilation: Symbols and Double Vision in *To the Lighthouse,*" In *Form and Meaning in Fiction,* ed. Norman Friedman, 240–58. Athens: University of Georgia Press, 1975.

Fromm, Gloria G. "Rebecca West: The Fictions of Fact and the Facts of Fiction." *New Criterion* 9.5 (1991): 45–53.

Fuss, Diana. *Essentially Speaking: Feminism, Nature and Difference.* New York: Routledge, 1989.

Fussell, B. H. "Woolf's Peculiar Comic World: Between the Acts." In *Virginia Woolf: Revaluation and Continuity,* ed. Ralph Freedman, 263–83. Berkeley: University of California Press, 1980.

Gerstenberger, Donna. "The Radical Narratives of Djuna Barnes' *Nightwood.*" In *Breaking the Sequence: Women's Experimental Fiction,* ed. Ellen G. Friedman and Miriam Fuchs, 129–39. Princeton: Princeton University Press, 1989.

Gilbert, Sandra M., and Susan Gubar. *No Man's Land: The Place of the Woman Writer in the Twentieth Century.* Volume 1: *The War of the Words.* New Haven: Yale University Press, 1988.

———. *The Norton Anthology of Literature by Women: The Tradition in English.* New York: Norton, 1985.

Gilligan, Carol. *In a Different Voice: Psychological Theory and Women's Development.* Cambridge, Mass.: Harvard University Press, 1982.

Ginsberg, Elaine K., and Laura Moss Gottlieb, eds. *Virginia Woolf: Centennial Essays.* Troy, N.Y.: Whitston Publishing Company, 1983.

Glendinning, Victoria. "Afterword." In West, *Sunflower,* 268–76.

———. "Introduction." In West, *Harriet Hume.*

———. *Rebecca West: A Life.* London: Weidenfeld and Nicolson, 1987.

Griffin, Susan. *Woman and Nature: The Roaring inside Her.* New York: Harper and Row, 1978.

Gunther, John. Letter to Rebecca West, West Collection, McFarlin Library, University of Tulsa.

Gustafson, Zadel Barnes (Buddington). "The Children's Night." *Harper's New Monthly Magazine* 296 (January 1875): 153–64.

———. *Meg: A Pastoral.* Boston: Lee and Shepard, 1879.

H. D. (Hilda Doolittle). *Bid Me to Live.* 1960. London: Virago, 1984.

———. *The Walls Do Not Fall.* 1944. In H. D., *Trilogy.* New York: New Directions, 1973.

Hall, Radclyffe. *The Well of Loneliness.* 1928. New York: Doubleday, 1990.

Haraway, Donna. "A Manifesto for Cyborgs: Science, Technology, and Socialist Feminism in the 1980s." In Nicholson, ed., *Feminism/Postmodernism,* 190–233.

Harrison, Jane. *Epilogomena to the Study of Greek Religion.* Cambridge: Cambridge University Press, 1921.

Haule, James M. "*To the Lighthouse* and the Great War." In Hussey, ed., *Virginia Woolf and War,* 164–79.

Henke, Suzette. "The Prime Minister: A Key to *Mrs. Dalloway.*" In Ginsberg and Gottlieb, eds., *Virginia Woolf,* 127–41.

Herzig, Carl. "Roots of Night: Emerging Style and Vision in the Early Journalism of Djuna Barnes." *Centennial Review* 31 (Summer 1987): 255–69.

Hussey, Mark, ed. *Virginia Woolf and War: Fiction, Reality, and Myth.* Syracuse: Syracuse University Press, 1991.

Hutchinson, G. E. "The Dome." In Hutchinson, *The Itinerant Ivory Tower: Scientific and Literary Essays,* 241–55. New Haven: Yale University Press, 1953.

Huyssen, Andreas. *After the Great Divide: Modernism, Mass Culture, Post-Modernism.* Bloomington: Indiana University Press, 1986.

Hynes, Samuel. "Introduction: In Communion with Reality." In West, *The Essential Rebecca West,* ix–xviii.

Jameson, Fredric. *Postmodernism, or the Cultural Logic of Late Capitalism.* Durham: Duke University Press, 1991.

Jardine, Alice. *Gynesis: Configurations of Woman and Modernity.* Ithaca: Cornell University Press, 1985.

Jehlen, Myra. "Archimedes and the Paradox of Feminist Criticism." *Signs* 6.4 (1981): 525–50.

Joyce, James. *Collected Poems.* New York: Viking, 1957.

———. *Dubliners.* Ed. Robert Scholes and A. Walton Litz. New York: Viking, 1969.

———. *Finnegans Wake.* New York: Viking, 1939.

———. *Letters of James Joyce.* 3 vols. Ed. Stuart Gilbert (vol. I) and Richard Ellmann (vols. II and III). New York: Viking, 1965–66.

———. *A Portrait of the Artist as a Young Man.* New York: Viking, 1968.

———. *Stephen Hero.* Ed. John J. Slocum and Herbert Cahoon. New York: New Directions, 1963.

———. *Ulysses: A Critical and Synoptic Edition.* Ed. Hans Walter Gabler. New York: Garland, 1984.

Kaivola, Karen. *All Contraries Confounded: The Lyrical Fiction of Virginia Woolf, Djuna Barnes and Marguerite Duras.* Iowa City: University of Iowa Press, 1991.

Kannenstine, Louis. *The Art of Djuna Barnes: Duality and Damnation.* New York: New York University Press, 1977.

Kristeva, Julia. "From 'Oscillation between Power and Denial.' " Trans. Marilyn A. August. In *New French Feminisms: An Anthology,* ed. Elaine Marks and Isabelle de Courtivron, 165–67. New York: Schocken, 1986.

———. *The Kristeva Reader.* Ed. Toril Moi. New York: Columbia University Press, 1986.

———. "Revolution in Poetic Language." In Kristeva, *The Kristeva Reader,* 89–136.

———. "Women's Time." In Kristeva, *The Kristeva Reader,* 187–213.

Lanser, Susan Snaider. "Speaking in Tongues: *Ladies Almanack* and the Discourse of Desire." In Broe, ed., *Silence and Power,* 156–69.

Larabee, Ann. "Early Attic Stage of Djuna Barnes." In Broe, ed., *Silence and Power,* 37–44.

Laurence, Patricia. "The Facts and Fugue of War." In Hussey, ed., *Virginia Woolf and War,* 225–45.

———. *The Reading of Silence: Virginia Woolf in the English Tradition.* Stanford: Stanford University Press, 1991.

Lawrence, D. H. *The Fox; The Captain's Doll; The Ladybird.* Ed. Dieter Mehl. Cambridge: Cambridge University Press, 1992.

———. *Lady Chatterley's Lover: A Propos of Lady Chatterley's Letter.* Ed. Michael Squires. Cambridge: Cambridge University Press, 1993.

———. *The Rainbow.* Ed. Mark Kindead-Weeks. Cambridge: Cambridge University Press, 1989.

Lessing, Doris. Letter to Rebecca West, West Collection, McFarlin Library, University of Tulsa.

Lewis, Wyndham. *Men without Art.* London: Cassell, 1934.

Lilienfeld, Jane. "The Genderization of Genre: The Lesbian Subtext of Virginia Woolf's *Mrs. Dalloway.*" Unpublished paper, MLA Convention, 1984.

London, Bette. "Guerrilla in Petticoats or Sans-culotte? Virginia Woolf and the Future of Feminist Criticism." *Diacritics* 21.2–3 (1991): 11–29.

Maika, Patricia. *Virginia Woolf's "Between the Acts" and Jane Harrson's Con/spiracy.* Ann Arbor: U.M.I. Research Press, 1987.

Marcus, Jane. "Acting Out." *Nation* 244 (4 April 1987): 438–40.

———. "Britannia Rules *The Waves.*" In Karen Lawrence, ed., *Decolonizing Tradition,* 136–62. Urbana: University of Illinois Press, 1992.

———. Introduction. In West, *The Judge.*

———. "Laughing at Leviticus: *Nightwood* as Woman's Circus Epic." In Broe, ed., *Silence and Power*, 221–50.

———. "A Speaking Sphinx." *Tulsa Studies in Women's Literature* 2 (1983): 151–54.

———. *Virginia Woolf and the Languages of Patriarchy.* Bloomington: Indiana University Press, 1987.

———. "A Wilderness of One's Own: Feminist Fantasy Novels of the Twenties—Rebecca West and Sylvia Townsend Warner." In *Women Writers and the City*, ed. Susan Merrill Squier, 134–60. Knoxville: University of Tennessee Press, 1984.

Marcus, Jane, ed. *New Feminist Essays on Virginia Woolf.* Lincoln: University of Nebraska Press, 1981.

———. *Virginia Woolf and Bloomsbury: A Centenary Celebration.* Bloomington: Indiana University Press, 1987.

Matro, Thomas G. "Only Relations: Vision and Achievement in *To the Lighthouse.*" *PMLA* 99.2 (1984): 212–24.

McNaron, Toni A. H. "Echoes of Virginia Woolf." *Women's Studies International Forum* 6.5 (1983): 501–507.

Messerli, Douglas. "The Newspaper Tales of Djuna Barnes." In Barnes, *Smoke and Other Early Stories*, vii–xix.

Miller, J. Hillis. *Fiction and Repetition.* Cambridge, Mass.: Harvard University Press, 1982.

Minow-Pinkney, Makiko. *Virginia Woolf and the Problem of the Subject.* New Brunswick: Rutgers University Press, 1987.

Moore, G. E. *Proof of an External World.* London: H. Milford, 1939.

Moore, Madeline. *The Short Season between Two Silences: The Mystical and the Political in the Novels of Virginia Woolf.* Boston: George Allen and Unwin, 1984.

Morrison, Toni. *Beloved.* New York: Knopf, 1987.

———. *Sula.* New York: Knopf, 1974.

Mulvey, Laura. "Visual Pleasure and Narrative Cinema." In *Feminisms*, ed. Robyn Warhol and Diane Price Herndl, 432–42. New Brunswick: Rutgers University Press, 1991.

Naremore, James. *The World without a Self: Virginia Woolf and the Novel.* New Haven: Yale University Press, 1973.

Neverow-Turk, Vara, and Mark Hussey, eds. *Virginia Woolf: Emerging Perspectives.* New York: Pace University Press, 1994.

Nicholson, Linda J., ed. *Feminism/Postmodernism.* New York: Routledge, 1990.

Nikolchina, Miglena. "Born from the Head: Reading Woolf via Kristeva." *Diacritics* 21.2–3 (1991): 30–42.

Norris, Margot. *Beasts of the Modern Imagination*. Baltimore: Johns Hopkins University Press, 1985.

———. *Joyce's Web: The Social Unraveling of Modernism*. Austin: University of Texas Press, 1992.

Orel, Harold. *The Literary Achievement of Rebecca West*. New York: St. Martin's Press, 1986.

Pearce, Richard. *The Politics of Narration*. New Brunswick, N.J.: Rutgers University Press, 1991.

Peterson, Shirley. "The Emancipation of the Heroine: The Suffragist in the British Novel (1907–1922)." Dissertation, University of Delaware, 1990.

Plumb, Cheryl. *Fancy's Craft: Art and Identity in the Early Works of Djuna Barnes*. Selinsgrove, Pa.: Susquehanna University Press, 1986.

Pochodo, Elizabeth. "Style's Hoax: A Reading of Djuna Barnes's *Nightwood*." *Twentieth Century Literature* 22 (1976): 179–91.

Ray, Gordon N. *H. G. Wells and Rebecca West*. New Haven: Yale University Press, 1974.

Raymont, Henry. "From the Avant Garde of the Thirties, Djuna Barnes." *New York Times* (24 May 1971): 24.

Retallack, Joan. "One Acts: Early Plays of Djuna Barnes." In Broe, ed., *Silence and Power*, 46–52.

Richardson, Dorothy. *Pilgrimage*. 1915–1938. 4 vols. London: Virago, 1979.

Richter, Harvena. *Virginia Woolf: The Inward Voyage*. Princeton: Princeton University Press, 1970.

Rosenbaum, S. P., ed. *Women and Fiction: The Manuscript Versions of "A Room of One's Own."* Oxford: Shakespeare Head Press, 1992.

Rossetti, Christina. *Goblin Market*. New York: Stonehill, 1975.

Schlack, Beverly Ann. *Continuing Presences: Virginia Woolf's Use of Literary Allusion*. University Park: Pennsylvania State University Press, 1979.

Scott, Bonnie Kime. *James Joyce*. Brighton: Harvester, 1987.

———. *Joyce and Feminism*. Bloomington: Indiana University Press, 1984.

———. " 'The Look in the Throat of a Stricken Animal': Joyce as Met by Djuna Barnes." *Joyce Studies* 2 (1991): 153–76.

———. "Refiguring the Binary, Breaking the Cycle: Rebecca West as Feminist Modernist." *Twentieth Century Literature* 37.2 (1991): 169–91.

———. "The Strange Necessity of Rebecca West." In *"Women Reading Women's Writing*, ed. Sue Roe, 264–86. Sussex: Harvester Press, 1987.

———. " 'The Word Split Its Husk': Woolf's Double Vision of Modernist Language." *Modern Fiction Studies* 32.3 (1988): 371–85.

Scott, Bonnie Kime, ed. *The Gender of Modernism*. Bloomington: Indiana University Press, 1990.

Scott, James B. *Djuna Barnes*. Boston: Twayne, 1976.

Sears, Sallie. "Theater of War: Virginia Woolf's *Between the Acts*." In *Virginia Woolf: A Feminist Slant*, ed. Jane Marcus, 212–35. Lincoln: University of Nebraska Press, 1983.

Shattuck, Sandra D. "The Stage of Scholarship: Crossing the Bridge from Harrison to Woolf." In Marcus, ed., *Virginia Woolf and Bloomsbury*, 278–98.

Showalter, Elaine. *A Literature of Their Own: British Women Novelists from Bronte to Lessing*. Princeton: Princeton University Press, 1977.

———. "On Hysterical Narrative." *Narrative* 1.1 (January 1993): 24–35.

Silver, Brenda R. " 'Anon' and 'The Reader': Virginia Woolf's Last Essays." *Twentieth Century Literature* 25 (1979): 356–441.

———. "Virginia Woolf: Cultural Critique." In Scott, ed., *The Gender of Modernism*, 646–58.

Singer, Alan. "The Horse Who Knew Too Much: Metaphor and the Narrative of Discontinuity in *Nightwood*." *Contemporary Literature* 25.1 (1984): 66–87.

Squier, Susan. "The City as Landscape." In *City Images: Perspectives from Literature, Philosophy and Film*, ed. Mary Ann Caws, 99–119. New York: Gordon and Breach, 1991.

Stetz, Margaret. "Rebecca West and the Visual Arts." *Tulsa Studies in Women's Literature* 8 (1989): 63–78.

Sypher, Eileen B. "*The Waves*: A Utopia of Androgyny." In Ginsberg and Gottlieb, eds., *Virginia Woolf*, 187–213.

Thomas, Sue. "Rebecca West's Second Thoughts on Feminism." *Genders* 13 (Spring 1992): 90–107.

Twain, Mark. *The Adventures of Huckleberry Finn*. Ed. Henry Nash Smith. Boston: Houghton Mifflin, 1958.

Weisstein, Ulrich. "Beast, Doll, and Woman: Djuna Barnes' Human Bestiary." *Renascence* 15.1 (Fall 1962): 3–11.

Wells, H. G. *H. G. Wells in Love*. Ed. G. P. Wells. London: Faber and Faber, 1984.

———. *The Outline of History: Being a Plain History of Life and Mankind*. New York: Macmillan, 1921.

———. *The Wife of Sir Isaac Harman*. London: Collins, 1930.

West, Rebecca. *The Birds Fall Down*. 1966. London: Virago, 1986.

———. *Black Lamb and Grey Falcon*. New York: Viking 1943.

———. "Bookshelf." Tape of radio interview, West Collection, McFarlin Library, University of Tulsa.

———. *The Court and the Castle*. London: Macmillan, 1957.

———. *Cousin Rosamund*. New York: Viking Penguin, 1986.

———. *The Essential Rebecca West*. Harmondsworth: Penguin, 1983. [Formerly titled *Rebecca West: A Celebration*. New York: Viking, 1977.]

———. *Family Memories*. London: Virago, 1987.

———. *The Fountain Overflows*. Harmondsworth: Penguin, 1987.

———. *Harriet Hume: A London Fantasy*. 1929; London: Virago, 1980.

———. *The Harsh Voice*. 1935; London: Virago, 1982.

———. *Henry James*. London: Nesbit, 1916.

———. "High Fountain of Genius." In Scott, ed., *The Gender of Modernism*, 592–96.

———. "If Worst Comes to Worst." Typescript, West Collection, Harry Ransom Humanities Research Center, University of Texas at Austin.

———. *The Judge*. 1922. London: Virago, 1980.

———. Letter to Colonel Charles Bridge, reporting on Yugoslavian tour for British Council, Archives, British Council, London.

———. Letter to Doris Lessing, West Collection, McFarlin Library, University of Tulsa.

———. Letter to J. B. Priestley, Harry Ransom Humanities Research Center, University of Texas, Austin.

———. Letter to S. L. Ratcliffe, West Collection, Beinecke Collection, Yale University.

———. Letter to Alexander Woollcott, Woollcott Collection, Houghton Library, Harvard University.

———. *The Meaning of Treason*. New York: Viking, 1947.

———. "Mr Setty and Mr Hume." In West, *The Essential Rebecca West*, 260–319.

———. "The New God." Ms., West Collection, McFarlin Library, University of Tulsa.

———. *1900*. New York: Viking, 1982.

———. "Notes on Novels" [review of *Jacob's Room*]. *New Statesman* 20 (4 November 1922): 142, 144.

———. *This Real Night*. 1984. London: Virago, 1987.

———. *The Return of the Soldier*. 1918. London: Virago, 1980.

———. *St. Augustine*. In West, *The Essential Rebecca West*, 159–236.

———. *The Strange Necessity*. 1928. London: Virago, 1987.

———. "The Strange Necessity." In West, *The Strange Necessity*, 13–198.

———. *Sunflower*. London: Virago, 1986.

———. *The Thinking Reed*. 1936. London: Virago, 1984.

———. "Trees of Gold." In Scott, ed., *The Gender of Modernism*, 570–73.

———. *The Young Rebecca: Writings of Rebecca West, 1911–1917*. Ed. Jane Marcus. London: Virago, 1983.

Williamson, Alan. "The Divided Image: The Quest for Identity in the Works of Djuna Barnes." *Critique: Studies in Modern Fiction* 7 (Spring 1964): 58–74.

Wolfe, Peter. *Rebecca West: Artist and Thinker*. Carbondale: Southern Illinois University Press, 1971.

Wolff, Larry. "Rebecca West: This Time Let's Listen." *New York Times Book Review* (10 February 1991): 1, 28–30.

Woolf, Virginia. *Between the Acts.* 1941. San Diego: Harcourt Brace Jovanovich, 1969.

———. *The Collected Essays of Virginia Woolf.* 4 vols. Ed. Leonard Woolf. London: Hogarth, 1966–67.

———. *The Common Reader.* New York: Harcourt Brace and World, 1953.

———. *The Death of the Moth.* 1942. New York: Harcourt Brace Jovanovich, 1970.

———. *The Diary of Virginia Woolf.* 5 vols. Ed. Anne Olivier Bell. San Diego: Harcourt Brace Jovanovich, 1977–84.

———. *The Essays of Virginia Woolf.* 4 vols. to date. Ed. Andrew McNeillie. San Diego: Harcourt Brace Jovanovich, 1986–94.

———. *Granite and Rainbow.* New York: Harcourt Brace, 1958.

———. *Jacob's Room.* 1922. San Diego: Harcourt Brace Jovanovich, 1960.

———. Letter to Rebecca West, 1928, West Collection, University of Tulsa.

———. *The Letters of Virginia Woolf.* 6 vols. Ed. Nigel Nicolson and Joanne Trautmann. San Diego: Harcourt Brace Jovanovich, 1975–80.

———. "Life and the Novelist." In Woolf, *Granite and Rainbow,* 41–47.

———. "The Mark on the Wall." In *A Haunted House and Other Short Stories,* 37–46. New York: Harcourt Brace and World, 1949.

———. *Moments of Being.* Ed. Jeanne Schulkind. New York: Harcourt Brace Jovanovich, 1976.

———. *Mrs. Dalloway.* 1925. New York: Harcourt Brace and World, 1953.

———. "The Narrow Bridge of Art." In Woolf, *The Collected Essays of Virginia Woolf,* vol. 2, 218–29.

———. *Night and Day.* New York: Harcourt Brace Jovanovich, 1948.

———. "The Novels of E. M. Forster." In Woolf, *The Death of the Moth and Other Essays,* 162–75.

———. *Orlando: A Biography.* 1928. San Diego: Harcourt Brace Jovanovich, 1956.

———. *A Passionate Apprentice: The Early Journals, 1897–1909.* Ed. Mitchell A. Leaska. San Diego: Harcourt Brace Jovanovich, 1990.

———. "Phases of Fiction." In Woolf, *Granite and Rainbow,* 93–145.

———. *Pointz Hall: The Earlier and Later Typescripts of "Between the Acts."* Ed. Mitchell A. Leaska. New York: University Publications, 1983.

———. "Professions for Women." In Woolf, *Collected Essays of Virginia Woolf,* vol. 2, 284–89.

———. *Roger Fry.* 1940. Harmondsworth: Penguin, 1979.

———. *A Room of One's Own.* 1929. San Diego: Harcourt Brace Jovanovich, 1957.

———. "A Sketch of the Past." In Woolf, *Moments of Being,* 64–137.

———. *Three Guineas.* 1938. New York: Harcourt Brace and World, 1966.

———. *To the Lighthouse.* 1927. New York: Harcourt Brace and World, 1964.

———. *The Voyage Out*. 1915. New York: Harcourt Brace and World, 1948.

———. *The Waves*. 1931. San Diego: Harcourt Brace Jovanovich, 1959.

———. *The Waves: The Two Holograph Drafts*. Ed. John W. Graham. Toronto: University of Toronto Press, 1976.

———. *Women and Writing*. Ed. Michèle Barrett. London: The Women's Press, 1979.

———. *The Years*. New York: Harcourt Brace Jovanovich, 1937.

Wordsworth, William. *The Prelude: 1799, 1905, 1850: A Norton Critical Edition*. Ed. M. H. Abrams and Stephen Gill. New York: Norton, 1979.

Yeats, William Butler. "The Circus Animals' Desertion." In Yeats, *The Poems of William Butler Yeats*, 346–48.

———. *The Poems of William Butler Yeats*. Ed. Richard Finneran. New York: Macmillan, 1989.

———. "The Second Coming." In Yeats, *The Poems of William Butler Yeats*, 187.

———. "Under Ben Bulben." In Yeats, *The Poems of William Butler Yeats*, 325–28.

# Index

BONNIE KIME SCOTT, Professor of English and Women's Studies at the University of Delaware, is general editor of *The Gender of Modernism*; she is also author of *Joyce and Feminism* and *James Joyce* (feminist readings series), and editor of *New Alliances in Joyce Studies*. She is presently editing the selected letters of Rebecca West.